# METHAMPHETAMINE
## ADDICTION

# METHAMPHETAMINE ADDICTION

## Biological Foundations, Psychological Factors, and Social Consequences

**Perry N. Halkitis**

**With Contributions by
Antonio E. Urbina and
Daniel J. Carragher**

American Psychological Association
Washington, DC

Published by
American Psychological Association
750 First Street, NE
Washington, DC 20002
www.apa.org

To order
APA Order Department
P.O. Box 92984
Washington, DC 20090-2984
Tel: (800) 374-2721; Direct: (202) 336-5510
Fax: (202) 336-5502; TDD/TTY: (202) 336-6123
Online: www.apa.org/books/
E-mail: order@apa.org

In the U.K., Europe, Africa, and the Middle East, copies may be ordered from
American Psychological Association
3 Henrietta Street
Covent Garden, London
WC2E 8LU England

Typeset in Goudy by Circle Graphics, Columbia, MD

Printer: Maple-Vail Books, York, PA
Cover Designer: Naylor Design, Washington, DC
Technical/Production Editor: Emily Welsh

The opinions and statements published are the responsibility of the authors, and such opinions and statements do not necessarily represent the policies of the American Psychological Association.

**Library of Congress Cataloging-in-Publication Data**

Halkitis, Perry N.
  Methamphetamine addiction: biological foundations, psychological factors, and social consequences / by Perry N. Halkitis. — 1st ed.
      p. ; cm.
  Includes bibliographical references and index.
  ISBN-13: 978-1-4338-0423-6
  ISBN-10: 1-4338-0423-9
  1. Methamphetamine abuse. I. American Psychological Association. II. Title.
  [DNLM: 1. Amphetamine-Related Disorders—therapy—United States. 2.
  Methamphetamine—United States. 3. Amphetamine-Related Disorders—psychology—
  United States. 4. Risk factors—United States. 5. Socioeconomic Factors—United States.
  6. Street Drugs—United States. WM 275 H173m 2009]
  RC568.A45H35 2009
  616.86'4—dc22
                                                        2008049682

**British Library Cataloguing-in-Publication Data**

A CIP record is available from the British Library.

*Printed in the United States of America*
*First Edition*

For my father,
Nicholas Halkitis,
who always said I could

# CONTENTS

# LIST OF FIGURES AND EXHIBITS

## EXHIBITS

# FOREWORD

CATHY J. REBACK

Methamphetamine is the drug of our time. Quick, accessible, affordable, and with an initial high that makes the user feel like a million bucks. The drug offers focused concentration, high-energy sex, and the ability to accomplish volumes of work in a relatively short period of time. For a fast-moving, quick-paced society, for a society that values a thin body and sexual expression, methamphetamine is the drug of our time. Every generation has had a drug that defines the culture, and every generation has used a drug as a social and sexual lubricant. Given this, what is it that makes methamphetamine different from other substances?

In 1994, I began working with gay and bisexual men, and other men who have sex with men (MSM), who use methamphetamine. I initially started by providing harm reduction outreach services and over the years increased the service and treatment modalities to offer those with higher intensity interventions coupled with research and evaluation studies. Through the years, what became evident in the data was the association among methamphetamine use, high-risk sexual behaviors, and, ultimately, HIV seroprevalence (Shoptaw & Reback, 2006). The data indicate that the more involved MSM are in their use of methamphetamine—as demonstrated by history of use and frequency of use over time—the higher the prevalence of HIV infection. This is what makes methamphetamine different. When any substance, from alcohol to marijuana to cocaine to heroin to methamphetamine (not necessarily in that order), is used at a level of abuse or dependence, there lies a substance-abuse problem. However, when HIV is added to the formula—as it is with methamphetamine use in particular populations—the substance-abuse problem becomes a public health crisis. Again, this is what makes methamphetamine different.

In my work as both a researcher and community provider, I offer a continuum of intervention and treatment options. To that end, I find it as important to provide risk reduction services to active, nontreatment-seeking methamphetamine users as it is to provide treatment options to those who wish to reduce or stop their methamphetamine use. Both prevention and treatment interventions should be a two-way interactive process between the participant and the staff member; the intervention should be client centered, meeting users "where they are" and providing the appropriate intervention that matches both users' need as well as their level of use.

In a similar way, *Methamphetamine Addiction: Biological Foundations, Psychological Factors, and Social Consequences* explores methamphetamine from a holistic perspective. It is a literary exploration that encompasses, as the title suggests, biological, psychological, and sociological perspectives. The examination of methamphetamine is expansive, from the development of the substance to the way methamphetamine is depicted in contemporary popular culture. Furthermore, one of the uniquely important aspects of the text is its inclusive examination of the varying methamphetamine-using population. In this sense, the individual user is considered with as much attention as the general trends that influence one person's use. For example, when addressing the "synergetic" relationship between methamphetamine use, mental health, and sexuality, which often leads to high-risk sexual behaviors among MSM, this complex subject is addressed from both the macroperspective as well as the microperspective. Methamphetamine is used within a cultural context and cannot be thoroughly understood devoid of the relevant cultural constructs and psychological and physiological responses. However, a thorough understanding does not stop at this level, and thus the individual user as well as differences among users is noted. In addition, in stark contradiction to the assertions of some colleagues, while the book explains the highly addictive properties of methamphetamine the author never assumes that every user of the drug is addicted.

Dr. Perry Halkitis has written a deeply personal as well as a comprehensive book about the many factors that influence and affect methamphetamine use in contemporary society. From the first few words in the Preface the reader understands the profound commitment Dr. Halkitis has toward his work. It is this commitment that guides his subsequent chapters. To explore the depth and range of issues regarding methamphetamine, the author takes his reader on a journey. This volume examines the history of methamphetamine use, as well as current trends, while contrasting different drugs and different drug-using populations. The reader learns of the pharmacological properties of methamphetamine and consequently the effects on a user's body and mind, physical, and mental health. Methamphetamine use, abuse, dependence, and addiction are understood as multilayered, as are the current treatment approaches.

Dr. Halkitis challenges himself and his colleagues by noting the limitations in the current literature. There is a gap in our understanding of the symbiotic relationship between sexual risk taking and methamphetamine use. Thus, by noting this limitation, Dr. Halkitis sets the direction for future work, both in research and the provision of services. I have often commented that for every individual who walks into one of my treatment clinics, there are one or more persons who are using methamphetamine for the first time. Efforts have to be placed on all fronts, from prevention to treatment. Understanding the complexity of an individual's use—be that individual a teenage girl, a heterosexual woman in her 40s, or a young gay man in his 20s—as well as patterns and trends in use, serves to create culturally appropriate research studies, prevention interventions, and treatment programs. Dr. Halkitis concludes his book by addressing new directions in our understanding of methamphetamine addiction.

This volume offers the opportunity to investigate and gain in-depth knowledge of methamphetamine and the individuals who use the drug. Given that the book addresses methamphetamine from different directions, the reader comes to understand methamphetamine from several perspectives. As the totality of the drug is considered, the totality of the drug user is also considered. In reading this volume, one comes to understand the toll methamphetamine takes on the individual body, mind, and soul as well as the effects on a society and public health.

# PREFACE

For more than a decade, much of my thinking has centered on the health of gay men. In that time, I have witnessed and examined the toll that risky behaviors have taken on each of us individually and as a community. In recent years, my own attention and that of other scientists has focused on the role that methamphetamine has played in the lives of many of these men, and how this drug, despite the numerous perceived benefits it seems to bestow on its users, ultimately exacerbates the burden on the physical, emotional, and social lives of those who walk this path of addiction. Despite our best efforts, use of methamphetamine is very present in the lives of so many in the United States—not just among gay men—but gay and straight, male and female, young and old, professional and working class, of diverse races, ethnicities, cultures, and of varying means and abilities. This powerful crystalline substance does not discriminate, and it functions as an equal opportunity destroyer of lives. Yet, its appeal to its users is undeniable.

We still have much to learn and much more work to undertake to confront the challenge of methamphetamine addiction, although an abundance of excellent scholarship in the natural and social sciences, medicine, education, and public health has cast some light on this pervasive drug addiction. Despite this myriad of knowledge, a comprehensive volume on the subject of methamphetamine addiction did not exist. Thus, my inspiration and ultimately my challenge was to somehow wrap my arms around the multitude of studies and volumes of generated knowledge regarding methamphetamine, and synthesize it in a manner that was both respectful to the original work while simultaneously contextualizing this knowledge in relation to the information generated by scholars, clinicians, and frontline staff working in the field. To this volume, I bring and honor the ideas of some of our nation's leading scientists, who through clinical trials, field studies, evaluation research, and ethnographic observation have sought to understand the use of methamphetamine and to develop strategies for treating the addiction. The efforts of community-based agencies are also considered, since individuals in these contexts have worked within political realities and economic constraints to help those who present at their sites seeking support. It is my hope that this volume effectively synthesizes all of these elements and presents a comprehensive, scientifically sound, and accessible understanding of all aspects of this drug and its use.

Three major tenets guided the writing of this volume. The first is the notion that, like all other health conditions, methamphetamine addiction must be understood using a biopsychosocial lens. In this regard, a complete appreciation for methamphetamine use cannot be achieved solely through a biomedical approach, but instead we must consider the biological bases and manifestations associated with using the drug, the psychological antecedents and responses to the drug, and the social and environmental transactions of the methamphetamine user. I revisit this idea numerous times throughout the book, as I believe a holistic approach to addiction in which we consider the physical, emotional, and social person will better equip us to understand the antecedents that predispose individuals to the use of methamphetamine. The holistic approach will better guide us in the development of prevention and intervention efforts in addressing this addiction.

The second theme guiding this volume is the belief that the most robust and powerful knowledge is generated on the hyphen of theory–practice. It is through the interaction and interplay of science with real-life situations, real-world practice, and real-world beliefs that we can ultimately attempt to arrive at the Platonic conception of "truth." In this regard, research that is conducted in the ivory tower, although important and most always rigorous, must not remain in the ivory tower; the knowledge generated must be translated into real-world applications. We, as researchers, have as much to learn from those in the communities we study as they have to learn from us. Therefore, questions must be formulated that are scientifically yet also practically meaningful. It is for this very reason that an effort is made in this volume to consider both scientific and community-based responses to the methamphetamine problem. These were my motivations for including two chapters written by health practitioners (Dr. Antonio Urbina, a physician, and Dr. Daniel Carragher, a counseling psychologist), who share firsthand accounts of their life experiences in working with methamphetamine users—one on work in medical settings and one in counseling settings. I know that these personal narratives help to illuminate many of the ideas that are discussed throughout the text.

The third tenet is the fundamental notion that methamphetamine addiction is not just a disease among the gay population, although the public and media hysteria in recent years has focused on just that. Although my own work in this domain has been nested in the context of life among the gay sector, I do not believe that a true understanding of this drug dilemma can be ascertained by focusing solely on this subpopulation. Moreover, such an approach would function to pathologize a segment of the population that has been overly pathologized. I will, however, note that much of the behavioral research that has been conducted in the last decade has focused on the gay and bisexual male population; thus, although this segment of the population may appear to be overrepresented in this volume, it is mainly because studies that focus on methamphetamine use among gay and bisexual men constitute the majority of scholarly work. As noted in the Foreword by Dr. Cathy Reback, the intersection between methamphetamine use and HIV transmission makes this drug addiction different from most others. Given that in North America, Europe, and Australia, gay men continue to constitute the population most affected by HIV, it is reasonable that the bulk of research on methamphetamine addiction would be disproportionately centered on this segment of the population.

Nonetheless, throughout the volume, all topics are considered in terms of methamphetamine users from all sociodemographic strata. What emerge are some common crosscutting themes, but nuanced understandings of the addiction that are particular to different segments of the population also emerge. The latter speak clearly for a need to develop a variety of diverse and focused prevention and intervention programs to address the range of lives in the methamphetamine-using world.

Writing this book was more than an intellectual exercise for me. As an academic, I find myself occasionally surrounded by those who conduct research for the sake of research. My dedication in the many behavioral studies I have undertaken with regard to methamphetamine use (as well as HIV and mental health) has been and will always be to generate knowledge that has utility and that seeks to improve all of our lives, individually and as a whole. It is my hope that this writing has resulted in a book that will be read by researchers, practitioners, students, staff in community-based agencies, and all others who are interested in or somehow affected by the realities of methamphetamine. It is also my hope that readers not only gain the knowledge that they are seeking but also that they are inspired and challenged to ask their own questions and take their own actions in addressing this public health dilemma. While much of the work, which is examined in this text, is based on empirical studies, the information is presented in a manner that, I believe, can be accessed by more than just my talented, dedicated, and inspired circle of peers.

Three more points need to be made. I have intentionally used the term *methamphetamine* throughout the book instead of the illicitly produced version of the drug *crystal meth*. I doubt anyone believes that the addiction, which exists in our country, is that of the minimally prescribed pharmaceutical formulation of methamphetamine, and thus when the term is used it refers to crystal meth and all of its varying manifestations. Second, I am a firm believer in interdisciplinary learning—it is the way of the world—and as much as possible my efforts have been to synthesize information from many disciplines—psychology, medicine, public health, journalism, and the arts. If truth be told, it is the "Renaissance man" who most impresses me. Finally, maybe in some small way this work will further push the federal government to take appropriate, meaningful, and respectful steps in addressing the methamphetamine problem. Making the purchasing of pseudoephedrine-based products (e.g., Sudafed, Claritin) a laborious task just doesn't cut it, but funding of innovative out-of-the-box thinking will.

This volume is structured linearly. The first three chapters provide an overview of methamphetamine, its historical bases, its biochemistry, and the illegal production of the drug in the United States. In chapter 4, I consider the biopsychosocial effects of the drug. I have intentionally included a separate section (chap. 5) on the associations between use of the drug and sexual behavior as so much of the research has focused on the complex intersections and synergies that exist between these behaviors. Chapter 6 delineates some of the potential explanations for why individuals become drawn to the drug and why a subset of them becomes methamphetamine dependent. In chapter 7, I provide an overview of what is known about treating methamphetamine addiction. Chapter 8 examines the prevention efforts made to stop the use of methamphetamine in the United States. Chapters 9 and 10, written by Drs. Antonio E. Urbina and Daniel J. Carragher, the former a physician and the latter a mental health clinician, have been purposefully included to help portray the real-life experiences of practitioners who are working with methamphetamine-using clients. I believe their stories help to humanize and illuminate the empirical research that is presented in this volume. Finally, I conclude this work in chapter 11 with thoughts to help guide our future work, both in terms of theory and practice.

Through the synthesis and dissemination of knowledge, I hope that those who read these pages feel empowered in their own lives to continue the discussion, keep it alive, and demand that a solution be sought. I will say that 25 years ago such discussions revolved around cocaine and before that LSD. Methamphetamine is the drug of the moment, and soon a new drug will rise to the top. Thus, it is my hope that one question you ask yourself while reading is less about "Why does methamphetamine addiction exist in our society?" but more about "Why do addictions exist in our society?"

# ACKNOWLEDGMENTS

I have dedicated this book to the individual who has most influenced my development. In spirit and in life he serves as my inspiration. I would be remiss not to acknowledge the others with whom I have had the pleasure of working and whose innovative and exciting modes of thinking have helped shape me. For helping me along my intellectual trajectory, I am very grateful to Drs. LaRue Allen, Paul Galatowitsch, Bruce Homer, Cathy Reback, David Rindskopf, Ron Stall, and Barbara Warren. To my colleagues at Terrence Higgins Trust in the United Kingdom, especially to Gerard McGuikin, it is you who have helped me see this work in a biopsychosocial manner. I am also very grateful to Drs. Antonio E. Urbina and Daniel J. Carragher, who have generously contributed the guest chapters to this volume. In addition, I thank Robert Massa, who once asked me, "Aristotle or Plato?"; not a day passes in which I do not think of you or about that question (the answer is still "Both!").

I am fortunate to be on the faculty of the world's global university ("the University of the Other," as our president, John Sexton, has described it), which equips me in many ways, the greatest of which is by providing me the opportunity to work with talented, dedicated, and intelligent students in the classroom and especially at my research center, the Center for Health, Identity, Behavior and Prevention Studies. The students' own passion for this work inspires me and frankly keeps my thinking fresh. I appreciate all the support and academic kinship I have experienced with the dozens of talented current and former students and colleagues who have constituted my research team. In particular, my deepest appreciation goes to Alex Dayton, Stephanie Doig, Lindsay Espinosa, Kelly Green, Beth Fischgrund, Buddy Hampton, Matthew Kiang, Sandra Kupprat, Ashley Manasse, Michael Marino, Robert Moeller, Paris Mourgues, Joseph Palamar, Molly Pappas, James Pollock, Michael Shrem, Daniel Siconolfi, Todd Solomon, and David Zade for their wisdom, their passion for this work, and for the rock-n-roll. I give special thanks to Alex (the keeper of the jpgs) and as always to Rob for organizing the team to help me pull this all together in the 23rd hour (as only Rob could).

This work is based on the myriad of studies undertaken by scientists throughout the United States and internationally. The field owes each of you a great deal of gratitude for your efforts to disentangle and address this public health dilemma. I have learned much from you.

In the end, every page was written with thoughts of Steven. It is my hope that this finds you sober and with happiness in your life.

# METHAMPHETAMINE ADDICTION

# 1

# METHAMPHETAMINE: SOCIOHISTORICAL CONTEXTS AND EPIDEMIOLOGICAL PATTERNS

*Crystal meth* is the popular name of the "street" version of the pharmacological compound methamphetamine. Crystal meth has captured the attention of the American public in recent years. A potent psychostimulant that has the potential to cause irreparable physical and psychological damage, crystal methamphetamine has infiltrated the mainstream and margins of American society as noted by numerous studies documenting use of this illegal drug among high school students, gay men in major urban areas, and "soccer moms," among others. Marcovitz (2006) reported that Quest Diagnostics, a medical testing laboratory, found a 68% increase in methamphetamine use among employees and job applicants in a 1-year period between 2002 and 2003. Successful, award-winning recording artists such as Fergie have spoken out on their abuse of crystal methamphetamine (Keegan, 2006). The 2006 announcement of "Jesus Camp" preacher Ted Haggard regarding his use of the drug (Banerjee, 2006) and the destroyed life and career of prominent AIDS doctor Ramon Torres, due to his methamphetamine addiction (France, 2008), are testaments to the pervasiveness and power of this substance, which *Newsweek* labeled "America's most dangerous drug" (Jefferson, 2005). The Substance Abuse and Mental Health Services Administration (SAMHSA; 2006) described methamphetamine as "America's homegrown drug epidemic."

The appeal of methamphetamine to such a wide range of individuals is easy to explain, as users report feelings of power and invulnerability, heightened sexual sensations, and euphoria. Because the drug is a stimulant, other desired effects include increased productivity and weight loss (von Mayrhauser, Brecht, & Anglin, 2002). Methamphetamine has been linked to "sex like you've never had," "more work that you could ever imagine doing," "feeling like the king of the world," and "a vacation from loneliness and sorrow."

However, the drug has also been referred to as "the evil one" because methamphetamine, a highly addictive stimulant, has the potential to destroy the physical, mental, economic, and social well-being of its users. The drug has many nicknames (Anglin, Burke, Perrochet, Stamper, & Dawd-Noursi, 2000). In addition to "crystal" (a name given to the illegally manufactured substance because of its crystalline nature), popular names for the drugs include "ice," "chalk," and "glass" (because of its appearance); "crank" (because of the section of the motorcycle where bikers who produced the drug hid the substance); "Tina" (derived from "Christina," which is derived from "crystal"); "go-fast" (because of its stimulant qualities); and "redneck cocaine" (because the drug was historically associated with rural drug addicts). Other less popular names include "chandelier" and "tweak." For those who have never used the drug, the images of emaciated bodies, destroyed teeth and gums, skin torn apart as a result of hallucinations of "crank bugs," and accelerated aging, severe enough to make a 25-year-old look like a 60-year-old, seem to provide sufficient deterrence from avoiding this substance (see Figure 1.1). But these physical outcomes, although real and powerful, are long-term effects that methamphetamine users do not experience early in their addiction or even consider as the drug is circulating throughout their bodies. The Department of Justice uses images of these physical outcomes as deterrents to methamphetamine use (U.S. Department of Justice, 2007). The effectiveness of such campaigns, however, has been minimal, as is evidenced by the continual growth of methamphetamine use in United States since 1995.

The diversity of methamphetamine users speaks to the need to understand addiction to this drug from a holistic and biopsychosocial perspective (G. L. Engel, 1977). No one trajectory is sufficient to explain why the 35-year-old single working mother in Des Moines with three jobs and four children uses the drug, why the 18-year-old gay man who has just emerged in the gay community of New York City depends on the drug to "get by," or why the 60-year-old trucker who regularly drives between Austin and Los Angeles has a methamphetamine addiction.

Understanding methamphetamine addiction requires a closer examination of the biological and neurophysiological manifestations of methamphetamine use; the psychological processes and social circumstances, which may function as antecedents to use; and the perceived emotional and physical benefits of use, all of which are nested in the contexts and environments

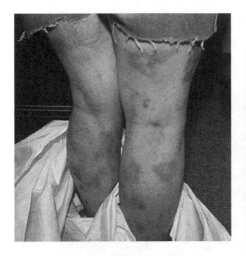
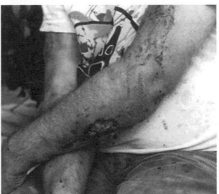
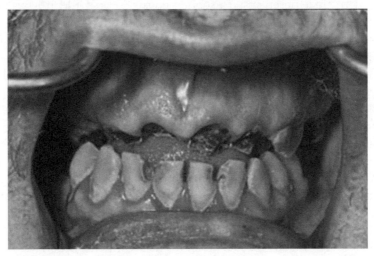

Figure 1.1. U.S. Department of Justice images of the effects of methamphetamine. From "Meth Awareness" prevention campaign, United States Department of Justice. Retrieved May 5, 2007, from http://www.usdoj.gov/methawareness. In the public domain.

through which the methamphetamine user navigates. This biopsychosocial perspective must also inform the design of treatments and/or interventions. This holistic understanding of methamphetamine use and addiction has been proposed by the Institute of Medicine (2001): "Health and disease are determined by a dynamic interaction among biological, psychological, behavioral, and societal factors. These interactions occur over time and throughout development" (p. 16).

In this chapter, the history of methamphetamine use in the United States is considered. Epidemiological trends for this drug use are then presented, accompanied by research examining use in subpopulations. Finally, as methamphetamine is rarely used in isolation, use of the drug is considered in relation to polydrug-using behaviors.

## HISTORICAL CONTEXTS OF METHAMPHETAMINE

Methamphetamine is a member of a class of drugs known as amphetamines. Amphetamines, also named stimulants and known colloquially as speed, were first developed in Germany in the late 1800s (Gahlinger, 2001). Initially, there were no specified medicinal uses of amphetamines. In the first third of the 20th century, amphetamine was introduced in the United States and marketed as a bronchial inhaler that could be used to treat allergies, asthma, and colds (Anglin et al., 2000). In 1937, an amphetamine tablet was developed to treat narcolepsy (a spontaneous sleep disorder); it was subsequently used as a treatment for hyperactive children and as an appetite suppressant for women trying to lose weight (Matsumoto, Miyakawa, Yabana, Iizuka, & Kishimoto, 2000).

The formulation of methamphetamine occurred shortly after the initial purification from plants of ephedrine, the substance on which the drug is based (Suwaki, Fukui, & Konuma, 1997), when scientists discovered that this form of speed could be easily made by using ephedrine as the base. The result was a crystalline powder that is water-soluble and could be administered via pill or injection (Marcovitz, 2006, p. 12). Shortly thereafter, in the United States, methamphetamine became available from pharmaceutical companies in the forms of Desoxyn and Methedrine as a drug to treat asthma.

In the 1950s, health care professionals began to prescribe Methedrine as a pain alleviator (Marcovitz, 2006, p. 15). This treatment, which was not controlled, was also available via injection (or in injectable form) and was widely used by homemakers, college students, truckers, and athletes, among others (D. Johnson, 2005, p. 7). In addition, during the apex of medicinal use during the 1950s and 1960s, methamphetamine was prescribed to treat narcolepsy, postencephalitic Parkinsonism, attention-deficit/hyperactivity disorder (ADHD), obesity, depression, and alcoholism. It was administered predominantly in the form of Desoxyn, which was first formulated by Abbot Laboratories in 1942 (see Figure 1.2).

The general class of amphetamines, which had long been available over the counter, was banned by the Food and Drug Administration in 1959; prescribed amphetamines, however, including methamphetamine, were made widely available to patients throughout the 1960s. In 1967 alone, 23 million prescriptions were filled, and 8 billion tablets of amphetamines were dispensed (Coleman, 2004). Of these prescriptions, 80% were for female patients.

*Figure 1.2.* Pharmaceutical formulation of Desoxyn. From "Meth Awareness" prevention campaign, United States Department of Justice. Retrieved May 5, 2007, from http://www.usdoj.gov/methawareness. In the public domain.

Today methamphetamine in the form of Desoxyn is a highly controlled substance that is not widely prescribed. This is true for all amphetamines, which are increasingly used for illicit purposes (Wolkoff, 1997). Methamphetamine is often a last resort treatment for ADHD, prescribed only after other stimulants such as methylphenidate (Ritalin), dextroamphetamine (Dexedrine), or mixed amphetamines (Adderall) have proven unsuccessful with the patient. When it is prescribed to treat ADHD in children over age 6, the starting dosage is 5 milligrams (mg) per day, which is raised over time to as much as 25 mg per day; for adults, dosing starts at 5 mg up to three times a day. When used to treat obesity in individuals ages 12 and older, prescriptions indicate one 5 mg tablet in the half hour before each meal (Healthyplace, 2002).

Amphetamine, as a chemical entity, is a molecular combination of two related structures, levoamphetamine and destroamphetamine. Levoamphetamine affects nasal pages and has no neurophysiological effects, whereas dextroamphetamine directly affects the brain. The substance methamphetamine, which was originally formulated for the medicinal purposes described earlier, is a methyl derivative of amphetamine with even stronger neurobiological effects.

Anecdotal evidence suggests that speed (amphetamine) was first used recreationally in the United States during the Depression and Prohibition when individuals sought a substitute for alcohol. Nonprescribed use was again seen during World War II, when German, Japanese, and American soldiers used the drug as a sleep inhibitor so that they could stay alert and energized (Iversen, 2006, pp. 71–73). Historical data also suggest that Adolf Hitler was addicted to the drug (Heston & Heston, 1979) and that the drug was made widely available to the Japanese public as a means of improving the productivity of workers involved in military support services (Anglin et al., 2000). American soldiers used amphetamines during the Vietnam War. In fact, American soldiers' use of amphetamine during the Vietnam War was higher than the rest of the world's total use during World War II (M. A. Miller, 1997).

The illegal production of methamphetamine has its historical roots in these initial abuses of speed (amphetamine) in general. The manufacturing of the drug that has come to be known as crystal meth was first recorded during the original "street speed scene" in San Francisco in the 1950s. Production then increased in the mid 1960s when products containing amphetamine were removed from the marketplace and prescription of amphetamines became more highly regulated. As noted earlier in this chapter, until 1951, amphetamine was available without a prescription, and amphetamine-based inhalers were not withdrawn from the market until 1959. Throughout the 1960s the drug was available via prescription and was used to treat depression.

Crystal methamphetamine was first illegally produced by outlawed "biker clubs," such as the Hell's Angels, many of whom were veterans of World War II and later the Korean and Vietnam wars. The nonnormative and sensational lifestyle of bikers, which included motorcycling, fighting, abundant partying, occurring on the fringes of society in the United States, was highly conducive to the manufacturing and use of the drug (Thompson, 1967). Fueled by the demand for pharmaceutical amphetamine, illicitly manufactured powdered methamphetamine was first developed and used by the various members of this counterculture street scene as a means of feeding the users' own addictions. The first crystal methamphetamine labs appeared in San Francisco in the 1960s. However, the development of more efficient methods of cooking crystal methamphetamine in Southern California shifted the center of the industry to San Diego, where the components used to create the drug could be easily trafficked from Mexico. In the 1980s a new form of methamphetamine became available mainly in Hawaii; it was known as "batu" and was imported from the Eastern Pacific (Cho, 1990). What is now known as crystal meth is a derivative of this version of the drug. Since 2000, due in part to the regulation of the materials and substances used to illegally manufacture methamphetamine, Mexico has become one major source of the drug that is abused by Americans (Colliver & Gfroerer, 2006). Describing the importation from Mexico to Washington state, *The Economist* ("Illegal Drugs," 2008) recently reported, "nearly all the meth is made in large Mexican labs and smuggled up Interstate 5, which runs through Pierce County. The product is imported crystalline, purer than the local powder, and more expensive" (¶ 5). These contextual considerations also provide a basis for understanding why the drug infiltrated the West Coast drug scene prior to its emergence in the eastern United States.

Since its initial emergence, there have been what can be considered three endemic periods of recognized methamphetamine use in the United States (Shrem & Halkitis, 2008). The first, post-World War II, has been associated with the abuse of the substance by war veterans. The second period, which began in the mid-1960s, followed a period in which amphetamines were heavily prescribed and available through products on the market. Most recently, the resurgence of methamphetamine use began in the mid-1990s. Abuse of crystal methamphetamine did not disappear from the American landscape during other periods. However, these are the epochs in which most attention had been directed toward the abuse of the drug.

Several factors distinguish the current period of increased methamphetamine prevalence from the previous epochs (Shrem & Halkitis, 2008). First, whereas methamphetamine use had been previously documented on the West Coast and in Midwest regions of the United States, use has spread rapidly to other geographic epicenters, including major eastern cities (Halkitis, Parsons, & Stirratt, 2001; Halkitis, Parsons, & Wilton, 2003b; Rawson, Anglin, & Ling, 2002). Second, the development of new production methods that require only household and store-bought materials and the rise of the Internet as a disseminator of information provide increased access to the means of production. Despite recent attempts through law enforcement and legislation to curtail this production, imports of the drug from Mexico have fueled this third period of crystal methamphetamine use (Colliver & Gfroerer, 2006). Finally, the current surge of methamphetamine use comes at a time when HIV prevalence continues to be a major health threat within the U.S. population (Centers for Disease Control and Prevention [CDC], 2005). Given the strong association between use of the drug and sexual risk taking, especially among certain segments of the population such as gay and bisexual men, where HIV is highly concentrated (Halkitis et al., 2001; Urbina & Jones, 2004; Wainberg, Kolodny, & Drescher, 2006), personal and public health threats extend beyond addiction to methamphetamine itself, creating the potential for a "dual epidemic." *The San Francisco Chronicle* reported (Heredia, 2003) that over 40% of gay men in San Francisco had tried crystal methamphetamine and that close to one third of new HIV seroconversions occurred in men who had used the drug in the recent past. A similar trend was noted in other locations, including New York City. Recognizing this potential, leading AIDS service organizations, such as Gay Men's Health Crisis (GMHC, 2004), convened task forces and implemented educational strategies to address the rising use of methamphetamine.

# NATIONAL TRENDS IN METHAMPHETAMINE USE

As has been previously stated, methamphetamine is used in all segments of American society. Numerous sources of epidemiological data collected at the national level support this assertion. According to the 2004 *National Survey on Drug Use and Health* (NSDUH; Office of Applied Statistics, 2007), a survey that annually samples individuals ages 12 and older to report on their use of illicit drugs in face-to-face interviews, nearly 12 million Americans have tried methamphetamine at some point in their lifetimes; this includes both the use of prescription drugs (i.e., Desoxyn and Methedrine) and non-prescription or illicit methamphetamine. In 2005, an estimated 1.3 million noninstitutionalized persons ages 12 or older (0.5% of the population) had used methamphetamine in the past year. Of this group, approximately 556,000 were female and 741,000 male. However, a decline in use between 2002 and 2005 has been noted (Office of Applied Statistics, 2007). Use also varies by geographic region; between 2002 and 2005, individuals living in the West (1.2%) were more likely to have used methamphetamine in the past year than persons in the Midwest (0.5%), South (0.5%), and Northeast (0.1%). Rates were comparable across gender within regions (see Figures 1.3 and 1.4). Additionally, 0.8% of individuals residing in nonmetropolitan areas reported use of methamphetamine in the last year, as compared with 0.7% in small metropolitan areas and 0.5% in large metropolitan areas, indicating widespread use of the drug outside the country's major cities.

Although regional differences in rates of abuse of crystal methamphetamine once existed (Freese, Obert, Dickow, Cohen, & Lord, 2000), these have disappeared over the last decade. Previously nested primarily on the West Coast of the United States and in the heartland of the country, the drug has since made its way into the major urban centers of the East Coast (Halkitis et al., 2001). Journalistic accounts have documented the emergence of methamphetamine in New York City among gay and bisexual men (Osborne, 2005). Seizures of crystal methamphetamine labs, where the drug is illegally manufactured, were once rare in states like New York, Virginia, Georgia, and Florida but have escalated in numbers between 1999 and 2006. Specifically, the number of clandestine lab incidents in these states rose from 59 in 1999 to 429 in 2006. A comparison of seizures across the United States is shown in Figures 1.5 and 1.6 (U.S. Drug Enforcement Administration, 2006). Although it can be suggested that this increase in seizures is due to greater awareness and law enforcement regarding methamphetamine, the increase in lab seizures has paralleled the rise of documented use of the drug in these regions.

Further evidence of the spread of methamphetamine use across the United States is provided by reports on treatment admissions for use of the substance from SAMHSA (Office of Applied Statistics, 2006b). Although

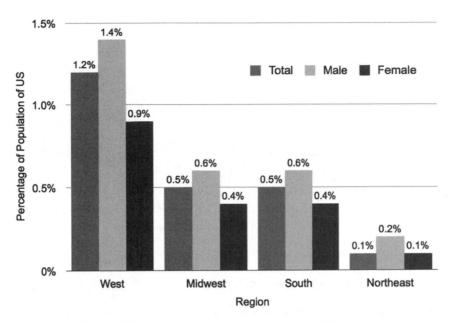

*Figure 1.3.* Methamphetamine use in the United States during 2005 by region as reported by the *National Survey on Drug Use and Health Report* (Office of Applied Statistics, 2007).

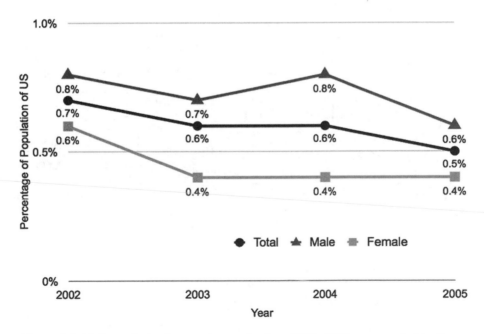

*Figure 1.4.* Methamphetamine use by gender from 2002–2005, as reported by the *National Survey on Drug Use and Health Report* (Office of Applied Statistics, 2007).

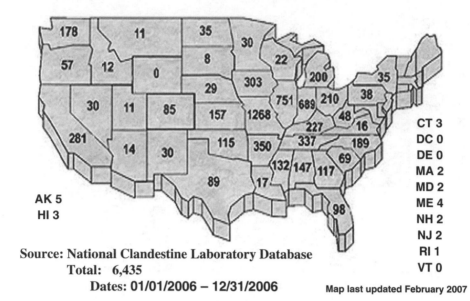

Source: National Clandestine Laboratory Database
Total: 6,435
Dates: 01/01/2006 – 12/31/2006

Map last updated February 2007

*Figure 1.5.* U.S. Drug Enforcement Administration seizures of clandestine laboratories in 2006. From "Maps of Methamphetamine Lab Incidents," U.S. Drug Enforcement Administration. Retrieved March 2, 2006, from http://www.usdoj.gov/dea/concern/map_lab_seizures.html. In the public domain.

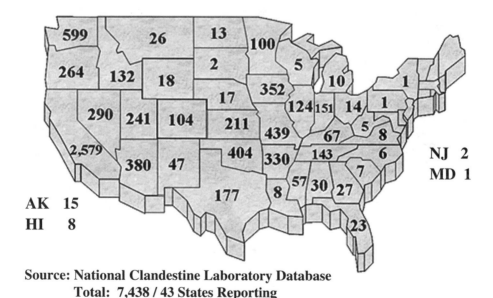

Source: National Clandestine Laboratory Database
Total: 7,438 / 43 States Reporting
Dates: 01/01/99 to 12/31/99

*Figure 1.6.* U.S. Drug Enforcement Administration seizures of clandestine laboratories in 1999. From "Maps of Methamphetamine Lab Incidents," U.S. Drug Enforcement Administration. In the public domain.

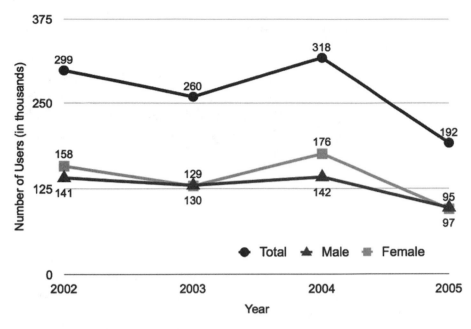

*Figure 1.7.* Initiation of methamphetamine use in 2002–2005 as reported by the *National Survey on Drug Use and Health Report* (Office of Applied Statistics, 2007).

there were 13 admissions per 100,000 individuals ages 12 or older in 1993, this number escalated to 56 per 100,000 by 2003. Dramatic increases in number of admissions were noted in various geographic regions of the country. In Oklahoma the number of admissions jumped from 19 to 117, in Minnesota from 8 to 200, in Hawaii from 52 to 241, and in Connecticut from 1 to 4.

The number of individuals who indicated that they had used methamphetamine for the first time remained relatively stable between 2002 and 2004 but decreased sharply between 2004 and 2005 (318,000 and 192,000 persons, respectively). *POZ* ("Crystal Meth Use Falls," 2007), the leading commercial publication for HIV-seropositive individuals, heralded this announcement. But 1 year does not make a trend. It should also be noted that the rate of decrease in the number of female initiates was steeper than that of male initiates in this 1 year (see Figure 1.7). While the number of male initiates decreased from 142,000 in 2004 to 97,000 in 2005, the number of female first-time users decreased from 176,000 in 2004 to 95,000 in 2005.

Complementary data in regard to the use of methamphetamine in the United States are given by the Treatment Episode Data Set (TEDS), which provide information on treatment admissions and discharges throughout the United States through a system of reporting on the state level to SAMHSA (Office of Applied Statistics, 2006a). Although a precise figure for number of

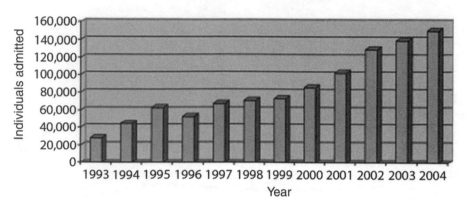

*Figure 1.8.* Data from Office of Applied Statistics, 2006b.

methamphetamine-related admissions cannot be ascertained, as reporting of amphetamines in general and methamphetamine are combined, these data complement those provided by the NSDUH. Figure 1.8 provides an overview of treatment admission for amphetamines and methamphetamine between 1994 and 2004. In 2004, 8% ($n = 151,409$) of all treatment admissions ($N = 1,875,026$) were for the abuse of stimulants, and 85% ($n = 129,079$) of all stimulant admissions and 7% of all total substance abuse admissions were for methamphetamine abuse. Nonmetropolitan areas had the highest rate of admissions (160 per 100,000 admissions for individuals age 12 and older), and large fringe metropolitan areas had the lowest rate (49 admissions per 100,000). Of the primary admissions to treatment for methamphetamine use, 45% were for women. In addition, the average age of those admitted was approximately 30 years old, with admission rates for emergent adults (ages 18–25) higher in rural counties than the most urbanized counties (32% vs. 26% of all amphetamine/methamphetamine admissions). The Drug Abuse Warning Network (DAWN) estimated that 73,400 of the 106 million emergency department visits in 2006 involved methamphetamine abuse (Office of Applied Statistics, 2006a).

The TEDS also provided statistics on the racial and ethnic makeup of methamphetamine users (Office of Applied Statistics, 2006a). Whereas White persons constitute between 77% and 87% of all admissions outside urban centers, they account for only 56% of admission in the inner cities. Admission rates of individuals in other racial or ethnic groups in large metropolitan areas are as follows: Latino (28%), Black (5%), and Asian–Pacific Islander (3%). These proportions are all much lower when admissions are examined outside of the large central metropolitan areas.

Findings from the TEDS are corroborated by recent anecdotal evidence provided by hospitals (Zernike, 2006). In a survey conducted by the National Association of Counties in late 2005, 73% of the 200 county and regional hospitals sampled indicated an increase in the number of methamphetamine-related emergency room visits over the period of 5 years. Moreover, over half of the hospital representatives indicated that they had experienced associated rises in costs in dealing with this segment of the population because many methamphetamine abusers are unemployed and uninsured.

Finally, the Drug Enforcement Administration reported a slight increase in methamphetamine-related arrests between 2004 and 2005, with the figures up from 5,893 to 6,055 (National Drug Intelligence Center, 2006). In addition, between the last quarter of 2004 and January of 2005 there were 1,136 federal offenses for methamphetamine-related charged in U.S. courts, 96% of which involved trafficking of the drug. This number escalated to 3,703 in the first 9 months of 2005, most of which again involved trafficking (U.S. Sentencing Commission, 2006).

National trends also document the rates of use among adolescents through the Youth Risk Behavior Surveillance Study funded by the CDC (2006). Data collected in 2005 indicated that 6.2% of all high school students surveyed had reported use of methamphetamine in their lifetimes, a figure that has been as high as 9.8% (in 2001), whereas 8.3% of emergent adults (ages 19–28) surveyed in 2005 indicated some use of the drug in their lifetimes, with 1.7% of college students indicating use in the last year and 0.1% indicating use in the past month (National Institute on Drug Abuse and University of Michigan, 2006).

## USE OF METHAMPHETAMINE IN POPULATION SUBGROUPS

Despite the media's focus on the pronounced use of methamphetamine among gay and bisexual men, the profile of users outside major metropolitan areas is dramatically different. For example, analyses of epidemiological and statistical reports, coupled with data collected from users and informed experts, suggest that in areas such as the Central Valley of California, users of methamphetamine are dissimilar in their demographics from those in large cities such as San Francisco. The former tend to be heterosexual, begin using in their early teen years, gravitate toward regular use as time progresses, and use until their 30s (Gibson, Leamon, & Flynn, 2002), and the latter group tend to be gay men.

The data from national surveys, records, and surveillance reports do not necessarily present a full picture of the methamphetamine problem in the United States. Numerous large- and small-scale behavioral investigations in segments of the population such as gay and bisexual men, including Black men who have sex with men (MSM), women, and adolescents—emergent adults, add to our understanding of methamphetamine use patterns in these groups.

## Gay and Bisexual Men

The issue of methamphetamine use among the gay and bisexual male population of the United States has garnered much attention in behavioral research undertakings and grassroots efforts. This attention is due in part to hysteria engendered by ad campaigns such as "Buy Crystal, Get HIV for Free" (Fierstein et al., 2006), which led to the publication of a manifesto as an advertisement in *The New York Times* (see Figure 1.9). Although no population-based data for methamphetamine use among gay, bisexual, and other MSM are available, estimates of methamphetamine use in this segment of the population have ranged from 7.4% (Stall et al., 2001) to 10.4% (Halkitis & Parsons, 2002) to as high as 62% in a self-identified drug-using sample (Halkitis, Green, & Mourgues, 2005). Iversen (2006, p. 100) indicated that use among gay men is twice that of the national average. Use among gay and bisexual men in the Northeastern United States has been estimated at 5% while use in the South-Central United States has been estimated at as high as 29% (Hirshfield, Remien, Humberstone, Walavalka, & Chiasson, 2004); on the West Coast rates as high as 36.9% have been noted (Reback & Grella, 1999). Methamphetamine use has been reported by MSM of varying races and ethnicities, with the highest levels documented among MSM who identify as White. However, this pattern among MSM is ever evolving. For example, in one Miami-based study (Fernández et al., 2005), a significantly greater proportion of Latino men than White men reported use of the drug. Use by Asian–Pacific Islander men has been reported at 10% (Choi et al., 2005). In a 2005 study conducted in New York City among a sample of gay, bisexual, and other MSM regularly attending gym facilities for health promotion, use of methamphetamine in the 6 months prior to assessment was noted in 24% of the total sample and in 30%, 28%, and 15% of the Latino, Black, and White samples, respectively (Halkitis et al., 2008).

More nuanced investigations have reported that binge use of methamphetamine is a common pattern among gay, bisexual, and other MSM. *Binge use* has been defined by study participants as "using large quantities of methamphetamine for a period of time—until you run out or just can't physically do it anymore" (Semple, Patterson, & Grant, 2003) and can also be defined as a spiking of use noted over a period of time (Halkitis & Shrem, 2006).

In the United Kingdom, use of the drug in this segment of the population also has begun to emerge. One recent study reported that 13% of men at HIV treatment clinics, 8% of men sampled at HIV testing clinics, and 20% of men surveyed at gyms indicated use in the prior 12 months (Bolding, Hart, Sherr, & Elford, 2006). Methamphetamine used in combination with other sexually disinhibiting substances such as inhalant nitrates (i.e., poppers) has been shown to increase risk of HIV seroconversion in this segment of the population (Plankey et al., 2007). Levels of polydrug use (especially combinations

# GAY MEN
# & CRYSTAL METH
## a manifesto

**Let's face it. There's a problem, and we all need to deal with it.**

Crystal meth poses a threat to many communities, both in this country and around the world. The U.N. says 35 million people use meth, making it the second most frequently used illicit drug behind marijuana. But while most meth use in the U.S. is among heterosexuals, here in New York City it's largely a problem among gay men.

While most gay men have never used meth, approximately 15% have. By chemically blocking inhibitions, it leads many to take sexual risks, resulting in more infections of HIV, syphilis and other diseases.

We've watched as meth worked its way into our lives as an "innocent" party drug and then established itself as a serious threat to our health and prosperity. We've seen it cripple our friends and loved ones, destroy the lives of our youth and mentors, and corrode the spiritual fabric of our community.

**Bottom line, meth is hurting gay men. How can we stand by and do nothing?**

We know that the failed approaches of our nation's "war on drugs" won't help. Addiction cannot be legislated away, and law enforcement is not the answer.

We know that treatment can work. Meth is highly addictive, and recovery is often difficult. While many will struggle, there is a growing army of gay men who have gotten off meth.

And most importantly, we know that love works. Yeah, that might sound corny to some. But love is what motivated gay men to care for one another when the AIDS epidemic hit 25 years ago. Love is what brought us together to fight America's silence and apathy. Love made us insist on safe sex, dramatically reducing new HIV infections.

Love supports without judgment. It challenges self-destruction. It strengthens community. And today, love is why one gay man will help another gay man quit using crystal meth.

**So, here's what we're going to do.**

**We will take responsibility** for our lives and for the health of our community. We will make informed choices about sex and partying, and urge our friends and lovers to do the same.

**We will not be silent.** We will talk to other gay men about the dangers of crystal meth. We will create honest prevention campaigns so that every gay man knows the real risks of meth use.

**We will show compassion** for those who are addicted. Meth is the problem, not those in its grasp. Addicts need treatment, not stigma. And if they're in denial, they need to be challenged by those who love them.

**We will fight** for more money for drug treatment. We will advocate for treatment programs tailored to the needs of gay men.

And finally, **we won't let crystal meth destroy another generation of gay men.** We will continue fighting the hatred that seeks to diminish our self-worth, our sexuality, and our relationships. We will continue to create and strengthen our political groups, our churches, our sports teams, our social clubs, and our families. **We will lead by example, as we have done before.**

*Signed, the Crystal Meth Working Group*

Daniel L. Carlson  Brian Gorman  Bruce Kellerhouse, PhD  Sasha O'Malley  Peter Staley  Bruce Steinberg

**Matthew Bank**
*CEO, HX Media, LLC*

**Lady Bunny**
*DJ/Entertainer*

**Richard D. Burns**
*Executive Director,
LGBT Community Center*

**Dennis deLeon**
*President, Latino Commission on AIDS*

**Hon. Thomas K. Duane**
*New York State Senate, 29th District*

**Gary English**
*Executive Director,
People of Color in Crisis*

**Harvey Fierstein**

**Matt Foreman**
*Executive Director,
National Gay and Lesbian Task Force*

**Howard A. Grossman, MD**
*Executive Director,
American Academy of HIV Medicine*

**Ronald S. Johnson**
*Associate Executive Director,
Gay Men's Health Crisis*

**The Reverend Charles King**
*President, Housing Works*

**Larry Kramer**

**Mark Krueger**

**Jay Laudato**
*Executive Director,
Callen-Lorde Community Health Center*

**Amanda Lepore**
*Transexual Performer*

**Petros Levounis, MD, MA**
*The Addiction Institute of New York*

**Michael Lucas**
*President, Lucas Entertainment*

**Martin Markowitz, MD**
*The Aaron Diamond AIDS Research Center*

**Craig R. Miller**
*Founder, AIDS Walk New York*

**David Mixner**

**Mark Nelson**
*Event Planner/Promoter*

**Tokes Osubu**
*Executive Director,
Gay Men of African Descent*

**Paul Schindler**
*Editor-in-chief, Gay City News*

**Jake Shears**
*Singer/Songsmith, Scissor Sisters*

**Michelangelo Signorile**

**Sean Strub**
*Founder, POZ Magazine*

**Andrew Sullivan**

**Henry van Ameringen**

**Alan Van Capelle**
*Executive Director,
Empire State Pride Agenda*

**Junior Vasquez**

**Tom Viola**
*Executive Director,
Broadway Cares/Equity Fights AIDS*

**Rufus Wainwright**

**Phill Wilson**
*Executive Director, Black AIDS Institute*

**Jeff Whitty**

*Organizational affiliations are listed for identification purposes only, and do not imply any endorsement by the organizations listed.*

*Figure 1.9.* Gay men and crystal meth: A manifesto. From "Crystal Meth Manifesto," by the Crystal Meth Working Group, New York, featured as a full-page ad in the *New York Times,* June 15, 2006. Copyright 2006 by The Crystal Meth Working Group. Reprinted with permission.

of methamphetamine, MDMA [3,4-methylenedioxymethamphetamine; i.e., Ecstasy], and ketamine) are particularly high for gay and bisexual men navigating circuit parties (i.e., raves or all-night dance parties; Lee, Galanter, Dermatis, & McDowell, 2003).

## Black Communities

Epidemiological and drug surveillance data indicate that methamphetamine abuse is a growing health concern in Black communities (Maxwell, 2004), yet this remains a highly understudied area. In a 2005 study of 311 "health-seeking" gay, bisexual, and other MSM attending New York City gyms, more Black men than White men reported methamphetamine use (28.1% vs. 15.2%; Halkitis et al., 2008). However, on the basis of data from the 2004 CDC National HIV Behavioral Surveillance System, methamphetamine-using MSM are more likely to be White than non-White men (50.4% vs. 43.5%; Mansergh, Purcell, et al., 2006). In a large-scale study of club drug use in New York City conducted between 2000 and 2005, 49% of the Black men ($n = 66$) in the sample indicated use of methamphetamine in the 4 months prior to assessment. Black methamphetamine users tended not to reside in neighborhoods considered traditionally gay, generally had lower levels of educational attainment and income, and were more likely to be HIV-positive than other methamphetamine users. In terms of frequency and reasons for use, however, Black methamphetamine users did not differ from users of other races in any substantive way (Halkitis & Jerome, 2008). Another study conducted among Black methamphetamine-using men in New York City revealed the following salient themes: (a) methamphetamine use as means of self-medication for depression and anxiety; (b) high levels of childhood trauma, including sexual abuse; (c) double and triple stigmatization stemming from sexual identity, race, and/or HIV status; (d) feelings of being excluded from both Black communities and White gay communities; (e) introduction of methamphetamine through navigation in White gay social circles; (f) high levels of sexual risk taking with both men and women while under the influence; and (g) use of methamphetamine in combination or conjunction with crack cocaine (Jerome, 2007).

Our knowledge about methamphetamine use and Black MSM is only beginning to develop. Empirical studies focusing on methamphetamine use in heterosexual Black communities are virtually absent from the literature. In one of the few studies that focuses on Black communities, injection use of methamphetamine is reported among Black heterosexually identified men in Los Angeles (Wohl et al., 2002). Those who injected methamphetamine were three times more likely than noninjector persons to also be HIV positive. Despite identification as heterosexual, 71 of the 272 men in the sample indicated engaging in anal intercourse with another man. In a more general sample of Black male and female injection drug users (IDUs; Somlai, Kelly, McAuliffe, Ksobiech, & Hackl, 2003), risk of HIV was highest among those who injected crack cocaine or methamphetamine.

## Women

Although women indicate use of methamphetamine at rates comparable to those of men, this segment of the population remains relatively understudied. Senjo (2007) noted, "the majority of substance abuse literature pertains to male alcoholism and male heroin addiction. Hence, the small number of studies on female meth users comes as no surprise" (p. 55).

Among incarcerated women, methamphetamine use has been associated with drug abuse in general, sexual assault, and concomitant psychiatric symptoms (Vik & Ross, 2003). Incarcerated female methamphetamine users tend to be White; to have low levels of educational attainment; to be mothers; and to be divorced, separated, or single. Women constituted 76 of the 204 individuals in a sample of methamphetamine users who had been arrested in Northern Utah in 2001 (Senjo, 2007). Of these female methamphetamine users, 86% were also White, and approximately 85% possessed a minimum of a high school degree. The women in the Utah sample indicated patterns of methamphetamine use that reflected a middle-class orientation to use of the substance and not a lifestyle of criminal activity.

In a somewhat restricted sample of women socializing in New York City dance clubs ($N = 1,104$; Kelly, Parsons, & Wells, 2006), lifetime methamphetamine use was reported by 13% of those surveyed. Women ages 30 or older were more likely to use the drug (53% vs. 39%), as were those who identified as lesbian or bisexual (47% vs. 37%). In a more general sample of heterosexual 18- to 25-year-olds in New York City from whom we collected data in 2006, use of methamphetamine in the prior 6 months was indicated by 8% of the women surveyed. Comparisons of female methamphetamine users with male methamphetamine users who presented at public treatment clinics in Los Angeles County in 1996 (Brecht, O'Brien, von Mayrhauser, & Anglin, 2004) indicated many similarities between the groups, including age at onset of methamphetamine use and any substance, polydrug use, and time between first use and chronic use of the drug. Women, however, were less likely to inject drugs such as methamphetamine (37% vs. 54%) and were more likely to identify a spouse or a boyfriend or girlfriend as the individual who had introduced them to methamphetamine (20% vs. 9%).

## Adolescents and Emergent Adults

Analyses of the 2002 NSDUH indicated a high level of methamphetamine use among adolescents and emergent adults (Wu, Schlenger, & Galvin,

2006). Of the 19,084 participants included in the analyses, 38.3% indicated some lifetime stimulant use, all of whom indicated that methamphetamine is one of stimulants they had used. Similarly, of the 43.7% who had used stimulants in the year prior to data collection, all had used methamphetamine. Results from the Study of Adolescent Health indicated that during 2001 to 2002, 2.8% of 14,322 18- to 26-year-olds had used methamphetamine and that 1.3% had used the drug in the month prior to assessment (Iritani, Hallfors, & Bauer, 2007). Data from a convenience sample of emergent adults (18–25) who attended social venues in New York City in 2002 (Parsons, Halkitis, & Bimbi, 2006) demonstrated that 9.4% had used methamphetamine in the prior 6 months. Rates were higher for men than for women (12.8% vs. 5.8%), but they were still highest among gay and bisexual men (14.2%). Rates for other groups were as follows: heterosexual men (10.7%), heterosexual women (6.5%), and lesbian–bisexual women (4.9%). In our 2006 sample of 261 primarily college-attending 18- to 25-year-olds, 3.4% reported lifetime methamphetamine use, and less than 1% reported use in the month prior to assessment. Degenhardt (2005) reported similar patterns when comparing gay–bisexual men and women to their heterosexual counterparts. Among 831 college students surveyed at two state universities, 42% indicated lifetime use of some club drug (including methamphetamine) and of these, 22.6% reported using seven or more times in the previous year (Simons, Gaher, Correia, & Bush, 2005). Patterns related to developmental stage and sexual identity have further confirmed higher rates of use of methamphetamine among high school gay and bisexual students in British Columbia, with 26.7% of the gay–bisexual students indicating use of methamphetamine in the year prior to assessment as compared with 1.8% of their heterosexual peers (Lampinen, McGhee, & Martin, 2006). Among treatment-seeking adolescents in Southern California (70% of whom were male and 55% of whom were White), older participants and female participants were more likely than those in their comparison cohorts to use methamphetamine (Rawson, Gonzales, Obert, McCann, & Brethen, 2005).

It should be noted that use of methamphetamine among adolescents and emergent adults is not a new phenomenon. Between 1989 and 1996, information regarding methamphetamine use was collected in schools throughout the United States (Oetting et al., 2000), using the American Drug and Alcohol Survey (Oetting, Beauvais, & Edwards, 1985). Rates of recent use and lifetime use remained stable between 1989 and 1992, but between 1992 and 1996 rates doubled, most drastically in the western United States. (As noted in chap. 2, this volume, some have suggested that this trend is due to the increased purity of the drug available.) Rates of use were slightly higher among males than females and among ethnic minorities, including American Indian, Latino, and Asian American people.

# METHAMPHETAMINE IN THE CONTEXT OF POLYDRUG USE

In considering the reality of methamphetamine use in the lives of men and women, young and old, gay and straight, it is also imperative to recognize that use of the drug occurs in the contexts of people's lives, in which multiple identities and a multitude of behaviors are being undertaken and negotiated. Furthermore, use of methamphetamine does not occur in a vacuum or only at one point in time; it is characterized by complex interrelationships between who people are, how they cope with life stressors, and the environments in which they navigate.

Perhaps one of the most important elements to consider is that methamphetamine users, more often than not, are polydrug users (Halkitis, Green, et al., 2005; Uys & Niesink, 2005). Methamphetamine is used in direct combination with multiple substances, simultaneously or "in tandem," as has been noted by Gorman, Nelson, Applegate, and Scrol (2004), or multiple drugs are used within a longer period of time, not necessarily concomitantly.

Many gay and bisexual men who use methamphetamine engage in polydrug use (Halkitis, Green, et al., 2005; Lee et al., 2003; Patterson, Semple, Zians, & Strathdee, 2005). Patterns of polydrug use cross ethnic and racial lines; such use has been noted in Latino (Fernández et al., 2005) and Asian–Pacific Islander MSM (Operario et al., 2006). It has also been noted among gay and bisexual high school students (Lampinen et al., 2006). In a longitudinal investigation of club drug-using men, patterns of methamphetamine use over the course of a 1-year period were found to be closely related to patterns of both Ecstasy and gamma-hydroxybutyrate (GHB) use (Halkitis, Palamar, & Pandey, 2007). Moreover, 64% of these men also reported use of alcohol, 55% reported use of Ecstasy, 45% reported use of ketamine, 38% reported use of marijuana, and 36% reported recreational use of Viagra in combination with methamphetamine (Halkitis, Green, et al., 2005). Finally, in documenting the sequence of methamphetamine use initiation in this sample, Halkitis and Palamar (2008) showed that methamphetamine users often use cocaine and Ecstasy prior to adding methamphetamine to their repertoire of drug-taking behaviors. Similarly, Lee et al. (2003) found that use of Ecstasy is associated with use of methamphetamine, as well as with ketamine and cocaine, among club-attending men. Semple et al. (2003) documented that binge-methamphetamine users reported consuming approximately four drinks per day during a 2-month period of assessment and that 12.2% of these men also reported using heroin during that period. In a study of 603 current "hard drug" (e.g., cocaine, methamphetamine) using MSM in North Carolina (Zule, Costenbader, Coomes, & Wechsberg, 2007), 97% of the methamphetamine users reported concurrent use of at least one other hard drug. Halkitis and Green (2007) reported that the combination of methamphetamine and Viagra is common but also environment driven; it is likely to be seen at sex and circuit parties and is less likely to be seen among Black methamphetamine users (Halkitis & Jerome, 2008). Among HIV-positive MSM who use methamphetamine, other commonly used drugs are alcohol (48%), marijuana (88%), and inhalant nitrates (76%; Semple, Patterson, & Grant, 2002). Among MSM, combined methamphetamine and inhalant nitrate use has been associated with a higher relative hazard for HIV seroconversion than use of either drug in isolation (Plankey et al., 2007).

Polydrug use patterns among women have also been noted. Brecht et al. (2004) indicated that 100% of methamphetamine-using women also reported use of alcohol, 99% use of marijuana, 87% use of cocaine, and 75% use of hallucinogens. In addition, among a sample of active methamphetamine-injecting women, 7% reported injection of other drugs in the period of assessment (2 months; Semple, Grant, & Patterson, 2004). In the same sample, 86% of the women also reported use of alcohol, and 69% reported use of marijuana. Among 39 incarcerated female felons who were interviewed, use of alcohol and marijuana was nearly universal; patterns of polydrug use included several substances, including methamphetamine (Kassebaum & Chandler, 1994). Lorvick, Martinez, Gee, and Kral (2006) examined the patterns of drug use among methamphetamine-injecting and noninjecting females between 2003 and 2005. In this sample of 477 methamphetamine users, 23% also drank alcohol daily, 72% had used crack in the 30 days prior to assessment, 87% had injected heroin, and 44% had injected speedball. Methamphetamine injectors were more likely to inject heroin and "speedball" than noninjectors but were equally likely to have used crack and to drink alcohol daily. Finally, pregnant women who had contacted the Motherisk Alcohol and Substance Use Helpline at The Hospital for Sick Children were examined with regard to their drug use patterns (Ho, Karimi-Tabesh, & Koren, 2001). In this study, women who had used Ecstasy ($n = 132$) were compared with a nonusing clinic sample ($n = 122$). Ecstasy users were also more likely than nonusers to have used amphetamines (including methamphetamine), ketamine, GHB, cocaine, and marijuana, again confirming the polydrug-using characteristics of women. In a more recent study of both Mexican and Mexican American women in the border counties of San Diego and Imperial, rates of methamphetamine use were among the highest in the country, and this use frequently occurred in the context of polydrug use (Rogala & Lopez-Zetina, 2008).

Among high school and college students, polydrug use patterns are most pronounced among methamphetamine users regardless of sexual orientation (Lampinen et al., 2006). Simons, Gaher, et al. (2005) corroborated similar patterns in a sample of college students. In the analyses undertaken by Wu et al., Gaher, (2006), 17.7% of 16- to 23-year-olds reported use of three or more club drugs in the previous year. Among those who reported use of methamphetamine, 46% indicated use of three or more club drugs in the period of assessment. In addition, 99% of methamphetamine users reported use of alcohol, 98% reported use of marijuana, and 56% reported use of inhalants.

In a sample of 113 adolescents who were 17 years old on average, 61% of whom were female and who were admitted to a treatment center in British Columbia for methamphetamine addiction treatment from March 2001 through December 2005, a review of medical records indicated a high rate of polydrug use (Callaghan, Brands, Taylor, & Lentz, 2007). Specifically, 67% also reported "problematic" use of alcohol in the 30 days prior to admission, 63% reported cocaine use, 89% reported marijuana use, 13% reported heroin use, and 64% reported hallucinogen use.

Methamphetamine users combine the drug with other substances to achieve a particular type of high or to balance the stimulant effects of the drug (Degenhardt & Topp, 2003; Palamar & Halkitis, 2006). Therefore, the use of substances such as marijuana in combination with methamphetamine is very common. The use of Viagra with methamphetamine serves to counter the erectile dysfunction (Halkitis et al., 2001) associated with the latter's use. However, for users of methamphetamine, the simultaneous use of illicit substances or prescribed substances increases health risks, including the risk of overdose through drug synergism; decreases cognitive function and inhibition; and may exacerbate associated risk behaviors such as unprotected sex, which could lead to the transmission of HIV and other bacterial and viral pathogens (Fernández et al., 2005; Halkitis & Parsons, 2002; Mattison, Ross, Wolfson, & Frankin, 2001; Operario et al., 2006; Palamar & Halkitis, 2006; Patterson et al., 2005).

## CONCLUSION

In 2002, Rawson et al. asked "Will the methamphetamine problem go away?" (p. 5). Since that time, this drug, which has captured the fascination of the American public and the American media, but not the American government, continues to be a problem that has not gone away. I have referred to the current state of methamphetamine abuse in the United States as one that fuels a "dual epidemic" because the synergy of addiction to methamphetamine and sexual risk taking is likely to exacerbate the transmissions of HIV and other viral and bacterial sexual pathogens (Halkitis et al., 2001). Although its "epidemic" nature is perhaps subject to debate, the drug is nonetheless very present in the lives of many Americans who struggle daily with the overlapping conditions of poor mental health, drug use, and sexual risk taking, which Stall et al. (2003) so eloquently labeled "syndemics." To their credit, Rawson et al. (2002) suggested that methamphetamine use and addiction may not be a long-term health challenge, but it does hold the potential to become more pervasive in the short term. The last several years have shown this statement to be true.

Unfortunately, much attention to the drug has focused on the drug culture of gay and bisexual men, who, as a segment of the population, have a long history of drug use and addiction fueled in part by the stigmatization and marginalization they face. But gay men as a group are just one facet of the methamphetamine problem in our country. As has been shown, the drug is a nondiscriminator, crossing the socially constructed barriers of gender, race, ethnicity, and sexual orientation. What may differ, however, are the factors that predispose individuals from different segments of the population to use this drug and the ultimate effects that methamphetamine has on each segment of the populace. Thus, an understanding of methamphetamine addiction in the United States requires an appreciation of the diversity of lives that the drug permeates, as well as an understanding of the symbiosis and interchange that exist between the biological, psychological, and sociological elements related to the use of this drug. The remainder of this volume is written from this biopsychosocial perspective in hopes of providing the reader with a holistic understanding of methamphetamine addiction in the United States and an appreciation of the struggles faced by those enthralled with the beauty of methamphetamine. In chapter 2, consideration is given to the chemistry of methamphetamine, its formulation, and most important the impact of the drug on the neurological system, an understanding of which may help clarify why so many are drawn to this drug.

# 2

# THE CHEMISTRY AND BIOLOGY
# OF METHAMPHETAMINE USE

A holistic understanding of methamphetamine addiction and its impact on lives and society is rooted, in part, on an appreciation of the chemical properties of the drug, as well as its impact on the biological system of the organism and the chemistry of the human brain. In this chapter the chemical structure of methamphetamine is fully considered. Thereafter, the impact of methamphetamine on the human brain is fully elucidated, as are the modes by which users introduce the drug into their systems.

## CHEMICAL STRUCTURE OF METHAMPHETAMINE

Methamphetamine, known also by its chemical names dextro-N-$\alpha$-dimethyl-phenethylamine and desoxyephedrine, is pharmacologically categorized under the phenylethylamine class of stimulant drugs and is a methyl derivative of amphetamine given by the chemical symbol $C_{10}H_{15}N$. In structure, methamphetamine is related to 3,4-methylenedioxymethamphetamine (MDMA; i.e., Ecstasy), with the former functioning as an enhancer of sexuality and the latter as an enhancer of sensuality. Methamphetamine also possesses a similar structure to amphetamine, with the only difference being the addition

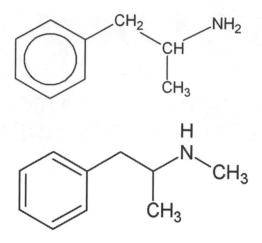

*Figure 2.1.* Chemical structure of amphetamine and methamphetamine.

of a methyl group (see Figure 2.1). The chemical composition of methamphetamine resembles that of ephedrine, a drug that has been used as stimulant and appetite suppressant. Ephedrine is also a key component of illegally manufactured methamphetamine and is found in the Chinese herb medicine Ma huang (*Ephedra sinica*). The structure is also related to pseudoephedrine, a component used to cook methamphetamine and the basis of the decongestant Sudafed; Ritalin, a pharmaceutical that is often prescribed to treat attention-deficit/hyperactivity disorder; and epinephrine. However, methamphetamine is the most powerful of this stimulant class of drugs. As a result, methamphetamine is a Schedule II drug under federal regulations because it has a high potential for abuse with a severe likelihood to cause dependence (Swan, 1996). A variant of methamphetamine, *l*-methamphetamine, is a major component of the Vicks Vapor Inhaler, which is sold as a nasal decongestant. However, this variation of methamphetamine has no psychoactive effects (Gahlinger, 2001, p. 208).

## CRYSTAL METH

In its purest form, illegally produced methamphetamine is a translucent crystal similar in appearance to rock candy or salt that can dissolve in water. This drug may be a 98% to 100% pure form of methamphetamine hydrochloride. Although it has an appearance similar to that of pure methamphetamine, it is rarely equal in purity to the pharmaceutical formulation manufactured in legal laboratories. Illegally produced methamphetamine is typically yellowish, brownish, or offwhite, although it is closer to a pure white powder, depending on its purity and the integrity of the cooking process, the filtering process

*Figure 2.2.* Crystal methamphetamine street versions. Retrieved March 1, 2008, from http://www.kci.org/meth_info/Meth_Pictures/pictures1.htm. Copyright 2008 by KCI: The Anti-Meth Site. Reprinted with permission.

(often undertaken with a coffee filter), and the substances from which it is made. Thus, for example, a street version of crystal methamphetamine may be pink if it is made from pink-colored pseudoephedrine medications (see Figure 2.2). The crystallization of the drug is due to its high salt content (Marcovitz, 2006, p. 24).

More recent formulations of the drug have been created in a pill format known as "yaba." These brightly colored tablets, which were first developed in the Eastern Pacific, are often flavored like candy or manufactured with caffeine (Iversen, 2006, p. 100). Like the crystalline formulation, these pills can be crushed into powder and may be administered via inhalation, injection, or smoking.

## METHAMPHETAMINE AND THE BRAIN

Like all drugs, the effects of methamphetamine on numerous bodily systems, as well as the associated emotional and physiological reactions to using the drug, are regulated through the chemical changes enacted in the brain.

Methamphetamine is a cationic lipophilic molecule that has dramatic effects on both the sympathetic and central nervous systems (CNS; Davidson, Gow, Lee, & Ellinwood, 2001) and is more potent than its parent compound, amphetamine, because its lipophilic nature allows for greater penetration of the CNS (Meredith, Jaffe, Ang-Lee, & Saxon, 2005). Methamphetamine and other stimulants cause the release of newly synthesized *catecholamine* in the CNS that partially blocks the presynaptic reuptake of these neurotransmitters (Cho & Melega, 2002). Catecholamines are chemical compounds, such as the neurotransmitters (chemicals that transmit signals in the neurons of the brain) *dopamine* and *norepinephrine,* which are derived from the amino acid tyrosine. With methamphetamine, the impact of the drug is due to the direct effect that the drug has on the neurotransmitter dopamine and the associated dopamine system; however, the drug also impacts the norepinephrine, epinephrine, and serotonin systems.

## METHAMPHETAMINE AND THE DOPAMINE SYSTEM

Dopamine is actively involved in controlling bodily movement, thought processes, emotions, and pleasure. This neurotransmitter is used primarily in the *mesencephalon* (also known as the midbrain; see Figure 2.3), a collection of approximately 40 nuclei and tracts that control various aspects of a person's personality and behavior (Holley, 2005, p. 31). Within the midbrain exists the *nucleus accumbens* (the pleasure center of the brain), where all sensations pleasurable, including sex, are regulated. Through the mesolimbic pathway, signals are mediated between the nucleus accumbens and the *ventral tegmental area* (see Figure 2.4). This creates a "brain-reward" circuit when dopamine is released. In addition, transmissions from this section of the midbrain are directed and sent to the frontal lobe and the prefrontal cortex, in particular. Here emotional information is processed and decisions are made with regard to the reaction to these emotions enacted by the pleasurable experiences. It is in this area of the brain where an individual's social cognitions are controlled. For example, this section of the brain regulates how an individual reacts to another's behavior or the manner with which one is able to detect the feelings of another. This ability to make quick and accurate assessments of social situations, which is essential for functioning, requires a complex understanding of the beliefs, desires, and emotions that motivate people's actions (Homer et al., 2008). The process of integration and comprehension of these domains has been called a *theory of mind* (Premack & Woodruff, 1978). As will be further explored in chapter 4, methamphetamine users have been shown to perform less effectively than their control counterparts on theory of mind tasks (Homer et al., 2008).

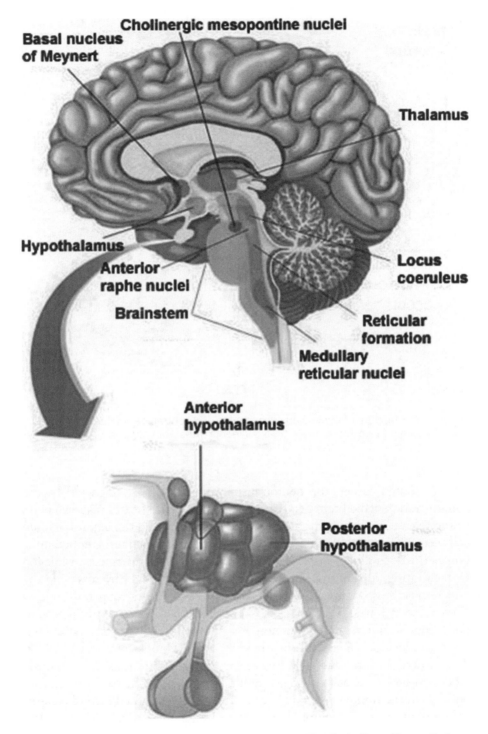

*Figure 2.3.* Structure of the midbrain. Retrieved from The Brain From Top to Bottom Web site: http://thebrain.mcgill.ca

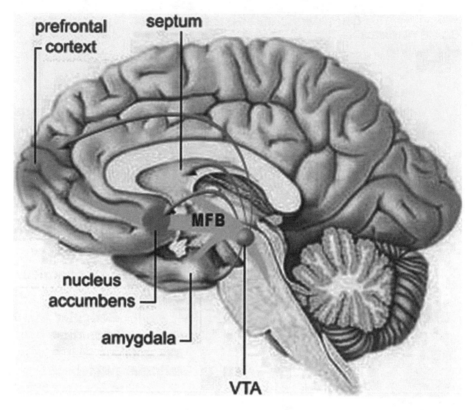

*Figure 2.4.* Structure of the nucleus accumbens and ventral tegmentum. Retrieved from The Brain From Top to Bottom Web site: http://thebrain.mcgill.ca

As noted earlier, the neurotransmitter that is most impacted by the administration of methamphetamine is dopamine. First, the drug causes a brain cell to release dopamine into the space between itself and the adjoining brain cell (Lee, 2006, p. 30). Animal studies also have shown that methamphetamine targets the dopamine transporter, which regulates dopaminergic transmission by facilitating dopamine reuptake (Davidson et al., 2001) by reversing the direction of the dopamine transporter, leading to an increased dopamine release (Giros, Jaber, Jones, Wightman, & Caron, 1996). In other words, methamphetamine stimulates the production of dopamine by the synapses in the mid-brain (under normal conditions, these synapses would reabsorb the excess dopamine that is produced); however, methamphetamine simultaneously blocks dopamine reuptake, and as a result, high levels of the neurotransmitter build up in the midbrain (see Figure 2.5), causing a sustained rush of pleasurable feelings. It should be noted that unlike methamphetamine, which causes both an increased release of dopamine and an obstruction of reuptake, cocaine impacts the dopamine system only through the reuptake process

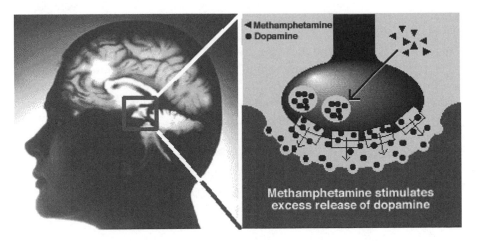

*Figure 2.5.* Dopamine release at synapses. From *Methamphetamine: Abuse and Addiction* by the National Institute on Drug Abuse (NIDA, 2002). In the public domain.

(Lee, 2006, p. 31). Because of the dual effects of methamphetamine on the dopamine system, levels of the neurotransmitter can be up to 1,500% higher than normal. When the effect of the drug finally decreases, however, dopamine levels gradually decrease. Methamphetamine users describe this sensation as "crashing," when feelings of euphoria and well-being are lost. This has also been referred to in the popular media as "Suicide Tuesday," after a weekend of partying with methamphetamine. Euphoric sensations do not reemerge until the dopamine system is restimulated. For many users, this is the trigger for the addictive cycle. Finally, continual overstimulation of dopamine neurons by methamphetamine can cause nerve cell death.

## THE EFFECT OF METHAMPHETAMINE ON OTHER NEUROTRANSMITTER SYSTEMS

In addition to impacting the dopamine system, methamphetamine affects, albeit less dramatically, the norepinephrine, epinephrine, and serotonin systems. Norepinephrine, also known as *noradrenaline*, is the neurotransmitter that provides the basis for maintaining alertness, attention, rest, and memory. It is also the chemical that the body uses to produce adrenaline. Methamphetamine prevents the reuptake of norepinephrine, but it does not increase the production of this neurotransmitter. This results in the ability of the methamphetamine user to go hours without any rest or sleep. It is unclear whether methamphetamine use causes the death of norepinephrine-producing neurons. Similarly, methamphetamine blocks the reuptake of epinephrine, also known as *adrenaline*, thus preventing users from feeling tired or overexerted. The high level of epinephrine in the synaptic gaps, in part, creates the high-energy level that methamphetamine users experience.

Finally, methamphetamine impacts the serotonin system. Serotonin is the neurotransmitter associated with mood, appetite, and sexual behavior, and unlike the other previously described neurotransmitters, it is a monamine neurotransmitter. As a result, the impact of methamphetamine on this system is slightly different. Whereas methamphetamine increases the production of dopamine, it interacts with neurons to decrease the release of serotonin. Because this neurotransmitter is key to regulating mood, low levels of the chemical may cause mood changes. Individuals with low levels of serotonin are more likely to experience anxiety, depression, and to demonstrate impulsive and violent behaviors.

## THE ADMINISTRATION OF METHAMPHETAMINE

Crystal methamphetamine is used in a variety of different ways. The drug usually appears in a crystalline form, and users often grind and crush the substance into a powder prior to use; however, the rock nature of the drug is appropriate for those who smoke the drug. The most common modes of administration include inhalation, ingestion, injection, and smoking (Anglin, Burke, Perrochet, Stamper, & Dawd-Noursi, 2000). Wolkoff (1997) indicated that much of the increased use of the drug in recent years is associated with the smoking of the crystallized methamphetamine, "ice." Some gay, bisexual, and other men who have sex with men insert methamphetamine into their rectums either by placing the substance directly into the anus or through use of a syringe in which dissolved methamphetamine is placed into the rectum. Using methamphetamine in this manner is referred to as a "booty bump" (Halkitis, Parsons, & Stirratt, 2001). Recently, in an effort to disguise their methamphetamine use while seeking sexual partners online, gay men have used the expression "to the poinT" in order to indicate they are injecting methamphetamine.

Smoking and injection of methamphetamine (also known as "slamming") produces the fastest rates of absorption, demonstrating a lag time of approximately 7 to 10 seconds if smoked, 15 to 30 seconds if injected intravenously, and 5 minutes if injected intramuscularly. Inhalation (snorting) creates a slow rate of absorption with a lag time of approximately 3 to 5 minutes, and ingestion–oral administration produces the slowest rate of absorption at approximately 20 to 30 minutes.

The use of methamphetamine via intranasal administration requires the use of straws or spoons similar to those paraphernalia used for cocaine, which holds a potential risk for the transmission of pathogens such as hepatitis C. Smokers use pipes (see Figure 2.6) similar to those used by individuals who use

*Figure 2.6.* Smoking methamphetamine. Retrieved March 1, 2008, from http://www. kci.org/meth_info/Meth_Pictures/pictures1.htm. Copyright 2008 by KCI: The Anti-Meth Site. Reprinted with permission.

crack cocaine. Of course, the use a syringe is required for either intramuscular or intravenous injection, which exacerbates the potential transmission of pathogens such as HIV if unsanitized needles are shared. The body of the syringe without the needle is used for booty bumping.

The route of methamphetamine administration chosen by the user is determined by numerous factors, including (a) purity of the substance, (b) social environments and contexts, and (c) level of addiction or history of use. Colliver and Gfroerer (2006) suggested that smoking is a favored route of administration when the drug is imported from Mexico because the purity of the substance is higher. The increased popularity of smoking methamphetamine is substantiated by the Treatment Episode Data Sets (TEDS) reported by the Substance Abuse and Mental Health Services Administration (Office of Applied Statistics, 2006c) as shown in Figure 2.7. TEDS data show that hospital emergency treatments for methamphetamine because of smoking of the substance rose consistently between 1993 and 2003, whereas all emergency visits because of other modes of administration decreased during that period. Among 260 individuals who sought treatment for methamphetamine at a Los Angeles facility in 1996, almost 50% reported inhalation as their main route of administration, whereas one quarter each reported smoking and injection (von Mayrhauser, Brecht, & Anglin, 2002). Regardless of route of administration, the ultimate effects of the drug on the brain and

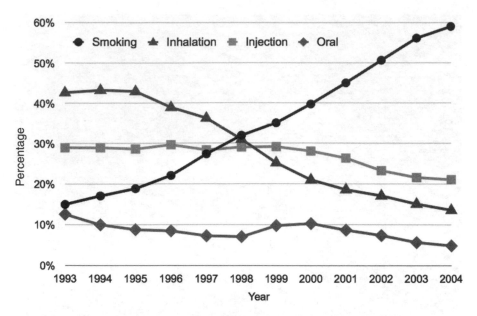

*Figure 2.7.* Mode of methamphetamine administration for treatment admissions between 1993–2004. Data from Office of Applied Statistics, 2006.

the neurotransmitter systems are similar. However, because illegally produced methamphetamine is rarely pure (see chap. 3, this volume), the manner in which the drug is administered may have differential effects on one's physical well-being, depending on the chemicals with which the drug is produced, adulterated, or both.

Support for how contextual and geographic factors relate to mode of methamphetamine administration can be seen by further examining data from the TEDS (Office of Applied Statistics, 2006a). A comparison of three geographic areas—San Diego, Minneapolis/St. Paul, and Texas—demonstrate differential patterns of inhaling, injecting, and smoking methamphetamine as shown in Figure 2.8. Further data suggest that a single mode of administration may dominate in a given environment. For gay and bisexual men, the use of crystal methamphetamine via a booty bump is often associated with sexual contexts (Halkitis et al., 2001; Halkitis, Shrem, & Martin, 2005). This method allows the individual to more easily engage in receptive anal intercourse, physically, by easing the discomfort associated with rectal insertion, and emotionally, by lowering inhibitions regarding anal penetration.

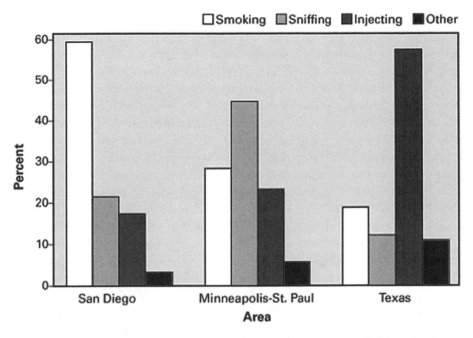

*Figure 2.8.* Treatment admission by mode of methamphetamine administration in San Diego, CA, Minneapolis/St. Paul, MO, and Texas in 2000–2001. Data from Office of Applied Statistics, 2006.

Although smoking has become an increasingly popular mode of administering methamphetamine, this type of use of the drug is relatively new and may be a characteristic of the present epidemic in the United States as well as in other regions of the world, such as Japan, where methamphetamine is widely abused (Matsumoto et al., 2002). "Methamphetamine smoking was first detected by treatment centers in Hawaii in the summer of 1986 with wider recognition of the problem coming later" (M. Miller, 1991, p. 72). An investigation that compared Japanese methamphetamine users who only smoked the drug with those who only injected the drug, and with a third group who initially smoked but later injected, indicated that those who smoke the drug are more likely than injectors to lose control when using the drug more frequently as well as to demonstrate psychotic episodes sooner from the initial use of methamphetamine (Matsumoto et al., 2002). In earlier work, Matsumoto (2000) showed an association between smoking methamphetamine and appetite control. Moreover, it is suggested that the smoking of methamphetamine may hold greater appeal for younger users and exacerbate the drug epidemic. Smoking has been previously associated with the expansion of other drug addictions, including cocaine (Gossop, Griffiths, Powis, & Strang, 1994) and heroin (Strang, Griffiths, & Gossop, 1997). Finally, smoked methamphetamine is more addictive than oral methamphetamine, which is twice as addictive as amphetamine (Beebe & Walley, 1995).

In addition to epidemiological reports, numerous behavioral studies document the manner in which methamphetamine is administered. In a sample of 311 gay, bisexual, and other men who have sex with men recruited at gym facilities in New York City, inhalation and smoking were the most commonly reported modes of administration; 24.3% reported that they inserted methamphetamine in the rectum (i.e., booty bump) and only 16% of men indicated using only one mode of administration (Halkitis et al., 2008). In a sample of both binge and nonbinge methamphetamine users, Semple, Patterson, and Grant (2003) identified approximately equal rates for inhaling, smoking, and injecting the drug, with inhalation being most popular (75.6%–79.6%) followed by smoking (71.4%–73.2%) and injection (30.0%–40.8%). Similarly, in a treatment-based sample (Brecht, O'Brien, von Mayrhauser, & Anglin, 2004), 44% of the 350 individuals reported inhalation of methamphetamine, 34% reported smoking, and 20% reported injection, with no differences between male and female individuals in terms of mode of administration. Among 98 methamphetamine-using women in San Diego, modes of administration for a period for 2 months prior to assessment were as follows: 83% smoking, 66% inhalation, 25% injection, 9% ingestion, and 9% insertion in the rectum (Semple, Grant, & Patterson, 2004).

## CONCLUSION

For methamphetamine users, the interaction of the drug with the dopamine system, as well as other neurotransmitter pathways in the brain, provides the basis for the enormous pleasure associated with use of the substance and inevitably the addiction, which manifests itself in a number of ways. For all users, such an enormous burden on these neurological systems may have long-term and irreversible physiological and psychological consequences. For those in the early stages of life (when the brain still remains relatively plastic and potentially more susceptible to long-term damage), the use of and exposure to methamphetamine may have even more pronounced long-term impacts. As if the addictive nature of the drug was not enough to ensure its infiltration into adolescent and emergent adult populations, recent formulations of methamphetamine in which the drug is cooked with cocoa, chocolate, Jell-O, or red energy drinks to disguise the bitter taste have been confiscated throughout numerous states (Gambrell, 2007). In chapter 3, further information is provided regarding the illegal production of methamphetamine in the United States, with an emphasis on how this enterprise may wreak havoc in individual lives and communities, as well as the legislative and judicial efforts to curtail the production of the drug in the United States.

# 3

# ILLEGAL PRODUCTION OF METHAMPHETAMINE IN THE UNITED STATES

Illicit drugs like cocaine are often imported to the United States. This is also true to some extent for marijuana. What distinguishes methamphetamine from other illicit substances is that this drug has, for the last 50 years, been illegally manufactured in the United States. As discussed in chapter 1, methamphetamine addiction is truly a home-grown American problem. Throughout the last several decades manufacturing of the drug has occurred in illegal operations throughout the United States, paralleling to some extent the manner in which alcohol was illegally produced during Prohibition. More recently, legislation has been enacted at the federal and local levels to curtail the production of the drug. This chapter provides an overview on how and where methamphetamine is illegally produced, as well as the impact such manufacturing has on individual lives and communities. In addition, an overview is provided of the legislative initiatives that have attempted to eradicate the production of methamphetamine in the United States.

# PRODUCING CRYSTAL METHAMPHETAMINE

Illegal production of methamphetamine boomed shortly after the regulation of the substance by the federal government in the 1950s. Given the pervasive use of the drug in various segments of the population, methamphetamine was in demand not only for its medicinal effects but also because of its psychoactive effects. The first documented illegal production was in San Francisco in 1962, where as noted earlier the substance was formulated in clandestine laboratories created by biker gangs (hence one nickname for the drug, "crank," originated from the practice of smuggling the drug in the crankcases of motorcycles).

The prevalence of methamphetamine was evident in 1967 during the "Summer of Love" in the Haight-Ashbury section of San Francisco, long considered a mecca for illegal drug trafficking. Even after the U.S. Congress passed the U.S. Controlled Substances Act in 1970, which is the legal foundation of the government's efforts against the abuse of drugs and other substances, the illegal production of methamphetamine continued to increase in the United States. Over the last 40 years illegal production of methamphetamine has spread to all geographic regions of the country, and methamphetamine is no longer (nor has it been for the last 2 decades) produced solely by biker gangs. Rather, the drug is produced by a wide array of individuals from all walks of life.

The cooking of methamphetamine is easily accomplished through the gathering of materials that generally are easy to obtain. Such materials include rubbing alcohol, table or rock salt, kerosene, gasoline, paint thinner, acetone, lye, and matches. Some of these products are shown in Figure 3.1 or are featured in recipes, which can be found abundantly on the Internet (see, e.g., http://www.totse.com/en/drugs/speedy_drugs/howtocookmethn191749.html). The substances are combined through a process refereed to as *cooking*. One of the most common methods for the formulation of crystal methamphetamine is the P2P amalgam method. This method uses phenyl-2-propanone, an additive to pesticides, although more recently, newer and more efficient means have been developed that use ephedrine and pseudoephedrine as the bases for the product. Gahlinger (2001, p. 215) reported that while less than 2% of methamphetamine seized in lab raids in 1992 used pseudoephedrine as a base, this percentage had risen to 55% by 1996. The toxicity of the chemicals used to create illegal methamphetamine has been cited in recent prevention campaigns by the Crystal Meth Working Group in New York City, as shown in Figure 3.2.

The illegal production of methamphetamine results in a substance that is rarely pure but that, nonetheless, induces the physiological and psychological effects sought by its users. Gahlinger (2001) indicated, "Drug seizures show an average purity of 54%, diluted with ingredients such as baking soda, lactose, Epsom salts, quinine, mannitol, procaine, ether, insecticides, MSG, photo developer, and strychnine" (p. 54). Other formulations are often cut with

## CHEMICALS

Alcohol (isopropyl or rubbing) ◇ Toluene (brake cleaner)
Ether (engine starter) ◇ Sulfuric Acid (drain cleaner)
Red Phosphorus (matches/road flares) ◇ Salt (table/rock)
Iodine (teat dip or flakes/crystal) ◇ Lithium (batteries)
Trichloroethane (gun scrubber) ◇ MSM (cutting agent)
Sodium Metal ◇ Methanol/Alcohol (gasoline additives)
Muriatic Acid ◇ Anhydrous Ammonia (farm fertilizer)
Sodium Hydroxide (lye) ◇ Pseudoephedrine (cold tablets)
Ephedrine (cold tablets) ◇ Acetone ◇ Kitty Litter

*Figure 3.1.* Chemical products used to illegally produce methamphetamine. From High Intensity Drug Trafficking Areas, Office of National Drug Control Policy Web site, http://www.hidta.org. In the public domain.

*Figure 3.2.* Prevention campaign of the Crystal Meth Working Group showing toxic chemicals used to produce methamphetamine. Copyright 2006 by The Crystal Meth Working Group. Reprinted with permission.

cocaine, heroin, or talc (Halkitis, Parsons, & Stirratt, 2001), and estimates suggest that homemade methamphetamine is rarely greater than 40% pure (Holley, 2005, p. 14). Grinspoon and Bakalar (1985) suggested that these chemicals may account for as much as 94% of the final product. This adulteration of the drug to include such harsh ingredients clearly then heightens the physical risks associated with the abuse of methamphetamine because these chemical precursors hold their own dangers for the integrity of the user. For HIV-positive individuals or those who are in some manner immunocompromised, the administration of these toxic substances may be particularly problematic. Furthermore, because street versions of methamphetamine are also likely to be cut with other illicit substances such as heroin and cocaine, addictions may develop for multiple substances, even if methamphetamine abusers belie that they are only using one drug. These adulterations of illegally produced methamphetamine and the resulting adverse effects of the nonpurity of the drug are further summarized as follows: Acute lead poisoning is a very real and documented potential risk for methamphetamine abusers, and individuals who have been poisoned in this manner can present symptoms of anemia, encephalopathy, hepatitis (Buchanan & Brown, 1988), and Parkinson's disease from attempted production of 1-methyl-4-phenul-propionoxy-piperidine. (Burton, 1991, p. 47). Because a common method of illegal methamphetamine production uses lead acetate as a reagent, production errors may result in methamphetamine contaminated with lead.

There have been numerous documented cases of acute lead poisoning in intravenous methamphetamine abusers (Burton, 1991, p. 56). For example, during a 1-month period in 1988, health officials in Marion County, Oregon, diagnosed eight intravenous methamphetamine users who were exposed to non-A or non-B hepatitis and who also had lead poisoning (Centers for Disease Control and Prevention, 1989).

## ILLEGAL METHAMPHETAMINE LABS

As has been noted, methods for cooking methamphetamine are easily accessed on the Internet, and the illegal production of methamphetamine occurs in a wide variety of different environments, from the back of pickup trucks to small makeshift operations known as "mom and pop" shops (see Figure 3.3) and super labs (see Figure 3.4), which can produce the drug in as little as 6 hours (Swetlow, 2003). "The trunk of a car is plenty of room for a lab" (Holley, 2005, p. 12), and thus labs are easily mobile. The development of more efficient processes for making crystal methamphetamine has allowed the drug to be produced in more populated areas, rather than the wide open spaces once required, which had resulted in the proliferation of laboratories in states like Utah and Colorado. In 2006, for example, a methamphetamine lab

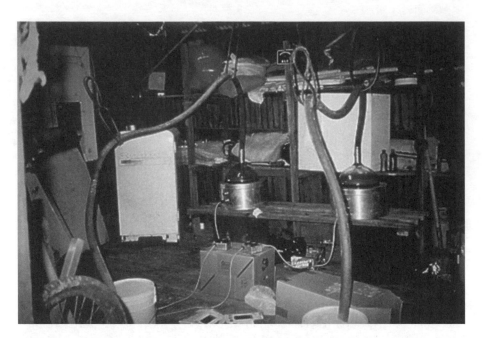

Figure 3.3. Image of "mom and pop" crystal methamphetamine lab. "Super Methamphetamine Lab Photo," by Robert Pennal. Copyright 2008 by the Institute for Intergovernmental Research. Reprinted with permission.

Figure 3.4. Image of crystal methamphetamine super lab. "Super Methamphetamine Lab Photo," by Robert Pennal. Copyright 2008 by Institute for Intergovernmental Research. Reprinted with permission.

was seized on a 28th floor penthouse apartment overlooking the United Nations in Manhattan (Burke & Marzulli, 2006). Furthermore, of the 8,290 clandestine labs seized in 2001, only 303 were super labs (Office of National Drug Control Policy, 2003).

The cooking of methamphetamine in illegal laboratories is highly dangerous in part because of the highly combustive nature of the cooking process. The production of the drug in these illegal conditions creates potential danger for the manufacturer (aka "the cook"), those in close proximity, and the environment in which the lab is located. However, the illegal production of crystal methamphetamine holds the potential for great profits to counterbalance the dangers:

> In some California cities, street drug dealers may pay as much as $900 for an ounce of crystal meth. In turn, they will sell it to their customers for $100 a gram. . . . With about twenty-eight grams to the pound, this means a street dealer can earn $2,800 or more by selling a single ounce of crystal. (Marcovitz, 2006, p. 24)

Short- and long-term illnesses for those who come in contact with a methamphetamine lab are a result of respiratory or skin exposures to the vapors, chemical residues, or both that inevitably accompany the cooking process (Clinard & Von Holtum, 2005). Individuals who are exposed to chemicals used in the production of the drug often experience cough, chest pain or tightness, shortness of breath, eye irritation, chemical burns, nausea, and/or lethargy. Exposure of the eyes to the chemicals may result in conjunctivitis or corneal injury. Depending on the chemicals, which are used to create the drug, exposure may lead to coma, respiratory failure, and death if hydrogen cyanide is present in the environment, and freezing injury to the skin if Freon is being use. In addition, exposure to infectious diseases, such as HIV, may be a risk for individuals who come in contact with paraphernalia used to administer methamphetamine often found in laboratories (Irvine & Chin, 1991, p. 36). These health consequences are not only a concern for those producing the drug but also for those in the social circles of the individuals who come in contact with the lab, as well as for health and law officials who may be involved in the seizing of illegal labs.

Fatalities are common in methamphetamine laboratories, where the use of highly volatile substances can lead to explosions and fires. Estimates suggest that one in every six methamphetamine labs seized is discovered because of a fire or an explosion associated with the handling and overheating of the materials used to make the drug (Mason, 2004).

> Meth makers sometimes wrap the interior of homes or apartments in a plastic sheath to trap the smell of fumes. But this also makes the toxic fumes more powerful and can make it difficult to escape an explosion. Doctors in burn units say they see meth cooks and users come in literally peeling melted plastic from their bodies. (D. Johnson, 2005, p. 21)

## Children in Illegal Methamphetamine Labs

Perhaps one of the greatest threats from illegal methamphetamine production stems from the exposure of children to the toxins of clandestine methamphetamine labs. In addition to all of the health consequences and dangers posed by the illegal production of methamphetamine, the presence of children in homes that function as makeshift labs creates the potential for the development of methamphetamine addiction in young children who crawl on floors and breathe the fumes created by the cooking process. The residues create an environment in which the child can easily ingest methamphetamine and inadvertently become poisoned, leading to a variety of complications, including the rapid breakdown of skeletal tissue (Kolecki, 1998). According to Mason (2004), some of the physical and behavioral characteristics of children that place them at increased risk for exposure to methamphetamine and exposure to other chemicals include (a) the tendency of young children to crawl on floors where some heavier gases created from the cooking processes and residual particles tend to be present; (b) the greater likelihood of faster absorption of chemicals through the skin of children, which is not as thick as that of adults; (c) the higher rates of metabolism of children; (d) the inclination of children to place things in their mouths; and (e) the inability of the developing nervous system to withstand exposure to chemicals. The last element has enormous ramifications for the cognitive and emotional development of children during a period of time when there exist high levels of plasticity in the brain (Rubia et al., 2000), also suggesting that methamphetamine use is potentially problematic for adolescents and young adults, for whom brain development is still occurring. The long-term exposure of these children to methamphetamine and methamphetamine production can create damage to the cardiovascular, digestive, and neurological systems (National Drug Intelligence Center [NDIC], 2002). Finally, as these children are likely being reared by caregivers who are themselves methamphetamine abusers, the potential for neglect and physical, sexual, and emotional abuse is high. All of these conditions compromise the biological, psychological, and social well-being of these children.

The number of children identified at clandestine methamphetamine labs in the United States doubled between 1999 and 2001 (NDIC, 2002), and the U.S. Drug Enforcement Administration (DEA; 2005) found that children are present in approximately 20% to 30% of the seized methamphetamine labs. Furthermore, the NDIC reported that 35% of children who are found in labs test positive for toxic levels of chemicals in their bodies, including but not limited to methamphetamine.

## Environmental Impact of Illegal Methamphetamine Labs

There are also enormous environmental consequences associated with the illegal production of methamphetamine in clandestine laboratories.

Butterfield (2004) estimated that for every pound of methamphetamine that is produced in these labs, approximately 5 to 7 pounds of toxic waste are simultaneously produced. Coupled with statistics from the Riverside County Department of Environmental Conservation (2005), which estimated that most "meth cooks" produce the drug between 48 and 72 times a year, the result is large amount of toxic waste produced by each lab annually. These toxic substances, which can be carcinogenic, are usually dumped in toilet systems or spilled on the ground (Holley, 2005, p. 13), and thus they hold the potential for contamination of water supplies, sewage treatment facilities, or both. Finally, according to the North Carolina Department of Justice (2004), typical costs for cleaning up a methamphetamine lab site can range from $4,000 to $10,000; it is estimated that in 2005, $50 million was spent on safely removing waste from such sites. However, even after a home is seized and cleaned, it is unclear whether the environment is truly free of toxins and potential carcinogens (D. Johnson, 2005, p. 22).

## LEGISLATION TO CURTAIL ILLEGAL METHAMPHETAMINE PRODUCTION

The key component in the production of crystal methamphetamine is either ephedrine or pseudoephedrine. Although these substances remain readily available in cold formulations such as Claritin, Sudafed, Actifed, and Tylenol Cold, recent legislation in various states has made the purchase of these over-the-counter treatments more difficult. In fact, most manufacturers have switched their formulations of these medications to phenylephrine. On the federal level, the Combat Methamphetamine Epidemic Act of 2005 (CMEA) was signed into law on March 9, 2006, and is found as Title VII of the USA PATRIOT Improvement and Reauthorization Act of 2005 (Public Law 109-177). The purpose of the act is to regulate retail over-the-counter sales of ephedrine, pseudoephedrine, and phenylpropanolamine products. Requirements of the Act are shown in Exhibit 3.1. Provisions of CMEA include daily sales limits and 30-day purchase limits per person, placement of products out of direct customer access, sales logbooks, customer ID verification, employee training, and self-certification of regulated sellers. It is believed that these regulations have shifted the production of illegal methamphetamine out of the United States. This drug, like cocaine, is now one that is smuggled from places outside of the United States, mostly from Mexico (Colliver & Gfroerer, 2006). However, this is not to say that production does not still occur in the United States, as is indicated by the map of laboratory seizures shown in chapter 1 and further confirmed by statistics, such as the following: In 1993 officials in Colorado seized 25 illegal methamphetamine labs, and in 2003 they seized 500 such labs, indicating an 1,800% increase within the decade (Holley, 2005, p. 12).

EXHIBIT 3.1
Requirements of Merchants in the Combat
Methamphetamine Epidemic Act of 2005

- A retrievable record of all purchases identifying the name and address of each party to be kept for 2 years
- Required verification of proof of identity of all purchasers
- Required protection and disclosure methods in the collection of personal information
- Reports to the Attorney General of any suspicious payments or disappearances of the regulated products
- Nonliquid dose form of regulated product may only be sold in unit dose blister packs
- Regulated products are to be sold behind the counter or in a locked cabinet in such a way as to restrict access
- Daily sales of regulated products are not to exceed 3.6 grams without regard to the number of transactions
- Monthly sales are not to exceed 9 grams of pseudoephedrine base in regulated products

The impact of ephedrine and pseudoephedrine regulations across the country has yet to be truly determined; however, Cunningham and Liu (2003) found some support for the regulations on the local level. Using a time-series analysis and data from California, Arizona, and Nevada, the investigators considered the impact of the legislation on methamphetamine-related acute-care hospital admissions. Findings suggest that regulation of the single ingredient ephedrine stopped a 4-year rise (1992–1995) in hospital admissions in all three states. Similarly, the regulation of pseudoephedrine was related to a decline in methamphetamine hospital admissions in all three states. The investigators concluded that regulations targeting precursors to methamphetamine used by large-scale producers of the substance reduced methamphetamine hospital admissions significantly but that these regulations had little effect when considered in terms of small-scale producers.

CONCLUSION

Once a widely prescribed drug in the United States for the treatment of depression, obesity, attention-deficit/hyperactivity disorder, and other conditions, methamphetamine is now illegal but remains widely available, albeit rarely pure, through the production of crystal methamphetamine in illegal labs or its importation from countries such as Mexico. Although recent legislation has attempted to curtail the production of methamphetamine through strict regulations of the purchase of base products such as pseudoephedrine, demand for the drug has not truly waned, and the ultimate effectiveness of such legislation remains to be seen. The detrimental effects of methamphetamine are seen not only among those who become addicted to the drug but also in the communities in which illegal crystal methamphetamine labs create ecological and financial burdens. Thus, the impact of the drug on the individual and society has been aptly labeled "a perfect storm of complications" (Lineberry & Bostwick, 2006, p. 77). Chapter 4 more fully considers the numerous damaging physiological and psychological effects of methamphetamine addiction and examines how this addiction destroys lives and can readily lead to death.

# 4

# BIOPSYCHOSOCIAL CONSEQUENCES OF METHAMPHETAMINE ADDICTION

Immediately after the administration of methamphetamine, users experience a number of highly desirable sensations arising from the interactions of the drug with various neurotransmitter systems, most primarily with the dopaminergic and secondarily with the epinephrine and norepinephrine systems. Most pronounced of all methamphetamine's effects is the great sense of euphoria. Euphoria is coupled with other "desirable" states and behaviors, including increased productivity, heightened attentiveness and curiosity, hypersexuality, decreased anxiety, and increased energy (Cretzmeyer, Sarrazin, Huber, Block, & Hall, 2003; Meredith, Jaffe, Ang-Lee, & Saxon, 2005). The euphoric feelings may vary in intensity and duration, depending on mode of administration, with smoking or intravenous injection leading to an intense but brief euphoria and oral ingestion or snorting leading to a slightly less intense but more long-lasting "high" (National Institute on Drug Abuse [NIDA], 2002; U.S. Department of Health and Human Services, 2004). Volkow et al. (1997) estimated that such effects may last anywhere from 4 to 24 hours. Users describe feeling "on top of the world," with few, if any, concerns. For individuals who experience depression, such feelings are masked, and thus the drug in some ways functions to self-medicate these undesirable states.

Despite the short-term desirable effects sought by the methamphetamine users, long-term use of the substance holds significant negative implications for the physiological, psychological, and social well-being of the individual. The detrimental effects of methamphetamine use are most evident among those who abuse or are dependent on the drug. The definition of addiction to and associated treatments for methamphetamine abuse and dependence are further described in chapters 6 and 7. Although the biological, psychological, and social sequelae associated with occasional use may not be as pronounced as those for the methamphetamine abuser and addict, the organism (i.e., people who are users but not addicts) is still at risk of the development of these complications.

The potential for addiction to methamphetamine transgresses all demographic states, and there is no "single, uniform career path that all chronic methamphetamine users follows" (Sommers, Baskin, & Baskin-Sommers, 2006, p. 1469). However, all users experience negative health and psychological and social outcomes, which lead to physical, social, emotional, and psychological deterioration. Abuse of the drug is highly related to criminal behavior, including violent criminal behavior, incarceration, as well as recidivism (Cartier, Farabee, & Prendergast, 2006). Deaths because of methamphetamine addiction are not always a direct result of the toxicity of the drug itself (Logan, Fligner, & Haddix, 1998). The combination of methamphetamine with other substances, as well as deaths because of homicide, suicide, and accidental causes, including those within the context of the meth lab, all contribute to the deadly nature of this drug.

This chapter provides an overview of the physiological impact of methamphetamine abuse and addiction with an emphasis on the impact of the drug on both the cardiovascular and neurological systems, two of the body systems most directly affected by chronic use of the drug. Next, the chapter outlines the cognitive and social–cognitive effects of the drug. These effects transgress the biological, psychological, and social domains. Finally, consideration is given to (a) the psychiatric consequences of methamphetamine abuse and addiction, (b) the decline in oral health, and (c) the complications that the use of methamphetamine may present for HIV-infected individuals. In the end, the stresses placed on the physical, emotional, and social domains of the methamphetamine abuser or addict often occur concurrently, placing enormous burden on the individual as well as on those who love and care for this person.

## OVERVIEW OF THE BIOLOGICAL, PSYCHOLOGICAL, AND SOCIAL SEQUELAE

The effects of chronic methamphetamine use are numerous and often pronounced. Brecht, O'Brien, von Mayrhauser, and Anglin (2004) found that in a sample of 350 individuals recruited from a publicly funded treatment site,

84% reported weight loss because of their methamphetamine use. Other problems included sleeplessness (78%), financial problems (73%), paranoia (67%), legal problems (63%), hallucinations (61%), work problems (60%), violent behavior (57%), dental problems (55%), and skin problems (36%). Such consequences of continued use of the drug result from the stress the drug places on the physical being of the individual. Also, behavioral outcomes associated with methamphetamine use in terms of impaired cognitions and emotions place additional stress on the homeostasis and well-being of the human organism. In one extreme case, a 44-year-old White man bisected his penis in a methamphetamine-induced psychosis (Israel & Lee, 2002).

The New York City Department of Health and Mental Hygiene (2004) described methamphetamine as being "so dangerous" because the drug is highly addictive and its use results in craving, loss of control, physical dependence, tolerance, cardiovascular burden, and numerous other physical manifestations including, but not limited to, periodontal disease, depression, aggressive or violent behavior, and potential death. In Hawaii, the number of deaths associated with methamphetamine use has more than doubled within 5 years, with 34 deaths reported in all of 2000 and 38 deaths reported through the first half of 2005 (DrugRehabs.org, 2005). What may be perceived as desirable effects experienced in the short term (increased attention, decreased fatigue, increased activity, decreased appetite, and euphoria) are eventually replaced by the long-term effects of methamphetamine use (dependence, addiction psychosis, paranoia, repetitive motor activity, heart attack, or stroke; Sheridan, Bennett, Coggan, Wheeler, & McMillan, 2006).

Ultimately, methamphetamine attacks an individual's life on numerous fronts, causing potential not only for irreparable physical damage and death but also for deterioration in one's cognitive, emotional, and social stability. The effect of the abuse of methamphetamine on sexual behavior can also act as a lubricator or facilitator for the transmission of HIV and other pathogens (Halkitis, Parsons, & Stirratt, 2001). This interaction is so pronounced that the effects of the drug on sex, sexuality, and sexual well-being are addressed separately in chapter 5.

## PHYSIOLOGICAL EFFECTS AND COMPLICATIONS

As noted previously, methamphetamine directly affects the functioning of the autonomic nervous system and central nervous system when taken in even small amounts (NIDA, 1997). The most direct physiological effects include increased heart rate, elevated blood pressure, and vasoconstriction (i.e., a narrowing of the blood vessels. Strokes, heart attacks, and irreversible damage to blood vessels are among the biological effects of methamphetamine on the cardiovascular system (NIDA, 1997). High doses of methamphetamine also have been shown to cause irreversible damage to neural cell endings in rats, pigs, cats, and nonhuman primates (NIDA, 1996; National Institutes of Health [NIH], 1996); long-term neurotoxicity in humans (Ernst, Chang, Leonido-Yee, & Speck, 2000); the development of Parkinson's-like symptoms later in life (Meredith et al., 2005); and acute liver failure (Kamijo, Soma, Nishida, Namera, & Ohwada, 2002). As has been depicted in numerous prevention campaigns, methamphetamine has significant effects on oral health as seen in those with "meth mouth." All of these physiological effects, however, have been attributed mostly to continuous use of methamphetamine (noted among those who are abusing or dependent), rather than one-time or occasional use of the substance. Figure 4.1 depicts the physiological "hot-spots" of sustained methamphetamine use.

The effects of methamphetamine on the body are long lasting because of the relatively slow nature with which the drug is metabolized (unlike cocaine, which is metabolized rather rapidly). Cocaine has a half-life of approximately 30 minutes, and 50% of the drug is removed from the body within 1 hour (Halkitis, 2006b). In contrast, methamphetamine has a half-life of 8 to 24 hours with 50% still remaining in the body after 24 hours. Under normal conditions, an examination of urine sample suggests that up to 43% of a methamphetamine dose is excreted as unchanged methamphetamine, 15% as p-hydroxymethamphetamine, 4% to 7% as amphetamine, and the remainder as minor amounts of the same metabolites found after amphetamine use. These figures can vary significantly as a result of differences in urine pH. Methamphetamine concentrations as high as 333,000 ng/ml have been reported in the urine of methamphetamine abusers. Methamphetamine is metabolized by the CYP2D6 isoform of the cytochrome P450 enzyme system, and because of the polymorphism associated with the system, there is a wide variability in how individuals respond to the drug. Because 3% to 10% of the White population is deficient in CYP2D6, however, this places them at greater risk for methamphetamine-related toxicity (Urbina & Jones, 2004). The physiological and psychiatric manifestations of the drug may differ from user to user in part because of variations in the ability to metabolize the drug effectively but also based on escalation in use and mode of administration (Meredith et al., 2005).

## CARDIOVASCULAR EFFECTS

Methamphetamine use causes numerous adverse effects to the cardiovascular system. These effects include chest pain, heart palpitations, shortness of breath, hypo- and hypertension, and ultimately, myocardial infarction (MI) and stroke. These ultimate and most severe complications have been well

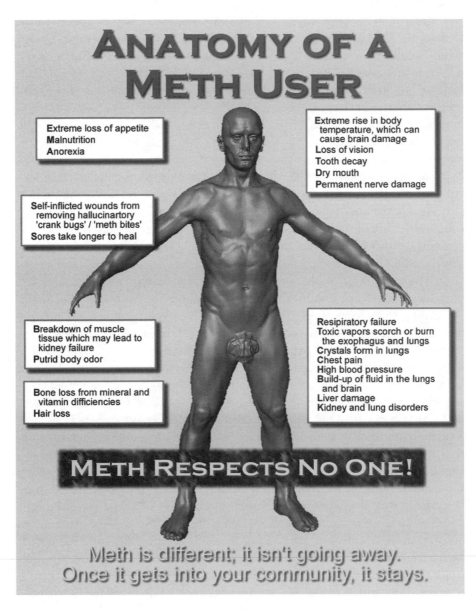

*Figure 4.1.* Physiological effects of methamphetamine use. Retrieved March 1, 2008, from http://www.kci.org. Copyright 2008 by KCI: The Anti-Meth Site. Reprinted with permission.

documented even among very young individuals (Urbina, 2006). Kalant and Kalant (1975) reported that stroke and heart attacks are the most likely causes of death after methamphetamine use.

In animals, chronic methamphetamine administration has been shown to lead to pathological cerebrovascular changes and signs of hemorrhage (Rumbaugh, 1977). In addition, as described by Meredith et al. (2005), deaths of methamphetamine users have been linked not only to cerebral hemorrhage but also to pulmonary edema and congestive heart failure. The use of methamphetamine has been related to the development of cardiac lesions as described by Matoba (2001), including the aorta, the largest artery in the human body (Swalwell & Davis, 1999). The complications of methamphetamine use on cardiovascular functioning are most evident among chronic users; however, binge use of the drug has also been shown to impact cardiovascular health. Because of the nature of binge use (i.e., cycles of time-limited periods of active methamphetamine use followed by nonuse), this type of drug use alters cardiovascular function and cardiovascular reflex functions, thus creating serous cardiac pathology (Varner, Ogden, Delcarpio, & Meleg-Smith, 2002).

The use of methamphetamine is associated with hypertension, which left untreated can result in cardiovascular abnormalities, hemorrhages, and death. According to B. Johnson et al. (2005), "Massive hypertensive crises relating to cerebrovascular accidents such as strokes or ruptured aneurysms, or cardiovascular dysfunction and toxicity, are an important cause of morbidity and mortality associated with cocaine or methamphetamine use" (p. 813). Chin, Channick, and Rubin (2006) noted methamphetamine as a pulmonary hypertension risk factor and found a diagnosis of the condition in approximately 30% of patients with a history of stimulant abuse. Moreover, patients with pulmonary hypertension were 10 times more likely to have used stimulants than patients who had the condition and other known risk factors. Hypertension stemming from the use of methamphetamine has also been linked to severe brain malfunctions. Moriya and Hashimoto (2002) described a case study of a massive hemorrhage in the cerebral ventricles of a 44-year-old methamphetamine user, who was likely injecting the drug. An autopsy of the man's body revealed that the lateral and fourth cerebral ventricles were filled with hematomas, and the hemorrhage likely occurred because of the hypertension induced by the man's methamphetamine use. The development of hypertension occurs regardless of route of administration of the drug and has been noted among those who ingest or inhale it (Schaiberger, Kennedy, Miller, & Petty, 1993) as well as among smokers of the drug (Hong, Matsuyama, & Nur, 1991). Hemorrhages experienced by chronic methamphetamine users are likely also encouraged by the elevated release of the catecholamines dopamine, epinephrine, and norepinephrine, which lead to elevated body temperatures (King & Ellinwood, 1997; Meredith et al., 2005).

Methamphetamine use can cause inflammation of the blood vessels, a condition known as arteriosclerosis (Rumbaugh et al., 1976). Arteriosclerosis, in effect, leads to inadequate blood flow that can result in either stroke or MI. In addition to this physiological impact on the cardiovascular system, methamphetamine use may lead to the development of blood clots (i.e., hypercoagulability) and epicardial coronary spasm, both of which may lead to heart attacks and strokes (J. Chen, 2007). In his review of the literature, DeSandre (2006) provided evidence of young individuals without cardiac risk factors, presenting in emergency rooms with chest pains after methamphetamine use, as well as the documentation of strokes among methamphetamine users at the same developmental stage. Wijetunga, Bhan, Lindsay, and Karch (2004) reported on eight case studies of young adults who developed unstable angina or acute MI in association with smoking methamphetamine. The smoking of methamphetamine, in particular, holds enormous potential for the development of pulmonary edema and a dilated cardiomyopathy, as well as vasospasm, which can lead to MI (Hong et al., 1991). However, MI has also been connected to the inhalation of the drug (Furst, Fallon, Reznik, & Shah, 1990).

Finally, a complex synergy occurs with chronic methamphetamine use and heart disease among HIV-infected individuals. Yu, Larson, and Watson (2003) suggested that concomitant methamphetamine use and HIV infection not only enhances immunosuppression but also increases the chance of heart disease, which is induced by both HIV and HIV antiviral medications. The debilitating effects of methamphetamine on the cardiovascular system were recently portrayed in the documentary *No More Sunsets: The Last Days of a Meth Addict,* which depicted addict Shawn Bridges, who by age 26 had suffered a heart attack and twice had to be shocked back to life. Bridges died at the age of 35 (Bridges, 2007). In addition to cardiovascular infarctions, intestinal infractions have also been documented as a result of methamphetamine use (Brannan, Soundararajan, & Houghton, 2004).

## NEUROLOGICAL COMPLICATIONS

The manner by which methamphetamine affects neuronal functioning through the interruption of the dopamine, epinephrine, and norepinephrine systems is described in chapter 2. The continuous overstimulation of these neural transmitters, however, has deleterious effects on the brain structurally, functionally, and behaviorally. Psychotic states such as paranoia and hallucinations are common, and such psychiatric manifestations may lead to extremely irrational behavior as well as suicidal and homicidal ideation (Wolkoff, 1997).

Chronic use of methamphetamine has been associated with long-term alterations to the dopamine system, including depletion of dopamine, a decrease in the number of dopamine transport pumps, and a degeneration of nerve endings (see De Vito & Wagner, 1989, for a review of the literature). Fleckenstein, Metzger, Gibb, and Hanson (1997) showed that after a single dose of methamphetamine, dopamine-transporter activities decrease by 48%. This decrease in transporter activity indicates the failure of the neurons to effectively reuptake the neurotransmitter, although normal activity returns after 24 hours. Using positron emission tomography scans, Volkow, Chang, Wang, Fowler, Leonido-Yee, et al. (2001) demonstrated a significantly lower number of dopamine transporters among methamphetamine abusers compared with control group nonusers. Moreover, such reductions were noted even in abusers who had been detoxified (i.e., sober) for 11 months. Comparisons are shown in Figure 4.2.

This reduction in dopamine transporters is associated behaviorally with poor motor activity, decreased memory performance, and reduced verbal learning. In addition, after detoxification from the substance, methamphetamine users experience low levels of motivation and decreases in the experience of pleasure in their lives. These states are linked to reductions in brain glucose metabolism, although, over the long term, abstinence from methamphetamine has been associated with a certain level of recovery in the brain (Wang et al., 2004). Even after a short period of abstinence (1–2 weeks), former methamphetamine users continue to demonstrate impairments across a variety of other neurocognitive domains, including attention and psychomotor speed and executive functioning (Kalechstein, Newton, & Green, 2003). The impact of methamphetamine on executive functioning has been corroborated by others

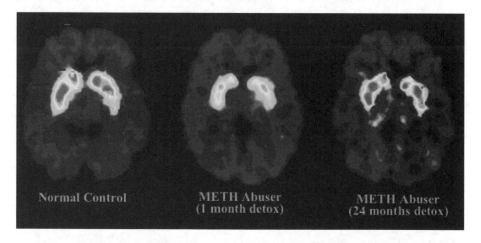

*Figure 4.2.* Effect of methamphetamine on dopamine transformers. From "Loss of Dopamine Transporters in Methamphetamine Abusers Recovers With Protracted Abstinence," by N. Volkow et al., 2001, *Journal of Neuroscience, 21,* p. 9415. Copyright 2001 by the Society for Neuroscience. Reprinted with permission.

(Paulus et al., 2002; Simon et al., 2002) and provides further support for the idea that the drug induces frontal lobe atrophy. This condition manifests in decision making that is driven more by the immediate outcomes rather than by task-related processes (Paulus, Hozack, Lawrence, Brown, & Schuckit, 2003). Other neurocognitive deficits include speed and information manipulation, as well as visual-motor scanning (Simon et al., 2002). All of these neurocognitive consequences appear to perpetuate over long periods of time, perhaps even worsening for a period after abstinence from the drug is achieved (see Meredith et al., 2005, for a review of the literature). Volkow, Chang, Wang, Fowler, Franceschi, et al. (2001) found that chronic abusers who have been abstinent for an average of 6 to 9 months still demonstrate significant reductions in striatal dopamine transporter density, which are correlated with years of use of the drug. Although the density of dopamine transporter appears to recover over time, the associated neurocognitive functions lag in their recovery, perhaps never reaching normal baseline states (Volkow, Chang, Wang, Fowler, Leonido-Yee, et al., 2001). Similarly, Chang et al. (2002) demonstrated both differences in cerebral blood flow and deficits in the performance of computerized tasks that require working memory among 20 previously methamphetamine-dependent individuals who had been abstinent for approximately 8 months. This result suggests that use of the drug is associated with persistent physiological changes to the brain that lead to slower reaction times in examinations of cognitive function. Chang et al. suggested that this state is indicative of subclinical Parkinsonism (i.e., Parkinson's disease); however, interactive effects of the drug by gender suggest that estrogen may play a neuroprotective role against the damages produced by methamphetamine abuse. Finally, high doses of methamphetamine in rats have been related to not only lowered dopamine concentrations but also to decreases in serotonin concentrations (Sabol, Roach, Broom, Ferreira, & Preau, 2001).

It has been shown that "clinical and preclinical observations suggest that methamphetamine may cause long-lasting injury to the brain" (Ernst et al., 2000, p. 1345). Such effects have been demonstrated over many years in animals (Pu & Vorhees, 1993; Woolverton, Ricaurte, Forno, & Seiden, 1989) and may be related to the production of molecules key to brain function. In their study of former methamphetamine abusers who had been abstinent for approximately 4 months, Ernst et al. (2000) further demonstrated the neurotoxic effects of methamphetamine by demonstrating a reduced production of N-Acetyl aspartate in both the basal ganglia (associated with motor control, cognition, and learning) and the frontal lobe of the brain (associated with impulse control, judgment, and language). Decreases in the production of this molecule are indicative of decreases in both neuronal and density content, thus suggesting atrophy in these regions of the brain. This chemical, which is produced only by neurons, has also been found at reduced levels in individuals

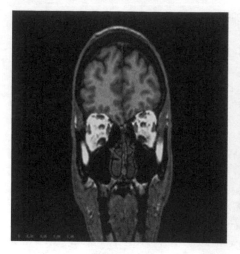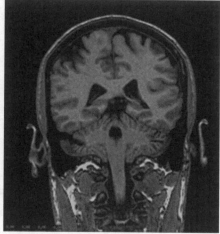

Figure 4.3. Brain scan of methamphetamine dependent male. From "Methamphetamine and Social Cognition: Findings From Project MASC," by P. N. Halkitis, B. D. Homer, R. W. Moeller, and T. M. Solomon, March 2007, New York University Developmental Psychology Colloquium. Reprinted with permission of authors.

with Alzheimer's disease and epilepsy, and in stroke victims. The brain scans shown in Figure 4.3 are magnetic resonance imaging images of a 47-year-old methamphetamine-dependent male that demonstrate frontal lobe atrophy. These images appear markedly different from the scan of an age-matched nonuser (Figure 4.4; Halkitis, Homer, Moeller, & Solomon, 2007). The dependent brain also demonstrates damage to the cerebellum and enlarged ventricles.

The neurotoxic effects of methamphetamine may be related to the further development of this drug addiction. In mice, the neurotoxicity of the drug has been associated with two behavioral outcomes: sensitization to the psychomotor-stimulating effects of the drug and desensitization to the rewarding properties of the drug (Itzhak & Ali, 2002). Such behavioral consequences may provide a foundation for compulsive drug-seeking behavior, whereby methamphetamine users continually crave and seek out the drug.

## Cognitive Deterioration

Direct effects of the neurotoxicity of methamphetamine include the cognitive impairments manifested in methamphetamine users. Although the short-term benefits in performance associated with amphetamine use have been well-documented (see Simon et al., 2000, for a review of the literature), the detrimental effects on the cognitive skills and abilities of long-term methamphetamine users have been minimally studied.

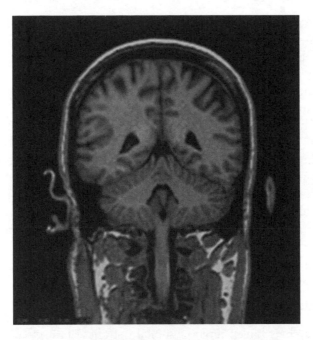

*Figure 4.4.* Brain scan of nonmethamphetamine dependent male. From "Methamphetamine and Social Cognition: Findings From Project MASC," by P. N. Halkitis, B. D. Homer, R. W. Moeller, and T. M. Solomon, March 2007, New York University Developmental Psychology Colloquium. Reprinted with permission of authors.

Recent work, however, has suggested that methamphetamine use is significantly related to cognitive impairment. Simon et al. (2000) compared 65 regular users of methamphetamine with a group of nonusers who were comparable in terms of age, gender, race–ethnicity, and educational attainment. The users in this study had been using the drug an average of 11 years, and over half reported daily use of methamphetamine. The users were found to be more impaired in numerous domains, including recall tasks, manipulation of information, abstract thinking, and ability to ignore irrelevant information; deficits were similar to those often seen in aging (Simon et al., 2000). They found no significant differences, however, in the verbal fluency or backward digit span of the two groups. Further evidence for distractibility and difficulty in focusing among recent methamphetamine uses was documented by Salo et al. (2002). Using the Stroop task, a test of selective attention, the investigative team compared performance of 8 former methamphetamine users who had been abstinent for 2 to 4 months with a group of 12 control participants who were equivalent in age. After controlling for educational attainment, the methamphetamine group took longer to reflect a response selection, which the investigators suggested arose "from an impaired ability to suppress irrelevant information" (Salo et al., 2002, p. 71).

Although methamphetamine users tend to demonstrate similar cognitive impairments to cocaine users, some differences do exist between users of these two substances. Specifically, methamphetamine users, more so than cocaine users, demonstrate greater problems manipulating information and with perseveration and set-shifting (i.e., changing points of view), indicating that "methamphetamine abusers would have trouble organizing information from more than one source and have difficulty switching points of view," which may underlie comprehension (Simon et al., 2002, p. 71). This pattern is noted in both current and former methamphetamine users, although cognitive problems are slightly more elevated among current users (Simon et al., 1999). Methamphetamine users display many of the behavioral characteristics associated with patients who suffer damage to the orbital prefrontal cortex of the brain, including lack of personal and social judgment, a reduced concern for the consequences of their actions, and difficulties in decision making (Rogers et al., 1999).

## Social Cognitions

To date, there have been no systematic studies of the effects of methamphetamine on social–cognitive functioning, although the role of methamphetamine on social interactions has been theorized (Homer et al., 2008). A number of animal and human studies, however, have noted changes in social behavior associated with chronic amphetamine exposure. For example, Clemens et al. (2006) found that rats given doses of methamphetamine demonstrated significantly lower levels of social interaction even weeks after administration of the drug. Similarly, Schiorring (1977) found that both acute and chronic methamphetamine exposure leads to extreme social withdrawal in monkeys. There is also evidence, from both animal and human studies, that in certain conditions chronic methamphetamine abuse can lead to an increase in aggressive behaviors. In a recent study, Sekine et al. (2006) linked increased aggression in abstinent methamphetamine abusers to a decrease in serotonin transporter density in the orbitofrontal cortex, anterior cingulated and temporal cortex. In addition to decreased inhibition, aggression has also been related to deficits in social–cognitive functioning (e.g., Holmes-Lonergan, 2003). These and related findings suggest that the changes in social behavior (i.e., social withdrawal, aggression) associated with chronic methamphetamine abuse may have a neurological basis and may, in part, be explained by impairments in social–cognitive functioning.

Because methamphetamine can induce damage to the prefrontal cortex through changes in dopaminergic function, executive functions—including social cognition—can become severely impaired. The result is an inability ". . . to organize or control a variety of component cognitive processes, such as those involving the maintenance of short-term information or the modulation of cognitive set, in order to complete more composite cognitive operations relating to deferred or distant goals" (Rogers et al., 1999, p. 323). Thus, decisions in everyday life may become a challenging task for methamphetamine users. Moreover, the interference with the social–cognitive processes associated with this region of the brain may lead to the development of faulty social interactions with family, friends, or strangers to the methamphetamine user.

In a comparison of 30 methamphetamine-dependent gay men with a comparable group of nonusers, the methamphetamine users demonstrated a significant dearth in social skills as evidenced by tests of social–cognitive functioning, such as the Mind's Eye and Social Faux pas tasks (Halkitis, Homer, et al., 2007). In the former, the individual is asked to "read" the emotions associated with sets of eyes; in the latter, the individual is asked about the awkwardness associated with social interaction, which is told in story form. In this study, performance on the Mind's Eye task by methamphetamine user was moderated by the presence of HIV, with HIV-positive participants doing significantly worse than both controls and dependent users without HIV. The decision-making patterns of methamphetamine users may be explained in part by the fact that the anticipated success or failures of actions may be less important or influential in the decision making of methamphetamine-dependent individuals (Paulus et al., 2003). However, recent findings suggest that the deficits in executive functioning of methamphetamine-dependent individuals may be explained in part by the fact that a large proportion of methamphetamine addicts had attention-deficit/hyperactivity disorder (ADHD) as children (e.g., Matsumoto, Kamijo, Yamaguchi, Iskei, & Hirayasu, 2005; Matsumoto, Yamaguchi, et al., 2005; ADHD is considered as a risk base for methamphetamine addiction in chap. 6, this volume). Moreover, this interactive effect may partially explain the predisposition of some individuals to use methamphetamine to self-medicate their condition. Finally, the instability of a group or social setting may function to accentuate the effects of methamphetamine, as noted in laboratory studies of rats (Syme & Syme, 1974). This finding suggests that the social contexts in which human methamphetamine users navigate may function synergistically with the drug to create the behavioral effects.

In a related line of research, Nina (2007) examined the relationship between two different models of personality characteristics (i.e., ego functions and five-factor personality traits) with drug of choice and degree of substance involvement in a sample ($N = 121$) of gay and bisexual men who used club drugs (methamphetamine, Ecstasy, and cocaine). Correlational analyses found that gay and bisexual men who abused or were dependent on methamphetamine had lower ego functioning in 8 of 12 areas, compared with a nonclinical sample. Abusers in this sample evidenced greater difficulties in living, including less relatedness to others, greater problems with evaluating the appropriateness of behaviors, lower sense of self in relation to the world, lower ability to manage impulses, less creative-thinking ability, less ability to control anxiety or depression, lower ability to deal with conflicting thoughts and affects, and reduced ability to perform or live up to their capabilities.

## Psychiatric Consequences

As noted previously in this chapter, the overstimulation of the sympathetic nervous system creates a number of undesirable physiological effects, including tachycardia, hypertension, papillary dilation, diaphoresis, tachypnea, peripheral hyperthermia, and hyperpyrexia (Meredith et al., 2005). Moreover, repeated use of methamphetamine results in a depletion of catecholamines and has been shown to produce withdrawal symptoms marked by psychiatric complaints (Meredith et al., 2005). This withdrawal, also known as "crashing," can produce a constellation of symptoms, including irritability, fatigue, depression, anxiety, impaired social functioning, aggression, and suicidal and homicidal ideation (Cantwell & McBride, 1998; Meredith et al., 2005; Newton, Kalechstein, Duran, Vansluis, & Ling, 2004). In a study of 1,016 methamphetamine users, 27% indicated at least one episode of attempting to commit suicide, and the majority reported depressive symptomatology (Zweben et al., 2004). Moreover, 68% of all women and 50% of all men who were seeking outpatient treatment for methamphetamine addiction reported a history of feeling depressed at some point in their lives. In the month prior to treatment entry, depressive symptoms were reported by 34% and 24% of women and men, respectively, and there was high level of association ($r = .25$) between depression scores (as measured by the Brief Symptom Inventory, Derogatis & Melisaratos, 1983) and number of days of methamphetamine use in the previous 30 days. In a study of methamphetamine-using gay and bisexual men, chronic users indicated a greater likelihood of using the drug to avoid unpleasant emotions than those who were occasional users of the drug (Halkitis & Shrem, 2006). Anxious and depressive states have been shown to continue for up to 3 years after abstinence from the drug is achieved (London et al., 2004). These psychiatric manifestations have been clinically noted (Urbina & Jones, 2004) and have been noted at more severe levels for female users (Lin et al., 2004; Zweben et al., 2004). The impact of the drug may be exacerbated by route of administration, with injection use more likely to induce these psychiatric states (Hall, Hando, Darke, & Ross, 1996). Recent studies of predominantly weekend-using gay men suggest continued use of the drug on Tuesdays to mask the undesired feelings brought forth by the withdrawal (Halkitis et al., 2009).

In addition, use of methamphetamine has been associated with psychotic states, including levels of paranoia and hallucinations. Such psychoses have been shown to last for several days or weeks as compared with cocaine-induced psychoses, which are much briefer in duration (Rawson et al., 2002). In one study, 90% of methamphetamine users with drug-induced psychoses required hospitalization, with the most consistent clinical features being organic delu-sional syndrome, with paranoid ideation and hallucinations (Szuster, 1990). One common hallucination is that of bugs crawling on one's skin, a condi-tion known as *formication* or "crank bugs." This hallucination may lead to excessive picking and tearing of the skin tissue (see chap. 1, this volume, Figure 1.1). These and other hallucinations are a common affliction of methamphetamine users.

Lee (2006, p. 39) indicated that there is a "kindling" effect of stimulant-induced psychosis (also known as *reverse tolerance*), whereby the more a person experiences psychotic symptoms, the more likely that person is to experience these conditions on subsequent uses of the drug, with both a heightening and lengthening in duration of the hallucinating experiences. In addition, the high levels of paranoia associated with use of the drug leads to social deterioration as the user may develop high levels of distrust for even the closest friends or family members. For chronic methamphetamine users, the damage to the receptor and transporter elements of the dopamine system are so severe that psychosis may become consistent, leading to a con-stant state of methamphetamine-induced psychosis (Holley, 2005, p. 75). It has been proposed that individuals who begin using the drug during ado-lescence and those using higher doses are more likely to develop the condi-tion. Methamphetamine abusers, even after termination of use, experience enhanced vulnerability to relapse of psychosis over a long period of time (Ujike & Sato, 2004).

For some clinicians, the characteristics of methamphetamine-induced psychosis are similar to those of schizophrenia, and paranoid schizophrenia in particular (Dore & Sweeting, 2006). Because of such similarities, recent NIDA-funded research has focused on using aripriprazole, a schizophrenia drug, as a treatment for methamphetamine addiction (Reid et al., 2006).

Despite the clinically proven relationship between methamphetamine and psychiatric disorders, it is difficult to disentangle the causal relations between the two because it is unclear whether the disorders are induced by the drug or are representative of primary disorders (Shoptaw, Peck, Reback, & Rotheram-Fuller, 2003). What is clear in the sample examined by Shoptaw et al. (2003) is that on entry into treatment, 26.5% of the sample met diagnos-tic criteria for anxiety, 52.9% had lifetime depressive disorders, and 24.7% indicated at least one lifetime suicide attempt. Moreover, 28.4% of the subjects met criteria for major depression compared with 4% with this condition in the general population. However, in a study of 21 methamphetamine users, Buffenstein, Heaster, and Ko (1999) found no indication of psychotic diagno-sis or symptoms before use of the drug was initiated. It is probably safe to say that methamphetamine users experience mental health issues at elevated rates, are often drawn to the drug as means for self-medication, and are likely to exacerbate their psychiatric conditions and develop more pronounced psychotic tendencies by becoming addicted to the drug. Although acute psychotic conditions tend to resolve after cessation of use, depressive symptoms tend to persist (Kalechstein et al., 2000). Whereas many users develop psychoses, others do not. C. Chen et al. (2005) found that those who developed psychoses more readily had a higher familial loading for schizophrenia. Nonetheless, Hartel-Petri, Rodler, Schmeisser, Steinmann, and Wolfersdorf (2005) indicated that treatments for methamphetamine must address both the addiction and the psychosis induced by the drug.

The development of methamphetamine-induced psychosis has been demonstrated to have physiological correlates (Sato, 1992). Ivo, Sekine, and Mori (2004) showed that abnormal cerebral blood flow patterns, reduction of brain dopamine transporter density, and metabolite alteration are all evident in methamphetamine users exhibiting psychoses. The longer that methamphetamine is used, the greater the severity of psychiatric symptoms and the greater the reduction in dopamine transporter density in the brain, which may be a long-lasting consequence (Sekine et al., 2001). Finally, the use of the drug has been associated with the development of focal perfusion deficits in the frontal, temporal, and parietal lobes, which have been associated with violent and aggressive behavior (Buffenstein et al., 1999).

## Oral and Dental Health

One of the most obvious and visible signs of methamphetamine abuse is the damage caused to the teeth and periodontal structures, commonly referred to as "meth mouth." Users of methamphetamine have been described as having teeth that are "blackened, stained, rotting, crumbling, or falling apart" (American Dental Association, 2005a; see chap. 1, this volume, Figure 1.1). This condition is due to both the physiological and behavioral impacts of the drug.

Chronic methamphetamine use is associated with large-scale tooth decay, also known as methamphetamine-induced caries (Klasser & Epstein, 2005). This health condition is induced by (a) the highly acidic nature of the drug; (b) the xerostomia (i.e., mouth dryness) caused by use of the drug, which reduces the protective saliva around the teach; (c) the consumption of sugar-based carbonated beverages stimulated by use of the drug; (d) the behavioral phenomenon of grinding and clenching of teeth when one uses the drug; and (e) the poor oral hygiene engendered while one is high on methamphetamine (American Dental Association, 2005b; Klasser & Epstein, 2005). The impact of methamphetamine on dental health has been clinically documented with regard to gingivitis, a form of gum disease, in a comparative study of 20 users versus 20 nonusers (Hasan & Ciancio, 2004), and overall tooth wear has been shown to be more pronounced among individuals who inhale the drug as compared with those who inject or smoke the substance (Richards & Brofeldt,

2000). Clinically, the emergence of dental caries has been shown to be highly elevated among children who undergo treatment with methamphetamine for ADHD or narcolepsy (Howe, 1995). The xerostomia caused by use of the drug has been associated with the reduction in salivary flow through the inhibition of the salutatory nuclei that is caused by a stimulation of the alpha-2 receptors in the brain (Saini et al., 2005).

## IMMUNE DETERIORATION AND COMPLICATIONS FOR HIV

The associations between methamphetamine use and sexual risk taking that can facilitate the transmission of HIV and other sexual pathogens have been widely examined, primarily but not exclusively, in populations of gay and bisexual men. The attention focused on gay and bisexual men, in academic circles as well as in the media (e.g., *Los Angeles Times*, "Preview of a Tragedy" [Eichenthal, 2001]; *San Francisco Chronicle*, "Dance of Death, Crystal Meth Fuels HIV" [Heredia, 2003]; *The New York Times*, "Battling H.I.V. Where Sex Meets Crystal Meth" [Jacobs, 2006]) may be due to two key elements: (a) the tendency of gay and bisexual men to engage in more sexual activity than their heterosexual counterparts, as noted in studies such as Molitor, Truax, Ruiz, and Sun (1998); and (b) the concentration of the HIV epidemic in the population of men who have sex with men population (i.e., 67% of all people living with AIDS in 2005 were infected through male-to-male sexual contact; Centers for Disease Control and Prevention [CDC], 2005). In addition, Shoptaw and Reback (2007b) indicated that methamphetamine-using MSM are more likely to contract both HIV and syphilis than are MSM who do not use the drug. In the end, methamphetamine addiction and HIV infection are comorbidities that can present further complications to the well-being of the individual.

The use of methamphetamine may have particularly pronounced effects for those who are immunocompromised with HIV infection. This is due in part to the impure nature of crystal methamphetamine, which often contains lead (see chap. 3, this volume) and may be cut with other materials that can be damaging to those with lower functioning immune systems. In addition, the impact of the drug on the various bodily systems can be more pronounced for those who are HIV positive. These individuals may be experiencing an increased burden on these systems because of HIV itself but also because of the antiviral treatments for the disease.

The deleterious interactive effects of HIV medications and methamphetamine have been previously documented, in particular, with individuals who have been undergoing treatment with the HIV antiviral ritonavir (see Urbina & Jones, 2004, for a review). In addition, methamphetamine use has been shown to interfere with HIV medication adherence. For example, Halkitis, Kutnick,

Borkowski, and Parsons (2002) showed that gay and bisexual men who had indicated the use of methamphetamine 2 months prior to assessments also indicated a greater number of missed doses of their protease-inhibitor treatment than those who did not indicate use of the drug (12 missed doses vs. 4 missed doses). Poor adherence behaviors such as these could lead to greater viral replication. Similar results were documented by Ellis et al. (2003), who identified higher viral loads in active HIV-positive subjects currently using methamphetamine than those who had never used or had used in the past. However, Ahmad (2002) indicated that even with optimal adherence, administration of methamphetamine was associated with greater HIV-viral replication in the brain, whereas Gavrilin, Mathes, and Podell (2002) showed similar patterns with regard to the feline immunodeficiency virus. In a recent investigation regarding affect regulation, stimulant use and viral load in 858 HIV-positive individuals on antiviral therapy, Carrico et al. (2007) further documented the effects of stimulant drugs such as methamphetamine on viral load and demonstrated a five-fold higher viral load among those who reported regular stimulant use than among those who did not. Moreover, the likelihood of stimulant use was related to depression, with a one-unit increase in the measure of affect regulation, which predicted a 23% decrease in the likelihood of use of stimulants. Moreover, stimulant users were twice as likely to be nonadherent than were nonusers.

In terms of HIV itself, Yu et al. (2002) documented adverse health consequences in laboratory mice that were retrovirus infected. Moreover, the synergistic effects of HIV and methamphetamine on the dopaminergic system may increase the HIV-positive user's susceptibility to neurotoxicity (Nath, Maragos, Avison, Schmitt, & Berger, 2001; Urbina, 2006). Specifically, methamphetamine abuse and HIV infection may cause alterations in the size of certain brain structures. In both cases, the changes may be associated with impaired cognitive functions, such as difficulties in learning new information, solving problems, and maintaining attention and quickly processing information (Jernigan et al., 2005). Thus, co-occurring methamphetamine abuse and HIV infection appears to result in greater impairment than each condition alone. In a comparison of the interactive effects of methamphetamine use and HIV, Rippeth et al. (2004) showed that rates of impairment to global neuropsychological functions were highest among HIV-positive methamphetamine users (58%); followed by HIV-negative methamphetamine users (40%), HIV-positive nonmethamphetamine users (38%), and HIV-negative, nonmethamphetamine users (18%). Finally, Tallóczy et al. (2008) showed that methamphetamine directly affects the ability of the body to effectively combat infections by exerting an immunosuppressive effect on dendritic cells and macrophages. Specifically, the drug has been shown to facilitate the replication and inhibit the intracellular destruction of two AIDS-related pathogens, *Candida albicans* (a fungal infection that affects the gastrointestinal system, aka "thrush") and

*Cryptococcus neoformans* (a fungus that can cause meningitis in HIV-infected individuals).

On a molecular level, magnetic response spectroscopy has indicated reduced levels of *N*-acetyl aspartate in those who are HIV positive and use stimulants, indicating more neuronal atrophy (Taylor et al., 2000). Similarly, Langford et al. (2003) found evidence for more elevated damage to the frontal cortex of those who are HIV positive and use methamphetamine than either of those two conditions in isolation, because of the additive damage induced by both to the calbindin-immunoreactive neurons.

## CONCLUSION

The short-term "desirable" effects of methamphetamine abuse are clearly outweighed by the numerous biological, physiological, behavioral, and social consequences of continual use of this drug. Physical, social–emotional, and financial deterioration in the lives of methamphetamine users is not uncommon, and although death from any of these impacts is possible, many methamphetamine users exist in a cycle of dependence and despair as their bodies and minds, and the connection between their bodies and minds, slowly give way to the harsh effects of the drug. It is not uncommon to see 20-year-old methamphetamine users with the appearance of adults in their 40s or 50s, because of the accelerated aging that is engendered by the use of methamphetamine and the continual stress that is placed on the bodily systems. Recent advances in cellular biology suggest that stress has a direct impact on health through the process of cellular aging. Stress has been linked to the shortening of telomeres, the buffer zone of DNA located at the end of chromosomes (Epel et al., 2004). Thus, it is feasible that the constant stress placed on the bodies of methamphetamine users has a direct effect on the aging process, and in turn on the aged appearance of methamphetamine addicts (Halkitis, Homer, et al., 2007).

A drug with the power to make one feel beautiful, powerful, and invincible insidiously masks the true appearance and behaviors of its users. Yet to the methamphetamine addict these biopsychosocial consequences are not readily evident because the drug alters thought processes, perceptions, and behaviors. In addition, although neurological systems appear to return to some level of normality after a period of abstinence, the detrimental behavioral and cognitive consequences of methamphetamine use may affect the user for much longer. Other effects, such as those on the mouth, may require intensive and expensive repair, and the emotional lives of former users may take extended periods of time to rebuild. Those wishing to break their dependence on methamphetamine must not only confront the addiction but also address the social and emotional advancements that predisposed the users to the addiction in the first place. The complex and potentially destructive synergy of biology and behavior creates a drug addiction that is often difficult to face, and that, even when addressed, will require years of support and care to return to a state of stability. For others, the increase in sexual adventurism and potential promiscuity enabled by the use of methamphetamine may have life-altering effects in an epoch in which pathogens such as HIV exist in all sectors of society. In chapter 5, the relation between methamphetamine use and sexual behavior is examined more closely. Consideration is given to the sexual pleasures experienced by users of the drug, as well as to the adverse consequences engendered by this heightened sexuality.

# 5

# METHAMPHETAMINE, SEX, SEXUALITY, AND SEXUAL RISK TAKING

Of the many reasons I had unsafe sex while high on crystal, I think the most profound was simply that I was lonely. Meth got me close to men at clubs and in bed. And unsafe sex allowed me the deepest connection possible. (Koffler, 2002, p. 42)

This quote from Kevin Koffler (2002), which appeared in the periodical *POZ*, encapsulates many of the psychosexual effects methamphetamine has on its users. It also demonstrates the sexual risk taking that often accompanies methamphetamine use, and the synergy that exists between use of the drug, mental health, and sexuality. Yet the connections between methamphetamine use, on the one hand, and sexual behavior and sexual risk taking, on the other hand, are not simple or linear, and the associations between these phenomena do not occur in isolation, in a decontextualized manner, or in a uniform, monolithic manner across users. Rather, the extant literature supports a complex interplay that, regardless of cause and effect, most certainly fuels the transmission of pathogens and potentially exacerbates the HIV epidemic. In this regard, the interconnectedness between methamphetamine use and the potential perpetuation of HIV through sexual risk taking behaviors aggravates a "dual epidemic" (Halkitis, Parsons, & Stirratt, 2001). Shrem and Halkitis (2008) posited that the current concern and alarm about the state of methamphetamine use in the United States is embedded in accompanying concerns about HIV disease.

Despite these co-occurring potential health hazards, methamphetamine is, for some, the ultimate sexual drug, creating a sense of disinhibition and facilitating the possibility of engaging in fantastical and desired sexual experiences. Methamphetamine creates an extreme and extended sense of euphoria, with some individuals using the drug as a means of amplifying their sexual experiences (Ellenhorn, Schonwald, Ordog, & Wasserberger, 1997). These potentially detrimental physical and mental health consequences, in turn, become outweighed by the pleasurable feelings that result from the hypersexuality and increased libido that the drug induces (Gibson, Leamon, & Flynn, 2002).

Although the effects of methamphetamine on sexuality and sexual risk taking have been documented across both male and female persons, the vast majority of research in this domain has focused on the behaviors of gay, bisexual, and other men who have sex with men (MSM). This research is due in part to the intimate link between the drug and the human immunodeficiency virus (HIV) and its overrepresentation in this segment of the population. However, according to the Centers for Disease Control and Prevention (CDC, 2007),

> What is becoming clear is that the use of methamphetamine can contribute to sexual risks, regardless of the sexual orientation of the users. Current data indicate a strong link between methamphetamine and sexual risk among MSM, and perhaps among heterosexual adults and youth. (¶ 4)

Across population strata (e.g., male–female, heterosexual–homosexual), Molitor, Truax, Ruiz, and Sun (1998) documented that methamphetamine users reported significantly more sexual partners than their nonusing counterparts.

In the remainder of chapter 5, the link between methamphetamine use and sexual behavior is considered fully across populations. First, the impact of the drug on impulsivity and its relation to sexual behavior are examined. Then, the "meth–sex" link is explored among gay, bisexual, and other MSM, in whom the preponderance of the behavioral research has been enacted. Finally, the existing research on heterosexual populations is presented.

## THE ROLE OF IMPULSIVITY

The use of methamphetamine is associated strongly with sexual risk taking in all segments of the population, as noted in numerous behavioral studies. However, the underlying processes between use of the drug and sexual risk taking have not been fully articulated. Rather, associations are based on correlational analyses, which have not fully delineated the pathways by which the drug may lower decision-making ability and increase impulsivity, which may lead to sexual risk taking. This state of knowledge exists even though methamphetamine use has been associated with higher levels of impulsivity (Patterson, Semple, Zians, & Strathdee, 2005; Semple, Zians, Grant, & Patterson, 2005, 2006a) and poor decision making (Rogers et al., 1999; Salo et al., 2002; Simon et al., 2000).

Among a sample of 261 HIV-positive, methamphetamine-using MSM, Semple et al. (2006a) showed that impulsivity was related to unprotected sexual acts and that this relation was moderated by level of impulsivity. The relation between unprotected sex and level of methamphetamine use was strongest among those with high levels of impulsivity. In a related line of research, Seal and Agostinelli (1994) demonstrated more sexual risk taking among individuals who demonstrated higher levels of impulsivity in making decisions. In a comparison of 40 abstinent, former methamphetamine users with age and gender matched controls, Hoffman et al. (2006) showed that the former methamphetamine users were highly impulsive as assessed by a delay-discounting task. These types of findings have been corroborated in treatment samples in rural facilities, where those who had indicated use of methamphetamine up to 90 days prior to treatment also demonstrated high levels of affect liability and impulsivity (Simons, Oliver, Gaher, Ebel, & Brummels, 2005). Moreover, such effects of methamphetamine may be exacerbated by HIV infection (E. M. Martin et al., 2004). Patterson et al. (2005) showed that HIV-positive, methamphetamine-using MSM who were "heavy" polydrug users (in that they used the drug in tandem with other drugs such as cocaine, ketamine, heroin, and hallucinogens), tended to demonstrate more sexual risk taking and higher levels of impulsivity than those who were methamphetamine-only users and "light" polydrug users.

As described in chapter 4, the use of methamphetamine has enormous consequences for frontal lobe functioning, an area of the brain posited to control decision-making ability and social cognition. Impulsive behaviors are determined, in part, by decision-making processes and thus are also likely regulated by the frontal lobe. Taken together, these elements suggest a mind–body paradigm for understanding the sexual risk taking stimulated by methamphetamine use. It is hypothesized that if frontal lobe function is compromised through the use of methamphetamine, then methamphetamine-using individuals will demonstrate deficits in judgment and decision making (i.e., deterioration in executive functioning and impulse inhibition) as well as deficits in social cognition, which would offer an explanation to the more pronounced sexual risk-taking behavior generated in methamphetamine users as compared with their nonusing counterparts. Such a model is shown in Figure 5.1 and provides basis

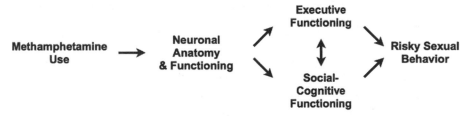

*Figure 5.1.* Proposed mediation pathway for methamphetamine use and sexual risk taking.

for considering the sexual behaviors of methamphetamine users described in the remainder of this chapter.

## METHAMPHETAMINE AND SEXUAL BEHAVIOR IN GAY, BISEXUAL, AND OTHER MEN WHO HAVE SEX WITH MEN

According to Guss (2000), use of methamphetamine among gay and bisexual men is intimately tied to hypersexual behavior, with many users understanding their drug use in these terms. In a mixed-methods investigation of active methamphetamine users, the majority understood and explained their drug use in sexual terms (Halkitis, Fischgrund, & Parsons, 2005). Because of its aphrodisiac qualities, methamphetamine is a quintessential drug for those seeking uninhibited and frequent sexual experiences because the drug may serve to initiate and enhance sexual encounters (Halkitis, Fischgrund, et al., 2005; Reback, Larkins, & Shoptaw, 2004). In direct comparisons of cocaine and methamphetamine users, the methamphetamine users were more likely to report a positive association between drug use and sex, whereas the cocaine users were more likely to indicate a negative association (A. H. Brown, Domier, & Rawson, 2005). Similarly, although heroin is also a public health concern, the link between heroin use and HIV is much less pronounced; in fact, methamphetamine users are more likely than heroin users to be HIV infected (Gibson et al., 2002). This may be because methamphetamine use, more so than any other drug use, decreases sexual inhibition and heightens sexual arousal, leading to sexual risk taking (Ireland et al., 1999; Reback, 1997).

Although research has demonstrated that methamphetamine use is linked to heightened sexual behavior in gay and bisexual men (Frosch, Shoptaw, Huber, Rawson, & Ling, 1996; Halkitis, Parsons, & Wilton, 2003b; Halkitis, Shrem, & Martin, 2005; Paul, Stall, & Davis, 1993; Reback, 1997), use of the drug is layered with complex behaviorally and psychologically driven motivations (e.g., desire for socialization and sexual promiscuity, decreased loneliness and depression) that vary depending on contextual factors and users' personality traits (Nina, 2007). Sexually related outcomes for methamphetamine use in this segment of the population include social and sexual disinhibition, enhanced sexual desire, extended sexual activity, and increased number of casual sex partners (Gorman, 1998; Halkitis, Shrem, et al., 2005; Hirshfield, Remien, & Chiasson, 2006). Green and Halkitis (2006) noted that the use of club drugs, such as Ecstasy, ketamine, and especially methamphetamine, is often used to facilitate sexual performance, which is of paramount importance in some segments of the gay population. However, the meth–sex link is not so easily explained by a cause–effect paradigm, as at least one investigation has shown that methamphetamine users report equal levels of sexual activity when sober as they are when they are high on methamphetamine (Halkitis, Shrem, et al., 2005). Another study has noted that the number of sexual acts does not differ between men who use the drug in binges and those who do not binge (Semple, Patterson, & Grant, 2003). Moreover, rates of sexual behavior, and in turn associated sexual risk, are equally high in both HIV seroconcordant and HIV serodiscordant sexual partnering (Semple, Zians, Grant, & Patterson, 2006b). However, in this segment of the population, the use of alcohol and drugs, whether methamphetamine or not, have long been associated with increased sexual promiscuity and associated sexual risk as was shown in the seminal work of Stall, McKusick, Wiley, Coates, and Ostrow (1986).

In a landmark study of methamphetamine use in Los Angeles among gay and bisexual men, Reback (1997) suggested that methamphetamine use not only enhances sexual pleasures but also reinforces the sexual identity of the user. This phenomenon is noted clearly in a case study in regard to methamphetamine documented in the *San Francisco Chronicle* (Heredia, 2003), which told the story of one young gay man: "Complicating matters was the fact that his remaining family members rejected him after he told them he was gay. Soon he was using drugs even more heavily as a way of partying and escaping his overwhelming emotions" (¶11).

The interconnectedness of sexuality, sexual identity, and methamphetamine use among gay and bisexual men has been further noted in clinical settings (Guss, 2000). In a sample of Black methamphetamine-using MSM, it was determined that the drug was used as a means for navigating one's sexual and racial identities (Jerome, 2007). Also, Kurtz (2005) explained the use of methamphetamine among men who attend circuit parties (i.e., large-scale, night-long dance parties) not only as means to lessen sexual inhibitions but also as a way to overcome loneliness and fear about declining physical attractiveness due to illness and aging. On the basis of interviews of 48 methamphetamine-using gay and bisexual men, Halkitis, Fischgrund, et al. (2005) indicated that approximately 70% of the sample reported they used the drug for its sexual effects, which include prolonged sexual experiences, heightened sexual feelings, and also as a means of reducing any negative attitudes that might be associated with sex. However, many of the men in the sample corroborate the ideas presented by Kurtz (2005), indicating other social, emotional, and behavioral motivations for use, including the fear of rejection from both within and outside of the gay community.

Among gay and bisexual men, the use of methamphetamine has also been associated with more extreme sexual practices. For example, in a sample of 25 HIV-positive MSM who participated in qualitative interviews in San Diego, many indicated group sexual activities (i.e., sex with more than one person at a time), water sports (i.e., sexual activities involving urine), fisting (i.e., anal penetration with a hand), and oral–anal contact. These findings were substantiated in a New York City-based sample of gay and bisexual methamphetamine users who, in addition to the above behaviors, expressed greater likelihood of also engaging in felching (i.e., the retrieval of ejaculate with the mouth from the anus) while high on the drug as compared with when they were sober (Halkitis, Shrem, et al., 2005). Finally, in an assessment of MSM injection drug users, researchers in Denver found that the injection of drugs such as methamphetamine stimulated sexual desires. Specifically, it was determined that sexual behavior was not only elevated with same-sex partners but also with female persons as well, with 82% of the sample of 100 participants indicating primary and nonprimary male partners and 20% reporting female sexual partners in the 6 months prior to assessment (Bull, Piper, & Rietmeijer, 2002).

Because of the sexual risk taking engendered by use of methamphetamine, most education campaigns targeting methamphetamine use have noted the connection between methamphetamine and HIV. In what is now a considered a "wake-up call" to the New York City Department of Health and Mental Hygiene, the poster campaign developed by AIDS activist Peter Staley, stating "BUY CRYSTAL, get HIV free," (Fierstein et al., 2006; see chap. 8, this volume) widely and bluntly alerted methamphetamine users to the synergies that exist between the methamphetamine and HIV epidemics, albeit years after researchers first noted this "dual epidemic" (Halkitis et al., 2001). Following this lead, numerous campaigns in major metropolitan areas have focused on the potential drug–HIV syndemic, using both appealing and nonappealing sexual images to broadcast the message (see Figure 5.2).

Sexual risk because of methamphetamine use in MSM has been quantified. Mansergh, Shouse, et al. (2006) recently estimated that methamphetamine use doubled the likelihood that MSM would engage in unprotected receptive anal intercourse. Among previously HIV-undiagnosed gay men, methamphetamine use was associated with 18 times more unprotected receptive anal intercourse in comparison with nonseroconverts (Halkitis, Green, & Carragher, 2006). However, Halkitis, Shrem, et al. (2005) showed that the type of sexual risk under the influence of methamphetamine is influenced by the serostatus of the study participant and the serostatus of his sexual partners, with less risk associated with HIV-serodiscordant partnering. Semple et al. (2006b) corroborated these findings. Wong, Chaw, Kent, and Klausner (2006) delineated that methamphetamine use increased the likelihood of contracting syphilis sixfold. Data from the Multicenter AIDS Cohort Study (MACS) presented by Plankey et al. (2007) considered the associations between HIV seroconversion and methamphetamine use among HIV-negative men. Results indicated that there was a 1.46 increase in the relative hazard for HIV seroconversion associated with methamphetamine use. In combination with the use of inhalant nitrates (i.e., poppers) the relative hazard was 3.05. The sexual

*Figure 5.2.* Methamphetamine prevention posters addressing the meth–sex link. Copyright 2006 by The Crystal Meth Working Group. Reprinted with permission.

risk associated with methamphetamine use is particularly pronounced among injection drug users, with MSM reporting inconsistent condom use with both female and male sexual partners for oral, anal, and vaginal sex (Bull et al., 2002). However, reductions in risk taking, as indicated by number of sexual partners, have been established for gay and bisexual men after receiving treatment for methamphetamine use (Reback et al., 2004). Within 1 year of treatment, the number of sexual partners in the month prior to assessment was reduced from 8.6 to 2.9.

Among gay, bisexual, and other MSM, methamphetamine heightens intentional unprotected insertive or receptive anal intercourse, known colloquially as "barebacking" (Halkitis, 2007; Halkitis, Parsons, & Wilton, 2003a). In multilevel models, patterns of methamphetamine use are highly associated with use of Viagra (Halkitis & Green, 2007), providing a proxy indication of the meth–sex link. (It should be noted that the combination of methamphet-amine with Viagra is common, due in part to the erectile dysfunction experi-enced by users of stimulants such as methamphetamine.) In metropolitan areas with large gay communities, which are also HIV epicenters, such as New York City, the drug is commonly used by MSM who frequent commercial and pub-lic sex environments, as well as private sex parties (Halkitis & Parsons, 2002; Halkitis, Shrem, et al., 2005), where use occurs in the context of sexual encoun-ters with anonymous partners of undisclosed HIV status.

Frosch et al. (1996) were among the first to document the association between sexual risk taking and methamphetamine use in gay and bisexual men. In a study of 16 methamphetamine-dependent or methamphetamine-abusing gay and bisexual men in Los Angeles, who were participating in a treatment demonstration project between 1989 and 1993, 62% reported unprotected insertive anal intercourse, 50% reported unprotected receptive anal inter-course, and 56% reported sexual intercourse with an HIV-positive partner. Such patterns have also been noted among male commercial sex workers in San Francisco catering to a male client base (Waldorf, Murphy, Lauderback, Reinarman, & Marotta, 1990). In the National Institute on Drug Abuse-funded Three Community Study of Methamphetamine Use, findings indicated that 76% of the sample reported increased sexual activity because of the use of the drug but that this relationship was more pronounced among the gay partic-ipants than the heterosexual participants; compared with their heterosexual counterparts, gay men reported a greater likelihood of multiple sexual partner-ing (72% vs. 57%) and a greater likelihood of having had 50 or more sexual partners in the period preceding the interview (Morgan, Beck, Joe, McDonnell, & Gutierrez, 1994). Greater validity in regard to the relation between metham-phetamine use and sexual risk taking is evidenced in a prospective longitudinal study of 736 men followed in San Francisco (Colfax et al., 2005). Over a 48-month period, high-risk sexual behavior was more likely during periods of higher levels of methamphetamine, powdered cocaine, and popper use.

For gay and bisexual men, who represent the segment of the population most affected by HIV (CDC, 2005), the risky sexual behavior associated with methamphetamine use increases the risk of HIV seroconversion. In a 1998 published study conducted at Los Angeles County's "Project Open-Window," a program aimed at early detection of HIV infection, of the 26 newly HIV-diagnosed MSM, 58% had indicated use of methamphetamine during the period in which HIV infection occurred (Senterfiti, Harawa, Whitfield, Kerndt, & Daar, 1998). Similarly, use of methamphetamine at least one time has been linked to a 2.3 times greater likelihood of seroconversion among gay men (Darrow et al., 1987). Among previously HIV-undiagnosed gay and bisexual men, those newly diagnosed men who used methamphetamine in the 4 months prior to assessment reported both an equivalent likelihood of hav-ing sex with nonprimary partners and an equivalent number of partners as those men who were confirmed to be HIV negative and had used methamphetamine (Halkitis, Green, & Mourgues, 2005). However, the newly diagnosed men were 18 times more likely to engage in unprotected receptive anal intercourse while high on methamphetamine than their seronegative counterparts, suggesting a complex interplay between use of the drug, sexual partnering, and sexual acts.

However, the sexual risk taking associated with methamphetamine use in MSM is not as monolithic as might be implied by some. In fact, recent investigations have documented serosorting strategies (i.e., strategies for selecting partners based on HIV serostatus) and sexual positioning (sexual roles given HIV serostatus; see Siconolfi & Moeller, 2007, for a review) among methamphetamine users. For example, Halkitis, Shrem, et al. (2005) found that HIV-negative, methamphetamine-using gay and bisexual men reported fewer acts of both anal receptive and oral receptive sexual behavior with partners who were known to be HIV positive, and that HIV-positive men reported more unprotected acts with their seroconcordant sexual nonprimary partners. Overall, the HIV-positive participants also reported unprotected anal intercourse of any kind at higher rates than their HIV-negative counterparts. This finding is similar to those indicated by Semple et al. (2006b), in which the 132 HIV-positive, methamphetamine-using MSM who constituted the sample reported fewer acts of unprotected insertive anal intercourse with HIV-negative as compared with HIV-positive partners. No differences were noted for either oral sexual activities or anal receptive activities across partner serostatus.

## METHAMPHETAMINE AND SEXUAL BEHAVIOR IN HETEROSEXUAL MEN AND WOMEN

This pattern of more frequent and more promiscuous sexual behaviors related to methamphetamine use is not limited to gay and bisexual men. Klee (1992) reported a heightened sex drive and level of desire among female methamphetamine users. In a sample of methamphetamine-injecting women in San Francisco studied between 2003 and 2005, the women who injected the drug were more likely than women who did not to report unprotected anal intercourse and a greater likelihood of multiple sexual partners (Lorvick, Martinez, Gee, & Kral, 2006). Molitor et al. (1999) also found that methamphetamine-injecting women who were not in treatment engaged in vaginal intercourse more frequently than their heroin-injecting counterparts. These findings corroborate earlier work (Semple, Grant, & Patterson, 2004) in which 31% of a sample of 98 heterosexually identified, methamphetamine-using women indicated an anonymous sexual partner in the 2 months prior to assessment. Moreover, the women additionally indicated an average of approximately 8 sexual partners in that same time frame. Furthermore, in an analysis of data collected at HIV testing sites in California, Molitor et al. (1998) documented higher rates of sex among women who used but did not inject methamphetamine, as well as greater number of sexual partners in the 12 months prior to assessment for heterosexual female methamphetamine users than nonusers (4.5 vs. 2.4). As is the case with gay and bisexual men, the synergies that surround methamphetamine use and sexuality for women are complex. In a panel conducted at the 2nd National Conference on Methamphetamine, HIV, and Hepatitis, Sheigla Murphy (2007) suggested an interplay between use of the drug by women who are often driven by a desire for weight loss and the accompanying feelings of attractiveness secondary to that weight loss. Furthermore, the euphoria engendered by methamphetamine use, coupled with these new feelings of attractiveness, plays a role in the associated sexual promiscuity. Morgan and Beck (1997) noted similar ideas. In a sample of 385 HIV-negative male and female heterosexual users, more frequent use of methamphetamine was found to be associated with using larger quantities of the drug and having a greater number of sexual partners (Semple et al., 2005).

There is a paucity of literature available that explores sexual promiscuity among heterosexual male methamphetamine users. However, one such study conducted between 2001 and 2003 among heterosexual men in Northern California found that methamphetamine users were more likely be sexually active with a female partner, have multiple female partners, have a casual or anonymous female partner, have anal intercourse with a casual or anonymous female partner, have a female partner who injected drugs, or to have received money or drugs for sex from a male or female partner than nonusers (CDC, March 17, 2006). In addition, in a sample of mostly male, White, heterosexual methamphetamine users, Semple, Patterson, and Grant (2004) found that within a 2-month period, approximately 22 acts of vaginal intercourse were reported, while 86% of the sample noted that they had engaged in long, continuous sexual experiences ("marathon sex") while high on the drug. In this sample, one third of the men reported having anal sex, using condoms only 25% percent of the time. In the previously noted Molitor et al. study (1998), more sexual partners were noted for heterosexual male methamphetamine users than their nonusing counterparts (4.5 vs. 2.9). In a sample of drug-injecting African American men, those who injected methamphetamine also indicated more sexual partners (Somlai, Kelly, McAuliffe, Ksobiech, & Hackl, 2003).

Although scant, the existing behavioral and biomedical literature on the relation between methamphetamine use and sexual risk taking among heterosexual men and women points to similar associations found in the research with gay and bisexual men. Given the vulnerability of women to HIV infection through heterosexual contact (CDC, 2005) as well as the transmission of other bacterial and viral pathogens between homosexual men and women, the hypersexuality engendered by use of the drug presents a health threat to this segment of the population. For example, in a sample of 272 African American heterosexually identified men in Los Angeles, being infected with HIV was associated with a three times greater likelihood of having a history of methamphetamine use (Wohl et al., 2002). Despite all of this, there are limited data with regard to HIV seroconversion and associated risk behaviors, especially for methamphetamine-using women (Murphy, 2007).

In one of the few behavioral investigations that exists, Semple, Grant, et al. (2004) documented high levels of sexual risk taking as indicated by the number of sexual partners, anonymous sexual partnering, and unprotected oral and vaginal intercourse in the period of 2 months prior to assessment among the 98 methamphetamine-using, heterosexually identified females. Users in the sample reported approximately 13 days of methamphetamine use. Furthermore, as many as 90% of casual and 76% of anonymous sexual partners reported to also be methamphetamine users, thus increasing the likelihood of unprotected sexual behaviors. In addition, the women reported an average of approximately 80 sexual acts, with approximately 70 of these acts being unprotected. Of the 34 vaginal acts, 27 were unprotected. Finally, slightly less than half of the sample reported receptive anal intercourse with an average of 8 such acts in the period of assessment. Similarly in a sample of 385 HIV-negative methamphetamine users, Semple et al. (2005) reported that those with higher levels of impulsivity had more sexual partners and engaged in more unprotected oral and vaginal sex than those with lower impulsivity scores. In an analysis of female and male methamphetamine users who had used 32 times in the prior 2 months, protection was reportedly used only one quarter of the time during anal sex, one third of the time for vaginal sex, and 7% of the time for oral sex in that same assessment window (Semple, Patterson, et al., 2004). Similarly, in a sample of 477 methamphetamine-using women (Lorvick et al., 2006), those who injected the drug indicated a higher likelihood than those noninjecting women to engage in both anal intercourse (22% vs. 11%) and unprotected anal intercourse (16% vs. 8%). However, rates of unprotected vaginal intercourse were equivalent. Moreover, whereas 33% of the injecting women reported 5 or more sexual partners in the 6 months prior to assessment, the probability was only 14% for noninjecting methamphetamine users. A current investigation is examining such sexual behavior patterns in Mexican and Mexican American female users who reside along the San Diego–Tijuana border (Rogala & Lopez-Zetina, 2008).

In HEY-Man, a population-based study of HIV infection, sexually transmitted diseases, and associated risk behaviors among heterosexual men ages 18 to 35 residing in the low income neighborhoods of Alameda, Contra Costa, San Francisco, San Joaquin, and San Mateo, California, methamphetamine use was associated with more sexual risk taking (CDC, March 17, 2006). Within the sample of 968 men, 9.6% reported use of the drug outside of the window of 6 months prior to assessment, whereas 6% reported recent use (within the 6 months prior to assessment). Both recent users and historical users of methamphetamine reported a greater likelihood of engaging in anal sex with a female partner than did nonusers. Moreover, recent users indicated a greater likelihood than historical users of having engaged in sex with a casual or anonymous female partners, reported having a greater likelihood of multiple partners, and a greater likelihood of having a partner who injected drugs. However, no associations between drug use and condom use were revealed, a condition confounded by the fact that there was infrequent condom use for vaginal sex in the entire sample.

The findings of Semple and her colleagues are also quantified by Molitor et al. (1998) in an analysis of methamphetamine use and sexual behavior data collected by the Office of AIDS in California. In this sample, heterosexual men who used the drug were two times more likely to have had sex with a sex worker than men who had not used the drug. They were also 1.4 times more likely to have had a sexually transmitted disease and 2.5 times more likely to have traded sex for drugs. Among the women in the sample, those who had used methamphetamine were 3.8 times more likely to have had sex with a sex worker, 1.7 times more likely to have had a sexually transmitted disease, and 6.7 times more likely to have traded sex for drugs. Moreover, the use of methamphetamine was associated with higher levels of sexual risk taking (i.e., lower rates of condom use for vaginal, anal receptive, and anal insertive intercourse) even after controlling for the use of cocaine, alcohol, and marijuana.

CONCLUSION

The relationship between methamphetamine use, sexuality, sexual behavior, and sexual risk taking is highly complex. Whether methamphetamine is directly responsible for increased levels of risk taking among users is certainly an area that requires further examination. There is no doubt that drug-using behavior and sexual promiscuity are highly associated. What is not so evident are the causal paths that help us understand these associations. Numerous behavioral investigations have found strong correlational evidence, but what remains unclear is whether the drug is the cause of the risk that accompanies it or whether it is simply a catalyst for sexual risk taking that would have occurred either with or without the use of this particular substance or with use of a different substance, such as cocaine, Ecstasy, or even alcohol. Perhaps there are underlying personality characteristics that drive certain individuals to use the drug for sexual enhancement, or perhaps the motivations for both drug use and sex are the same. For example, Nina (2007) documented lower levels of self-esteem among those who are drawn to methamphetamine, compared with those who are drawn to either cocaine or Ecstasy. For the gay population, perhaps the sociocultural norms in regard to sexual behavior and performance are at the crux of this complex phenomenon. Despite the lack of clarity on what the causal routes are, it seems safe to say that the association between sex and methamphetamine is one that is not fully understood by the users themselves or by those who are working with this drug-using population. In this regard, such orientations to the drug itself suggest that research must continue to focus on the enmeshment that exists between the two and that treatment modalities continue to address the interactive effects of sex and methamphetamine use. This phenomenon creates an immediate and urgent public health concern, which stems from two sources: (a) methamphetamine use in and of itself and the potential for abuse and dependence; and (b) the potential transmission of pathogens, such as HIV and other sexually transmitted infections, which are facilitated by the intimate link that exists between methamphetamine use and sexual risk taking—the dual epidemic. (Halkitis et al., 2001).

In this chapter, I examined enhanced sexuality and sexual promiscuity as motivation for methamphetamine use. However, there are numerous other factors that may predispose an individual to use and become addicted to the drug. In the following chapter, I explore more fully the biological, psychological, and social antecedents to methamphetamine use.

# 6

## MOTIVATIONS AND ANTECEDENTS OF METHAMPHETAMINE USE: RISK BASES

The path to methamphetamine addiction is a nonlinear, nonuniform process that varies from person to person. Like all other paths to drug dependency, such behavior neither exists in a vacuum nor manifests itself in an easily predictive fashion; rather a complex array of biological, psychological, and social processes interact to drive it. In addition, it is imperative to recognize that not all individuals who use a drug will become addicted. Some will choose to use it once and never again, others will become recreational users, and a smaller subset will become dependent on the substance in some way or another. The path to methamphetamine addiction is a complex one, with no single factor being solely responsible for the development of this health problem. Also, treatment for the addiction must take into consideration the various factors that predispose an individual to this behavior. Because of these realities, an understanding of the processes that fuel the initial use of methamphetamine in a person's life is crucial. It is also important to appreciate the resiliencies that some individuals embody, which act as protective factors for deterring the process of becoming addicted to methamphetamine. Understanding these protective factors may be useful in enacting future prevention efforts.

In chapter 4, the biopsychosocial effects of methamphetamine use and addiction were considered. In this chapter, consideration is given to the biopsychosocial antecedents of this drug addiction. First, the concept of addiction–dependence is presented to frame the discussion. Next, medical and biological factors that may lead to methamphetamine dependence are described, followed by a consideration of mental health vulnerabilities that may predispose the individual to this addiction. Finally, the role of social influences in regard to methamphetamine addition is fully delineated.

## METHAMPHETAMINE ADDICTION

At this point, it is important to further clarify what is meant by the term *addiction*. According to Lee (2006), "the fundamental concept of substance dependence is that a person no longer has control of the drug or the use of it—rather, the drug is controlling the person, whether by psychological or physiological means" (p. 46). Lee's definition is a paraphrase of the definition of addiction as delineated in the *Diagnostic and Statistical Manual of Mental Disorders* (4th ed., text rev., *DSM–IV–TR*; American Psychiatric Association, 2000). Nora Volkow, director of the National Institute in Drug Abuse, further illuminated this concept of addiction and suggested, "The use of drugs has been recorded since the beginning of civilization. Humans in my view will always want to experiment with things that make them feel good" (Lemonick, 2007, ¶ 7).

However, it is important to differentiate levels of drug use. As has been noted throughout this volume, the use of methamphetamine can be characterized as falling along a continuum from occasional or social use to abuse to addiction or dependence (American Psychiatric Association, 2000). A methamphetamine abuser is characterized by at least one of the following behaviors: failure to fulfill major obligations; use of the drug when physically hazardous; recurrent legal problems; recurrent social or interpersonal problems, or both. The methamphetamine-addicted individual may experience one or more of these conditions and is also characterized as dependent when three or more of the following criteria are evidenced: tolerance to the substance; withdrawal of the substance; large amounts of drug use over a long period; unsuccessful efforts to cut down use of the drug; spending time in obtaining the substance, which replaces social, occupational, or recreational activities; and/or continued use of the drug despite adverse consequences.

For the methamphetamine user, the onset of dependence may be a slow and gradual process or it may be more immediate. In our society, a belief about the drug suggests that using methamphetamine once will lead to an addiction. This idea may be overinflated and is often considered to be a fear tactic used by some educational campaigns (see chap. 8, this volume). Like the development of many other addictions, drug and nondrug alike, the process of developing a methamphetamine addiction is complex. An understanding of the potential risk factors that lead to dependence may illuminate the varying trajectories related to addiction that manifest across individuals. That "the complex interrelations between society, culture, psych, and soma shape methamphetamine use over time" was indicated by von Mayrhauser, von Brecht, and Anglin (2002, p. 46).

An understanding of the motivations for methamphetamine is illustrated well by the words and stories of users. Gay Men's Health Crisis (2007), an AIDS service organization in New York City, recently published an educational booklet titled *Hurricane Tina*. Within the pages of the booklet, testimonials of methamphetamine-using gay men suggest possible explanations for use of the drug—"Because of loneliness," "Cause I was young and had to experiment," "I just wanted a momentary separation of mind and body . . . ," "Depression. Depression" (see Figure 6.1). Although these fragmented ideas do not provide a thorough explanation of the potential antecedents of methamphetamine use, they do provide insights into many of the feelings that users express in regard to their need for this drug. Gay and bisexual male users have indicated that in addition to sexual disinhibition, which drives many to use it, other motivations include the development of physical and emotional prowess, as well as enhancement of socialization (Halkitis, Fischgrund, & Parsons, 2005). In addition, for HIV-positive individuals, the desire to address the negative affect associated with their serostatus may provide the impetus for use of the drug (Semple, Patterson, & Grant, 2002). Among heterosexuals, the desire for more energy, to get high, and to party have been cited as factors associated with use of the drug (Semple, Grant, & Patterson, 2004), and for women, such motivations may include the "need to get it all done" and manage multiple roles (Murphy, 2007). A recent storyline on *ER* portrayed a soccer mom driven to methamphetamine use in order to meet the demands of her life. "Soccer moms use it so that they feel they can achieve the Soccer Mom image" (The City of White Rock, 2006, ¶ 14). In chapters 9 and 10 of this volume, medical and mental health practitioners, respectively, share their own case studies of working with methamphetamine-using individuals and provide further insights into the potential motivations for use of the drug.

Of course, the use of other drugs such as marijuana, alcohol, and nicotine may provide a gateway to the use of methamphetamine. In fact, Holley (2005) included an entire chapter of her book on understanding how the use of such substances may lead to the eventual use of methamphetamine, stating "methamphetamine is not usually the first drug abused by the addict" (p. 109). More recently, Halkitis and Palamar (2008) found that in gay and bisexual men, the use of methamphetamine usually follows the onset of cocaine, Ecstasy, and ketamine. Specifically, in club-drug using gay and bisexual men, 59% of 437 men in this New York City-based sample reported cocaine as the first club drug that they had used, whereas the majority of those who had used methamphetamine indicated it was the fourth drug in their sequence of initiation,

*Figure 6.1.* Testimonials of methamphetamine use from Gay Men's Health Crisis Hurricane Tina [brochure]. From "Hurricane Tina," Gay Men's Health Crisis. Copyright 2007 by Laura Horwitz and Francisco Roque. Reprinted with permission of Gay Men's Health Crisis.

following Ecstasy and ketamine, but preceding gamma-hydroxybutyrate. Nonetheless, it is unclear whether such "stepping stone" or gateway theories (H. Cohen, 1972; Kandel & Faust, 1975) are fundamental to truly understanding the path to methamphetamine dependence. Given the high level of polysubstance use that is evidenced in methamphetamine-using populations (see chap. 1, this volume), it is likely that the vulnerabilities that predispose individuals to methamphetamine use are the same vulnerabilities that place these individuals at risk of drug dependence in general. Knowledge of risk bases is crucial to our understanding of addiction in general and of methamphetamine addiction in particular.

Despite all of these insights in regard to the potential motivations for methamphetamine use and addiction, there is still a very limited understanding in regard to the trajectories of these behaviors. Stories in the popular press, such as *Newsweek* (Jefferson, 2005), describe methamphetamine as "America's Most Dangerous Drug" and provide images and stories of users from all races, ethnicities, and socioeconomic groups. However, these articles never fully examine or delineate the deep-rooted factors that lead to methamphetamine addiction beyond the understanding that the drug enhances feelings of pleasure and increases energy. If our prevention and intervention efforts are centered on such simplistic explanations of the motivations for use, we will find ourselves hardpressed to effectively treat this addiction. Enhancement of pleasure and increasing energy levels are not necessarily such damaging desires in our fast-paced and demanding society. This idea is consistent with those of Hawkins, Catalano, and Miller (1992), who outlined the risk factors that may predispose adolescent and emergent adults to the use of alcohol and other drugs. In their work, the emphasis is multifaceted and encompasses the understanding of physiological, psychological, and social bases of the development of these drug-use trajectories. What follows is a discussion of more intrinsic and intrapersonal factors that may motivate an individual to use methamphetamine or place him or her at risk of becoming addicted to the drug.

## BIOLOGICAL AND MEDICAL BASES

As indicated in chapter 1, methamphetamine has historically been used as a treatment for attention-deficit/hyperactivity disorder (ADHD). Although use of methamphetamine as a treatment for this condition is typically not initiated until other treatment methods have failed (Halpern, 1999), the ability of the drug to alleviate symptoms associated with ADHD provides a potential explanation of why some individuals are drawn to and may become addicted to methamphetamine.

ADHD is a neurological impairment and is associated with a persistent pattern of inattention, hyperactivity, or both; forgetfulness; impulsivity; and distractibility (American Psychiatric Association, 2000), which can lead to faulty social relations and decreased levels of self-esteem. The condition is estimated to affect approximately 5% of adults (Holley, 2005, p. 138). Methamphetamine effectively masks the negative behaviors and feelings that are associated with ADHD. Because of the various neurological effects of the drug, which were previously described, it may empower individuals with ADHD to feel focused, confident, and empowered in their ability to navigate social relations. For this reason, individuals who are undiagnosed or untreated for ADHD may be vulnerable to methamphetamine addiction. According to Khantzian (1985), the illicit use of methamphetamine can be understood in terms of self-medication for individuals with ADHD. Similarly, Holley (2005) stated, "the National Institutes of Health consensus conference found that the appropriate use of Ritalin or Adderal, both of which are amphetamine derivatives, does not increase the risk for methamphetamine addiction. Untreated ADHD most certainly does" (p. 138).

The idea presented in this quote is further supported by existing literature, as numerous studies have associated childhood ADHD with substance-abuse disorders (Horner & Scheibe, 1997; Wilens, Biederman, Mick, Farone, & Spencer, 1997). In an investigation that included 413 Japanese prisoners without drug addiction and 282 with addictions, Matsumoto, Kamijo, Yamaguchi, Iskei, and Hirayasu (2005) found a very significant association between childhood ADHD tendencies and illicit drug use. Specifically, those who were drug abusing and had childhood ADHD were more likely to be abusing methamphetamine than any other illicit drugs, including toluene (i.e., methylbenzene or phenylmethane, a benzene solvent) or marijuana. Such findings have been further corroborated by Matsumoto et al. (2005), who found that more than half of 54 methamphetamine users had higher scores than the requisite score needed to diagnose ADHD as indicated by the Wender Utah Rating Scale. Similarly, Sim et al. (2002) compared the cognitive deficits of methamphetamine users with and without an ADHD symptomatology. In all, 29 methamphetamine abusers with ADHD were compared with 41 abusers without ADHD symptoms. Although both groups demonstrated impairments in cognitive functioning such as abstract thinking and psychomotor speed, methamphetamine abusers with ADHD also demonstrated additional deficits in attention and executive functions. These additional deficits seem to relate to the finding that many of the methamphetamine addicts had ADHD symptomatology as children. Even though ADHD may provide a medical basis for methamphetamine addiction, and untreated ADHD may exacerbate the abuse of the drug, chronic use of the drug heightens impulsivity and decreases attention and other executive functions in adult populations, as described in chapters 4 and 5 of this volume.

The vulnerability of individuals with untreated ADHD to methamphetamine addiction can also be explained on a neurogenetic level. According to

Volkow, "Some people have a genetic predisposition to addiction" (Lemonick, 2007, ¶ 8). In particular, genetic defects have been associated with ADHD and, in particular, with the coding of defective dopamine receptors. Variations in genes that code for both the dopaminergic D2 and D4 receptors have been associated with impulsive, addictive, and compulsive behavior, leading to a "reward deficiency syndrome" (Holley, 2005, p. 140). As a result, a proclivity toward the use and abuse of methamphetamine by individuals with untreated ADHD may be explained by a need to compensate for reduction in feelings of pleasure that are due to the genetic variations that affect the dopamine receptors. Studies have indicated that individuals who are vulnerable to addictions such as methamphetamine (Volkow, Chang, Wang, Fowler, Ding, et al., 2001) have reduced levels of dopamine receptors. Because of this condition, individuals may be more apt to seek out methamphetamine to compensate for the irregularities that exist in the dopaminergic system. Similar findings have been associated with individuals who may be vulnerable to heroin (Wang et al., 1997) and cocaine addictions (Volkow et al., 1993). As illustrated in chapter 4 of this volume, methamphetamine has direct effects on the dopamine system, flooding the brain with the neurotransmitter and preventing its reuptake, thus resulting in elevated feelings of pleasure. The flooding of the brain with dopamine because of methamphetamine use, enhanced by certain genetic circumstances, may be a possible reason for the development of the addiction. As Lee (2006) suggested, "the more often a drug stimulates the brain-reward circuit, the primitive brain becomes more strongly programmed to the repeat the behavior of using the drug" (p. 51).

Another perspective, which considers the biological aspects for developing addictions with psychological processes, is given by Robinson and Berridge (1993) in a theoretical conceptualization known as incentive-sensitization theory. Although this paradigm does not, in and of itself, explain the onset of drug use, it does postulate that the effects of drugs such as methamphetamine on dopamine neurotransmission are key to understanding the development of drug use. Moreover, these effects on the dopamine system may affect neural adaptations in some individuals, rendering them increasingly and potentially sensitized to the drugs and their associated stimuli. All of these neural effects are coupled with associative learning, which may lead to greater dependence on the substance. Thus, if individuals are rendered vulnerable to methamphetamine because of biological states, the onset of use and the potential biological, psychological, and cognitive impacts as delineated by Robinson and Berridge (1993) provide a basis for considering the development of the ongoing addiction.

In recent years, the biological bases for methamphetamine use and addiction have been studied through the implementation of human brain imaging with magnetic resonance spectroscopy, structural magnetic resonance imaging, functional magnetic resonance imaging, positron emission tomography, and single positive emission computed tomography scans. These are thoroughly described in Fowler, Volkow, Kassed, and Chang (2007). According to Chang and Linde (2007), the combination of genes, genetic markers, and imaging can reveal something about who is at risk and who might respond to an addictive drug in a certain way; however, this area of research is relatively new and exploratory in nature.

In addition, genetic vulnerabilities are associated with methamphetamine abuse (London et al., 2004). Barr et al. (2006) provided a summary of genes that may predispose individuals to the use of methamphetamine and noted that these studies have been primarily undertaken with East Asian populations. These studies suggest that there are numerous associations with genetic variations and that tendencies toward methamphetamine use include but are not limited to genes that control dopamine transporters and receptors, as well as receptors associated with gamma aminobutyric acid (GABA), an inhibitory neurotransmitter in the central nervous system. GABA is associated with an upbeat mood and positive self-image, which is a side effect often described by methamphetamine users. If genetic variations in the production, transmission, and transport of GABA result in faulty signaling, then the administration of methamphetamine may help to compensate for this atypical physiological state. Recently GABA has been considered as a treatment for addictions (Lemonick, 2007).

Predisposition to methamphetamine use and dependence also may be understood in terms of mood disturbances and metabolic abnormalities evidenced in the cerebrum of methamphetamine users. London et al. (2004) compared 17 individuals who had been abstaining from methamphetamine use for 4 to 7 days with 18 control subjects with regard to depression and anxiety as well as glucose metabolism in various areas of the brain to consider the associations between abnormalities in glucose metabolism and these mood disturbances. Findings indicated that methamphetamine users not only reported higher levels of depression and anxiety than the control subjects but also that these states covaried with irregularities in the metabolism of glucose in certain areas of the brain. These findings suggest that such abnormal metabolism of glucose may provide a risk base for the use and abuse of methamphetamine.

Finally, although it is beyond the scope of this particular understanding of biological bases for methamphetamine use, it is worth noting that certain chronic conditions, the treatments associated with these conditions, or both, may indirectly impact the onset of methamphetamine use. In particular, the physical burden of HIV disease and HIV antiretroviral treatment have been cited as factors associated with use of methamphetamine among HIV-positive men who have sex with men (Colfax & Shoptaw, 2005; Halkitis, Fischgrund, et al., 2005; Semple et al., 2002). More recently, consideration has been given to the condition of hepatitis C and associated interferon therapy, as the burdens of both the treatment and the disease may cause some to initiate the use of methamphetamine (Lampinen, Greatheart, Schilder, & Kowdley, 2007).

# MENTAL HEALTH BASES

For many of its users, dependence on methamphetamine is often understood in terms of emotional or mental health states, including depression, self-esteem, anxiety, and stress. For others, these may be underlying conditions of which they are not fully aware, which are eased by the administration of methamphetamine. "For some people, drugs are a way that they have found to deal with the reality of day to day living" (Lee, 2006, p. 52). Such psychiatric states among methamphetamine users have been noted in direct comparisons with those with cocaine addiction (Copeland & Sorensen, 2001). Specifically, among 345 individuals who sought outpatient treatment for stimulant abuse, methamphetamine users were more likely to report both addiction-unrelated psychiatric diagnoses and to be taking psychiatric medications. As Volkow (2001) indicated, the comorbidity of drugs such as methamphetamine and psychiatric states indicates both a risk for individuals to use drugs and a high level of psychopathology that is induced by the use of substances. As a result, the psychological, psychiatric, and mental health precursors of methamphetamine use are not easily delineated.

## Depression

One of the most commonly indicated mental health bases of methamphetamine use is depression, which may lead both to the onset of drug use and the potential development of dependence. Methamphetamine use and depression are often viewed as comorbid conditions that must be considered in conjunction during treatment for this drug addiction (Jaffe, Shoptaw, Stein, Reback, & Rotheram-Fuller, 2007; Sadek, Vigil, Grant, Heaton, & The HNRC Group, 2007). Levels of depression range widely in the population, from major depression to minor depression, the latter being characterized by less acute symptoms than are evident in major depression. Even moderate to mild levels of depression may serve as an impetus for methamphetamine use if left untreated. "Untreated depression preceding the onset of drug abuse is temporarily relieved by methamphetamine" (Holley, 2005, p. 149). This is supported by the findings of Kalechstein et al. (2000), who reported that among 1,580 individuals who had been arrested, depressive symptoms were more likely to be reported among those who reported methamphetamine dependence than those who did not report this addiction. Zweben et al. (2004) corroborated such findings in an assessment of 1,016 individuals enrolled in the Methamphetamine Treatment project, where individuals reported high levels of depression as well as other psychiatric complications, including attempted suicide. Similarly, among 590 high school students in Canada, gay, lesbian, and bisexual students were more likely both to report methamphetamine use and to report depression in the month prior to assessment (Lampinen, McGhee, & Martin, 2006).

Among 98 heterosexually identified female methamphetamine users, depression was the most frequently reported psychiatric diagnosis, with 53 of the women in this sample reporting this state (Semple, Grant, et al., 2004). On the basis of clinical diagnosis using the Beck Depression Inventory, approximately one third of the women in the study by Beck, Steer, and Brown (1996) were classified as moderately depressed and approximately one fifth of the women as severely depressed. Finally, in a comparison of 224 cocaine users with 500 methamphetamine users admitted for outpatient treatment between 1989 and 1995 in a treatment facility in California, methamphetamine users were more likely than cocaine users to report being "depressed a lot" (19.3% vs. 12.1%, respectively; Rawson, Huber, Brethen, Obert, Gulati, et al., 2002). However, it should be noted that among methamphetamine users, depressive symptoms are equivalent between binge and nonbinge users (Semple, Patterson, & Grant, 2003). Such homogeneity in depressive symptomatology among methamphetamine users is also supported in longitudinal investigations among gay and bisexual men in whom this psychological state fails to differentiate level of use at onset and pattern of use across the course of the year (Halkitis, Mukherjee, & Palamar, 2007).

The use of methamphetamine as a form of self-medication for depressive symptoms may ultimately serve only to exacerbate the condition (Meredith, Jaffe, Ang-Lee, & Saxon, 2005; Rawson, Gonzales, & Brethen, 2002), given the physiological and psychological reactions of the body when users are coming down from their high. Such feelings may be so severe that they may be associated with suicidal ideation. This dual-edged sword of methamphetamine use with regard to depression is summarized effectively by Rabkin (2006), who stated, "depression is both a precursor and a consequence of chronic MA [methamphetamine] use" (p. 4).

Not only may methamphetamine directly impact depression by alleviating the mood disturbances engendered by this condition, but it also may mask feelings of fatigue as well as lack of concentration, both characteristic of a depressive state (American Psychiatric Association, 2000). Methamphetamine may help to both increase energy levels and allow the individual to be more focused and able to concentrate on tasks, as has been previously described in relation to ADHD. Thus, a desire to overcome these states may provide additional impetus for the users of methamphetamine.

For HIV-positive individuals, the negative affect and depression that are often associated with this health condition are cited as factors that may predispose some men to use methamphetamine (Semple et al., 2002). HIV-positive individuals are more prone to depressive symptomatology, and levels of major depression are elevated in this segment of the population (Rabkin, 2006). Evans et al. (2005) estimated that depression among HIV-positive individuals may range from 5% to 20%, depending on the manner in which the condition is assessed. The use of methamphetamine by seropositive individuals may be initiated or exacerbated by an HIV diagnosis as a means of coping with the feelings that are due to the determination of sero-conversion. In a study of 48 gay and bisexual men, 15% of those men who were HIV-positive indicated that emotional support for negative mood was a key factor in driving their methamphetamine use, even though many recognized the only temporary "beneficial" effects of the drug (Halkitis, Fischgrund, et al., 2005).

Even when depression per se is not assessed, bases for use of methamphetamine appear to be related to the negative affect imposed by a depressive state. For example, in their assessment of 350 methamphetamine users, Brecht, O'Brien, von Mayrhauser, and Anglin (2004) reported that 24% of users indicate that the drug is used as an escape and that this understanding is equally present among male and female users. For all of the reasons given earlier, treatment for methamphetamine dependence with antidepressant medications, which is more fully described in chapter 7, has yielded some effectiveness.

## Stress and Coping

The role of stress as a factor, which may influence the onset of substance use, as well as a factor that may increase the probability of relapse, has been abundantly articulated. The stress response exists as part of the body's regulatory system, very primal in nature, and was crucial to the survival of our prehistoric ancestors as means of survival (Canon, 1936). Chrousos (1998) further articulated the stress response as a rapid and pervasive adjustment of the internal states of an organism in light of a threat. Throughout the course of evolution, threats to our lives have changed, and today stress is viewed as a biological and biobehavioral process that can either protect or cause damage (Institute of Medicine, 2001).

With regard to drug use, stress has been related to self-administration of substances in animal studies as well as human laboratory studies (Sinha, 2001). The use of substances, including methamphetamine, by individuals, has been postulated to occur as a means of reducing feelings of stress (Dawes et al., 2000; Kosten, Rounsaville, & Kleber, 1986). This is evidenced even among people who have demonstrated extended periods of abstinence. It is hypothesized that stress causes a biological response in the brain through the release of a peptide corticotrophin-releasing factor (CRF), which may in turn impact on stress-related behaviors, including substance use (Jacobsen, Southwick, & Kosten, 2001). Furthermore, some initial work has shown that the neural connections associated with CRF are also the ones through which stress is realized (Piazza & Le Moal, 1996).

Stress as a predisposing factor in explaining methamphetamine use is particularly relevant in consideration of the prevalence of this drug use among gay men. The use of drugs by gay and bisexual men has been linked to a desire to relieve stress and strain (Barrett et al., 1995; Leigh & Stall, 1993; Wills, 1985). In particular, the drugs are used as a mechanism for coping with the oppression from homophobia, racism, and poverty as articulated by Latino men (Diaz, 1998) and as evidenced in sample of Black methamphetamine users in New York City who expressed the power of the drug to overcome the oppression they experience both in the Black communities and the gay circles in which they navigate (Halkitis & Jerome, 2008). Drug use has been directly attributed to the desire of gay and bisexual men to avoid difficult situations (Paul, Stall, Crosby, Barrett, & Midanik, 1994). Among methamphetamine-using gay and bisexual men, use of the drug has been reported as a means of coping with the loneliness that these men feel in their lives or as a coping mechanism for the realties of HIV for both HIV-positive and HIV-negative gay men (Halkitis, Parsons, & Wilton, 2003b). Lewis and Ross (1995, p. 103) reported use of methamphetamine as a means of coping with HIV disease on both individual and community levels. Use of recreational drugs as a mechanism for coping with HIV illness has been reported elsewhere among a sample of 156 HIV-positive gay and bisexual men and was related significantly to risky sexual behaviors (Robins, Dew, Davidson, & Penkower, 1994). The frequency of methamphetamine use among gay and bisexual men has been associated with the desire to escape the stress created by social situations (Halkitis, Parsons, & Wilton, 2003a). The need to escape the perceived pressures experienced in social contexts has been noted as a primary reason that gay and bisexual men actually use this substance (Halkitis, Fischgrund, et al., 2005; Halkitis, Parsons, & Stirrat, 2001).

In addition, stress may be applicable to understanding the use of methamphetamine across all other segments of the population. The prevalence of the drug among both the rural and semirural low-income or low-SES populations might be explained in part by the economic realities confronted by such individuals. Moreover, "depressed economic conditions in rural and semi-rural areas have contributed to methamphetamine's appeal as a source of income" (Wermuth, 2000, p. 423). For the mother who is raising multiple children and trying to balance the demands of her life and the multiple roles she is asked to undertake, the stress induced by these conditions may also lead to the use of the drug. Urban racial and ethnic minority groups experience heightened levels of stress because of immigration status, limited access to resources, and poor economic conditions that may exacerbate perceptions of minimal control. Such findings have been documented among Filipino methamphetamine users in San Francisco (Nemoto, Operario, & Soma, 2002). In this sample of 83 male and female users, frequency of methamphetamine use in the 30 days prior to assessment was significantly related with levels of psychological control, with those indicating less control also reporting more use of the drug. Moreover, depression may exacerbate the tendency to use the drug before sex (Derogatis, Lipman, Rickels, Uhlenhuth, & Covi, 1974).

## Posttraumatic Stress Disorder

In addition to generalized stress, which has been implicated in the onset of drug abuse, posttraumatic stress disorder (PTSD), a condition of chronic stress, has garnered much attention as a risk base for drug abuse. According to the American Psychiatric Association (2000), PTSD develops in response to events that are threatening to life or bodily integrity, witnessing threatening or deadly events, and hearing of violence to or the unexpected or violent death of close associates. Events that could qualify as traumatic, according to the *DSM–IV–TR*, include combat, sexual and physical assault, being held hostage or imprisoned, terrorism, torture, natural and man made disasters, accidents, and receiving a diagnosis of a life threatening illness. The symptoms of PTSD include chronic insomnia; obsessive and compulsive behaviors; high levels of anxiety; depression; and flashbacks, nightmares, or both; and the *DSM–IV–TR* diagnosis of PTSD categorizes these symptoms along three domains: re-experiencing symptoms, avoidance symptoms, and arousal symptoms. PTSD is a condition that has long been evidenced in combat veterans of wars (National Institute of Mental Health, 2006). However, this state, which is a relatively new diagnosis, has also been identified among those who are abused as children or adolescents, in addition to those who have survived disasters caused either by natural phenomena or as a result of war and terrorism. The Oklahoma City bombings and the World Trade Center attacks of 9/11 have been considered in relation to the development of PTSD among survivors and rescue workers, and some behavioral studies have been linked to drug abuse behaviors. In addition, because of the emotional and physical pain endured by some lesbian and gay individuals during the course of their development, some have suggested that lesbian, gay, bisexual, and transgender persons may experience higher rates of PTSD than the general population.

PTSD is a likely condition for the development of methamphetamine dependence in some individuals (Jacobsen et al., 2001; Stewart, Pihl, Conrod, & Dongier, 1998). In their review of the literature, Jacobsen et al. (2001) indicated that among individuals with substance-use disorders, diagnosis of PTSD is found in 21.6% to 43% of such individuals as compared with rates of 8.1% to 24.7% for those without substance-use disorders. Cottler, Compton, Mager, Spitznagel, and Janca (1992) indicated that abusers of cocaine or opiates are three times more likely than comparison subjects who do not meet criteria for substance use to report a traumatic event, report more symptoms and events, and more likely to meet the clinical diagnosis for PTSD. Among 84 patients admitted for detoxification at a private New England hospital, approximately 25% were found to present with significant PTSD symptomatology, and the women in the sample were more likely to report traumatic events in their lives and in effect were more likely to be classified as having PTSD. Despite the implication of PTSD in the development of substance-use disorders, it appears to be underdiagnosed by clinical staff who are working with this population (Dansky, Roitzsch, Brady, & Saladin, 1997).

However, the relation between PTSD and substance use is not unidirectional. Although PTSD may certainly act as a risk base for the development of abuse of drugs such as methamphetamine, the use of the substances themselves may elevate PTSD symptoms. This condition is similar to that with regard to methamphetamine use and depression whereby methamphetamine is used to alleviate feelings of depression; withdrawal from the drug and long-term effects may cause an elevation in depressive symptomatology. Such effects can be understood in relation to the neurobiological implications of methamphetamine use and the stress circuits in the brain that are impacted by both the abuse of drugs and PTSD (Volkow, 2001; see chap. 3, this volume). However, research evidence points, more often than not, to PTSD as a risk base for the development of substance-use disorders, rather than the converse. Such support is given by Chilcoat and Breslau (1998), who examined the causal pathways between PTSD and substance use and showed that exposure to trauma, which did not result in increased levels of PTSD, in turn did not increase the risk of developing substance-abuse disorders. Previously, such understandings have also been shown by Keane, Gerardi, Lyons, and Wolfe (1988) to suggest that PTSD often precedes, and sometimes parallels, the onset of substance abuse. However, such overlapping conditions—and in turn potentially overlapping epidemics in our society—can also be considered in light of the theory of syndemics posited by Stall et al. (2003), inasmuch as drug abuse and mental health issues exacerbate each other. To this understanding, which has been applied primarily to gay men, Stall et al. also considered the overlay of the HIV epidemic in fueling each of these sets of conditions. Yet these ideas are highly applicable to all populations. For example, in considering the impact of early trauma in the form of childhood sexual abuse in women, Wilsnack, Vogeltanz, Klassen, and Harris (1997) documented strong associations between these early life events leading to PTSD and other mental health issues such as depression and anxiety, problem drinking, use of illicit substances such as psychoactive drugs, as well as sexual promiscuity.

Holley (2005, p. 143) indicated that the majority of drug users in the United States are victims of childhood abuse, be it sexual, emotional, or physical, which leads to the development of PTSD and in turn serves as a risk base for the development of drug addiction. This relation is particularly pronounced for women; 2.6% of a national sample indicated having experienced serious assaults in childhood primarily from fathers or stepfathers (Duncan, Saunders, Kilpatrick, Hanson, & Resnick, 1996). Najavits, Weiss, and Shaw (1997) reported that women substance abusers often have dual diagnosis of drug use and PTSD, ranging from 30% to 59%, and the PTSD is most often related to repetitive childhood physical assault, sexual assault, or both. Duncan et al. (1996) corroborated such findings and indicated a much greater likelihood of substance abuse, PTSD, and depression among women who had been victimized in their childhood. Fullilove et al. (1993) found that 104 of 105 women in addictions treatment reported lifetime traumatic events across 14 different categories.

Both large- and small-scale studies have provided further evidence for the relation between PTSD due to childhood violence and ensuing substance disorders. An assessment of 33 individuals with comorbid PTSD and cocaine dependence determined that for those for whom the PTSD preceded the cocaine addition, the foundation for the stressor was primarily childhood abuse (Brady, Dansky, Sonne, & Saladin, 1998). In addition, those women who experienced childhood abuse were also more likely to report abuse of benzodoazepine and opiates. Further evidence on the effects of trauma in early childhood are realized in a study of adolescents, ages 12 to 17, who constituted a household probability telephone-interviewed sample of 4,023 individuals (Kilpatrick et al., 2003). Overall, 6-month PTSD was reported in 6.3% of the girls and 3.7% of the boys in the sample. Moreover, 13.5% of the boys reported comorbidities of PTSD and substance abuse or dependence; among the girls, this comorbidity was 24.6%. Finally, as depression was also assessed, it is important to point out that approximately three quarters of those who met the criteria for PTSD reported at least one other comorbidity, with substance use or depression. In terms of the comorbidity between substance use and PTSD, this dual diagnosis was more likely to be present among those who witnessed violence or who experienced sexual or physical assault.

Further evidence for PTSD as a risk base for methamphetamine use is given by Vik and Ross (2003), who undertook behavioral and psychological assessments of 77 incarcerated women who either reported regular drug use or met the criterion for drug dependence. When compared with nonstimulant users in this sample, the women who reported injection methamphetamine use as well as the women who reported noninjection use of the drug were more likely to report sexual assault in both their childhood and adulthood. Specifically, although only 7% of the nonstimulant users reported these assaults, 42% of the noninjection methamphetamine users and 48% of the injection methamphetamine users reported both child and adult sexual assault. Psychological function also indicated that the two methamphetamine-using groups of women demonstrated higher levels of global severity, positive symptoms, and positive symptom distress. The injection methamphetamine users were twice as likely to meet the criteria for PTSD as the noninjection users and three times more likely than the nonstimulant users (42% vs. 20% vs. 13%, respectively). Finally, von Mayrhauser et al. (2002) indicated that among 260 methamphetamine users (male and female and of varying races and ethnicities) motivation for use of the drug was understood as a crutch for dealing with mental illness, past trauma, and other mental distress or discomfort.

De Bellis (2002) posited a developmental traumatology model as a mechanism by which to understand substance-use disorders. In his view, maltreatment in childhood, whether it is physical, emotional, sexual, or all of the above, induces a dysregulation of the biological stress-response symptoms. This dysregulation in turn acts as an antecedent to the development of PTSD and depressive symptoms, which in turn through a bidirectional relation induce alcohol- and substance-use disorders. De Bellis further posited that drug- and alcohol-use disorders further exacerbate the dysregulation of the biological stress systems (see chap. 4, this volume, for neural effects of methamphetamine use), creating a cyclical pattern that "feeds" the drug abuse, the dysregulation, and the depression and PTSD. This pathway is shown in Figure 6.2.

The development of substance-abuse disorders among men is often related to PTSD induced by combat or crime trauma (Najivits et al., 1997). In a comparison of 122 male and female cocaine-dependent individuals, all users reported a large number of traumatic events in their lifetimes, but whereas for the women traumatic events were related to physical and sexual abuse, for the men events were due to general disasters and crime-related events (Najavits et al., 1998). An association between war-related PTSD and drug dependence is highly evident among Vietnam War veterans. In a study of 61 such veterans, Bremner, Southwick, Darnell, and Charney (1996) indicated that symptoms of PTSD typically occurred at the time of exposure to combat and leveled off a few years after the war and were characterized by hyperarousal as well as avoidant symptoms. Use of illicit substances was in sync with the onset of PTSD. The impact of war and combat on drug use is mediated by the development of PTSD, as has been shown by McFall, Mackay, and Donovan (1992). In a comparison of Vietnam veterans with combat involvement to those without war-zone duty, all were equivalent in terms of their levels of drug and alcohol abuse. However, those who were involved with combat and who were diagnosed as having PTSD experienced more severe drug-abuse problems and were at a greater risk of having both alcohol and drug abuse. The effects also clearly impact those who reside in the combat zones, and such individuals are also likely to develop PTSD. In turn, substance abuse as has been shown in studies of children who lived in the regions impacted by the Vietnam War (Xian et al., 2000).

Further support for the role that PTSD plays in terms of drug-use disorders is given by findings in regard to the behaviors of those affected by the events of 9/11 and the Oklahoma City bombings. The Center for Epidemiological Studies at the New York Academy of Medicine has followed the well-being of New York City residents since 9/11. One month after 9/11 rates of PTSD were reported in 7.5% of the Manhattan residents who were surveyed, but they decreased to less than 1% after 6 months (Galea et al., 2003). In examinations of 988 Manhattan residents who were residing in the southern part of Manhattan, Vlahov et al. (2002) found a 9.7% increase in cigarette

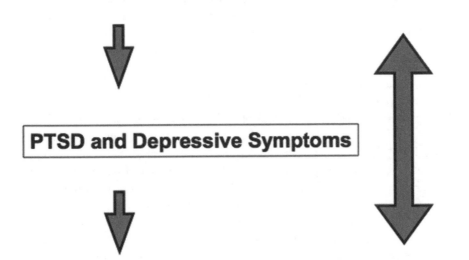

**Maltreatment in Childhood**

**Dysregulation of Biological Stress Systems**

**PTSD and Depressive Symptoms**

**Alcohol and Substance Use Disorders**

*Figure 6.2.* De Bellis's developmental traumatology model. Data from DeBellis, 2002.

smoking, 24.6% increase in alcohol consumption, and a 3.2% increase in marijuana use. Furthermore, those who increased their smoking and marijuana use were more likely to have been experiencing PTSD during this time than those who did not. Evidence of stress right after 9/11 has also been documented among HIV-positive individuals who declined in their antiviral medication adherence behaviors post-9/11 (Halkitis, Kutnick, Rosof, Slater, & Parsons, 2003) and among residents throughout the United States (Schuster et al., 2001). With regard to the Oklahoma City bombing, a higher proportion of individuals who survived the attack and were diagnosed with PTSD and other comorbidities (i.e., depression, anxiety, panic disorder) used alcohol postbombings than those with only PTSD (32.4% vs. 13%, respectively; North et al., 1999).

In the book *The Politics of Crystal Meth*, Kenneth Cimino (2005) considered another manifestation of PTSD and its relation to methamphetamine use—that of gay men who live in a society that stigmatizes them for their same-sex desires and within a reality of trauma brought forth by the AIDS epidemic. Many, including myself, have long argued that mental health issues are more highly elevated in this segment of the population, thus, creating a strong risk base for the development of methamphetamine and other drug use among gay men. To this point, Cimino shared the stories of numerous gay men. One gay man, David, suggested, "One of the big hurdles we must overcome is helping a generation or more that have lived years of trauma and years of loss. The reality is, gay men are using meth to cope" (Cimino, 2005, p. 13). J. L. Martin, Dean, Garcia, and Hall (1989) indicated the effects of the AIDS epidemic early in the history of this disease and noted a close relation between the trauma and the exacerbation of alcohol and drug use. This state has also been documented among those gay men who survived AIDS but who nonetheless indicated high levels of PTSD symptoms as part of a larger set of pathologies known as AIDS survivor syndrome. This idea of trauma in the gay community extends beyond the AIDS epidemic and has also been examined further by others who indicate that lesbians, gay men, and bisexual (LGB) individuals experiences a series of losses and trauma throughout their lives and that such trauma and loss are in fact quite common in the experience of LGB individuals (L. S. Brown, 2003). D'Augelli, Grossman, and Starks (2006) quantified such realities, indicating that because of the victimizations they faced, LGB youth experience trauma at extremely high rates. Nearly 80% of the 528 individuals they assessed reported verbal victimization, 11% physical victimization, and 9% sexual victimization, with the onset of these events approximately at age 13 but often as early as age 6. With regard to PTSD, 9% of the youth assessed were diagnosed for this condition, which was often associated with past physical victimization. Among 74 gay-male, sexual-assault survivors, high levels of PTSD were also noted and are related to depressive symptomatology and to internalized feelings of homophobia (Gold, Marx, & Lexington, 2007). For these reasons, LGB individuals may be more prone to illicit drug use and dependence; moreover, such understandings provide one frame of consideration for the prevalence of methamphetamine use in urban gay social circles.

Although the previously discussed work indicated the role that PTSD may play in the development of drug disorders generally, and although PTSD has been studied specifically in relation to addictions such as cocaine (e.g., Brady et al., 1998; Najavits et al., 1998), research emphasizing the relation between PTSD and methamphetamine abuse has been more circumscribed.

Yet, on the basis of the evidence provided here, this area of research is one worthy of further examination. Further support for this idea is provided by the findings of J. B. Cohen et al. (2003), who studied 1,016 methamphetamine users who participated in a multisite study in California, Hawaii, and Montana between 1999 and 2001. Numerous indicators suggest that early traumatic life experiences may lead individuals to methamphetamine use. In particular, 35% of the women and 42.4% of the men in the study reported parental physical violence, and a smaller yet substantial proportion (14.2% for women, and 11.3% of the men) indicated sexual abuse violence from a parent. Overall, approximately 60% of the methamphetamine-using women reported some lifetime experience of sexual abuse, whereas 16% of the men reported this life event. In addition to parents, other predators included siblings, partners, friends, and strangers. Exacerbating these realities is the tendency of methamphetamine users to report physical abuse in their current lives even as they were entering treatment for this particular study. Such indicators suggest that PTSD is very likely a powerful risk base for methamphetamine use among many individuals.

## SOCIAL INFLUENCES

Although biological and psychological realities provide some understanding with regard to the risk bases for methamphetamine use, abuse, and dependence, it is important to remember that use of this illicit substance, or any other drug, does not occur in a vacuum. Rather, these behaviors are manifested in the contexts of realities in which individuals hold multiple roles and identities and navigate social environments. Thus, the influence of these contexts is delineated in this section. However, consideration is given first to the primary social circle in which almost all human beings are engaged—the family—and the role that family risk bases may play in the development of a methamphetamine use disorder. Thereafter, the roles of peers are delineated in relation to substance use.

### Family

Several features of the family structure and dynamics may influence the development of methamphetamine abuse in children, adolescents, or both. Use during these primary developmental stages may then create a trajectory for abuse of the drug into emergent adulthood and the later stages of life. These features include the overlapping synergies of the biological bases, which may be inherited from the parents; the social environment of the family, including the levels of attachment; communication; and conflict; as well as the mental health of the individual within the context of this family structure and the extent to which the mental health of the individual is nurtured. One of these sets of factors is likely insufficient in and of itself to lead to the onset of substance use, and these factors work in conjunction to create a vulnerability for children to develop a substance-use disorder either in adolescence or as they emerge into adulthood.

In their review of the empirical research in regard to the risk bases for the development of drug abuse in adolescents and young adults, Hawkins et al. (1992) documented a series of family-centered factors, including (a) family alcohol and drug behavior attitudes, (b) poor and inconsistent family management practices, (c) family conflict, and (d) poor attachment to family. These ideas are further supported by the work of Brook, Brook, Gordan, Whiteman, and Cohen (1990), and the reader is referred to the article by Hawkins et al. (1992) for a more comprehensive review of these ideas. Suffice it to say that the vulnerability of a child to the eventual development of methamphetamine or other substance use will be determined in part by the extent to which the family models drug use behavior. If alcohol and drug use attitudes are highly favorable, or if family members, especially parents, use substances, then the potential initiation of use by the adolescent is heightened (McDermott, 1984). The familial transmission of no-alcohol and drugs has also been documented by Miles et al., (1998). In direct comparisons of male adolescent probands in treatment with matched controls, higher levels of conduct disorder and antisocial personality disorder were also noted in the relatives of those adolescents who were in treatment. Similarly, Meller, Rinehart, Cadoret, and Troughton (1988) found that adults who had been admitted for treatment for drug abuse were more likely to have a family history of drug abuse than those who had been admitted solely for alcohol abuse and dependence. These ideas were substantiated by Rounsaville, Kosten, and Weissman (1991), who found that first-degree relatives of individuals admitted for opiate addiction reported higher rates of alcohol and drug abuse than those of normal controls. Penning and Barnes (1982) also showed that where issues of discipline were inconsistent, the likelihood of drug use development was also greater. The extent to which parents effectively implement practices for managing behavior that are authoritative but not authoritarian, or not permissive, will likely affect the child's eventual relationship to illicit substances. Also, positive and healthy attachment to parents has been demonstrated numerous times over to reduce the likelihood of drug-use initiation (see Hawkins et al., 1992). Finally, Simcha-Fagan, Gersten, and Langner (1986) demonstrated a positive relation between the use of heroin and other illegal drugs and parental marital discord. Although the popular belief may be that children from divorced homes are more vulnerable to the use of substances, this has not been substantiated; rather, the level of conflict between parents, whether they are married, separated, or divorced, is likely a much better indicator of the potential development of drug abuse in children.

The roles that family dynamics play in the development of methamphetamine and other drug abuse might also be considered in light of the interplay between risk and resiliency. Although predisposing family risk factors may lead to the development of substance-use behaviors, resiliencies within the individual may function to counter such risk, and in combination these elements may be better suited to explain the development of these maladaptive behaviors. For example, Moon, Jackson, and Hecht (2000) indicated that among both male and female adolescents, risk and resiliency each contributed to an understanding of substance use. In particular, for male adolescents resiliency had an indirect effect on overall substance use through age at first use, whereas risk had an effect on overall substance use. For female adolescents, resiliency was found to have a direct effect on overall substance use and risk and an indirect effect through the age of first use, further suggesting that not only might risk and resiliency work in tandem but that gender (and perhaps gender identity, sexual orientation, or both) may moderate the extent to which these factors manifest. Resiliency may also be a factor in helping to explain the "natural recovery" from drug use in gay men noted by Stall and Biernacki (1986).

Among methamphetamine users, the role of family-centered factors has also been examined, albeit in a more limited number of studies. Matsumoto et al. (2002) examined the life backgrounds of methamphetamine-using, treatment-seeking outpatients in Japan; in particular, they contrasted the characteristics of those who smoked the drug ($N = 42$) versus those who injected ($N = 57$) versus those who smoked and injected ($N = 17$). Although clinical characteristics and family-level risk factors were high across groups, the injection group reported higher levels of both parental absence and family history of alcoholism. A comparison of methamphetamine-using adolescents with other substance-using adolescents in Southern California who sought outpatient treatment (Rawson, Gonzales, Obert, McCann, & Brethen, 2005) found that both groups reported family-level risk factors but that the groups did not differ from each other. Specifically, 64% noted that they had parents who used drugs, and 60% reported coming from divorced homes, with most indicating that they "did not get along" or had "poor relationships" with their stepparents. In direct comparisons of cocaine users with methamphetamine users, Simon, Domier, Sim, Richardson, Rawson, and Ling (2002) reported that methamphetamine users were more likely to report a family history of suicide and were more likely to have parents or siblings who used alcohol or other drugs.

## Peers

Like families, peers can function in the role of either risk or protection with regard to methamphetamine and other substance abuse. For example, Rawson et al. (2005) indicated that methamphetamine and other substance-using adolescents tend to report peers who also use drugs, with 66% of their sample of 305 reporting this social condition. The role of peers in influencing drug use has been noted as early as fifth and sixth grades (ages 10–12), where Dielman, Campanelli, Shope, and Butchart (1987) showed that adolescent substance use, misuse, and intention to use are all highly related to susceptibility to peer pressure. Such findings have been corroborated in a sample of 49 predominantly gay and bisexual methamphetamine-using men, where approximately one third indicated that most of their friends used the drug and about two thirds indicated that some of their friends used the drug (Halkitis et al., 2003b).

The social basis for methamphetamine use has been most extensively examined with regard to gay, bisexual, and other MSM. Social bases for use are described by these men as a means of having a pleasant time with others, enhancing social situations, and lessening the tension or conflict that they might experience in social venues (e.g., Halkitis, Fischgrund, et al., 2005; Halkitis, Green, & Carragher, 2006). This is also noted among African American men (Halkitis & Jerome, 2008). Although these social transactions for gay and bisexual men often center on sexual exchange (e.g., Halkitis, Shrem, & Martin, 2005; Semple et al., 2002), this is not the sole social base for use of the drug. In fact, use of the drug has been described as a means of avoiding loneliness and alienation (Kurtz, 2005).

The social venues in which gay and bisexual men navigate facilitate the use of methamphetamine. In particular, use of methamphetamine and other club drugs such as Ecstasy has been associated with large circuit parties also known as "raves," where sociosexual transactions are at the heart of this type of venue. Lewis and Ross (1995) effectively documented this social scene in *The Select Body: The Gay Dance Party Subculture and the HIV-AIDS Pandemic*. Along these lines, Green and Halkitis (2006) suggested that self-esteem and social awkwardness are related to methamphetamine use among gay men and that "these factors arise in and are exacerbated by interactional pressures attendant to Manhattan's gay subculture, which revolve around the expectation of peak sexual performance" (p. 317). This understanding is in sync with the model for cognitive escape postulated by McKirnan, Ostrow, and Hope (1996), in which the use of substances such as methamphetamine interacting with social, often sexually charged, settings is believed to create a cognitive disengagement through which individuals enact automated scripts and are more responsive to external pressures toward risk. Such ideas regarding the social bases of methamphetamine user are also evident in the seminal work of Reback (1997) in which the following points are made:

- Social networks and subcommunities of crystal users are formed across class and ethnic boundaries.
- The demographic patterns indicate that user groups are formed around socioeconomic rather than racial similarities; however,

these socioeconomically based subcommunities are fluid and easily expanded to include individuals in a particular subcommunity where crystal and/or sex is included.

- Many of the effects associated with crystal use complement those aspects of gay culture that are valued by many gay and bisexual men.
- The creation of social settings where crystal use is common—or expected—serves to normalize crystal in gay culture.
- The use of crystal in gay communities is facilitated through various gay institutions such as phone sex lines, personal ads, computer networks, circuit parties, bars, and clubs. (pp. xi–xiii).

However, the desire "to party" and escape is not restricted to this segment of the methamphetamine-using population. Semple, Patterson, and Grant (2004) reported similar indices among heterosexual methamphetamine users, with approximately 45% of these HIV-negative heterosexual adults indicating that the desire to party was the main reason they started using the drug and 29% indicating that this was the factor explaining their current use.

## CONCLUSION

What drives a man or woman to use methamphetamine? In this chapter, I examined a set of evidence-based motivations or antecedents for use of the drug, encompassing the biological, psychological, and social realities of the person. Not one of these factors or sets of factors seems sufficient in providing a fully articulated explanation for methamphetamine addiction. Instead, this array or constellation of causes may predispose some to use this drug or any other of a number of illicit substances.

Although this simple linear path between cause (x) and methamphetamine addiction (y) may not be so easily articulated, it is safe to say that numerous behavior studies have demonstrated two major patterns: (a) that the vast majority of individuals do not develop addictions; and (b) that even among users of drugs such as methamphetamine, patterns of use are as diverse as the users themselves. To this first point, it is important to reemphasize some statistics: For example, whereas one study may find that 22% of gay men use methamphetamine, the flip side of this proportion suggests that 78% of these men do not use the drug. Thus, perhaps, we have as much to learn from those who are free of methamphetamine use as those who are addicted to the substance. What factors predispose the former to not use methamphetamine, to avoid addiction, or to limit themselves to casual use of the substance? Some might suggest that the resiliencies an individual possesses may be the most powerful force in avoiding such problematic behavior. If that is the case, then how do these resiliencies develop? Moreover, how can we study and document them as a basis for developing interventions for those who lack these abilities and are in turn susceptible to methamphetamine addiction? There is much to learn about resiliency especially from gay men, who in the United States have not only had to battle stigma, prejudice, and social isolation, but also have had the devastation of an incurable disease. In fact, the literature on this subpopulation has emphasized the problems without parallel consideration to the roles of coping and resilience (Hunter, 1999).

With regard to the second point—that of the varying levels of drug use within the methamphetamine-using population—it is vitally important to note that little work has been undertaken to differentiate the potentially differing factors that predispose some individuals to infrequent use, some to casual use, and yet a small subset set to chronic use or addiction. The extent to which variations in biological, psychological, and social processes determine this variation in level of use is worth examination, especially because it is likely that varying patterns of antecedent factors predisposing individuals to use would dictate varying types of interventions for the many types of methamphetamine users.

In recent years, there has been a major shift in the landscape of addiction research, emphasizing the biomedical underpinnings of these behaviors and a reliance on the development of pharmacological substances to treat a variety of different addictions from alcohol to methamphetamine. Although such efforts are both scientifically sound and potentially useful, it is important to remember that no addiction, or any health behavior for that matter, can be fully understood from a purely biomedical perspective. Human beings are more than a collection of cells, and thus understanding methamphetamine addiction necessitates the use of strategies that are true to the lives of the users. Methamphetamine addicts do not articulate their need as driven by a faulty dopaminergic system, but rather they articulate a desire characterized by feeling depressed, isolated, or out of sync. In addition, although providing medications to correct the dopaminergic system may be an effective first step, we must also consider the behaviors that individuals have learned throughout their lives to cope with this biomedical deficit, and we must provide support to the emotional and social lives of these individuals. This argument becomes particularly important as we consider the treatment approaches to methamphetamine addiction described in chapter 7.

# 7
## TREATMENT CONSIDERATIONS FOR METHAMPHETAMINE ADDICTION

According to the Substance Abuse and Mental Health Services Administration (SAMHSA, 2006) more than 228,000 or 12% of all drug treatment admissions in the United States in 2004 were because of the primary, secondary, or tertiary abuse of methamphetamine. More recent data (SAMHSA, 2008, p. 2) indicated that treatment admissions increased 127% between 1995 and 2005. In 1995 there were 30 drug admissions per population of 100,000 people ages 12 years and older, which rose to 68 per 100,000 in 2005. These patterns indicate the continual presence of methamphetamine in our society and an increasing number of individuals in need of treatment. However, the complex synergy between intrapsychic, environmental, and behavioral factors makes methamphetamine addiction an extremely difficult disorder to treat (Shrem & Halkitis, 2008). The precursors to use, when coupled with the perceived benefits of methamphetamine, are exacerbated by severe anhedonia, depression, insomnia, agitation, and fatigue (National Institute on Drug Abuse [NIDA], 1998), as well as intense cravings, which can make efforts to terminate use "long and treacherous" (Wolkoff & Burns, 1997). Compounding this situation is that conventional therapies have shown limited effectiveness for the treatment of methamphetamine addiction (Rawson & Huber, 1996), and "treatment programs and personnel that have for decades delivered traditional

12-step-based alcoholism treatment are unprepared for the influx of MA [methamphetamine] users" (Rawson, Gonzales, & Brethen, 2002, p. 147). Although rumors about the ability to treat this drug dependence do exist (i.e., only 5% will ever really recover), these rumors are in fact mythologies (Disney, 2007). Dependence on the drug is challenging to treat, but recent approaches have shown promise, especially those that capture the biopsychosocial synergies.

In this chapter, consideration is given to the treatment of methamphetamine addiction. Numerous modalities for addressing methamphetamine addiction are reviewed, including cognitive–behavioral approaches, the "matrix model," motivational interviewing, contingency management, 12-step, and medication approaches. Finally, treatments that address the meth–sex link are explored, positing the intimate connection between methamphetamine treatment and HIV prevention.

## CONSIDERATIONS FOR THE TREATMENT OF METHAMPHETAMINE ADDICTION

Attempts to overcome methamphetamine addiction are often characterized as a vicious cycle whereby methamphetamine users revert back to their use to combat the intense dysphoric experience associated with withdrawal (Shrem & Halkitis, 2008). In reality, these cycles perpetuate the dependence on methamphetamine and increase the likelihood that users will experience more frequent depressive symptomology, further intensifying their craving for the drug, influencing them to return to methamphetamine as a form of self-medication to alleviate depressive withdrawal symptoms.

The motivations and consequences of methamphetamine use examined in previous chapters clearly suggest that treatment models should be holistic in their approach and imbue a biospsychosocial paradigm that considers mind–body connections. Biopsychosocial methodologies consider the interplay between the intrapsychic and biological processes of persons, their behaviors, the physical and mental health consequences of these behaviors, and individual environmental influences. Such treatment approaches support the view of addiction as a chronic brain disease (Leshner, 1997). Specifically, imaging research has concluded that the methamphetamine-addicted brain has depleted dopamine function, reduced celluar activity in the frontal cortex, which affects decision making, and that reduced dopamine receptor levels may create a higher level of vulnerability to methamphetamine abuse and addiction (Fowler, Volkow, Kassed, & Chang, 2007). Taken together, these elements indicate treatment modalities that underscore the biological elements of addiction, in addition to intrapsychic, behavioral, and environmental processes.

To date, no one modality to treat methamphetamine addiction has proven full efficacy in community-based, clinical, or research settings. However, numerous frameworks, which include cognitive–behavioral therapy, motivational interviewing, contingency management, and 12-step–12-step facilitation, have been applied to the treatment of dependency on the drug. Others have used aversion therapy as well as psychoeducational approaches, adopted by numerous community-based organizations to address the addiction. Pharmaceutical therapies remain relatively elusive. At present, the matrix model (Anglin & Rawson, 2000a) remains one of the most publicized and well-respected approaches to addressing methamphetamine addiction. The difficulty in treating methamphetamine addiction is evidenced in part by relatively noncommittal stance of the National Institute on Drug Abuse as noted in a report first published in 2002 and reprinted in 2006:

> At this time, the most effective treatments for methamphetamine addiction are behavioral therapies such as cognitive behavioral and contingency management interventions. For example, the Matrix Model, a comprehensive behavioral treatment approach that combines behavioral therapy, family education, individual counseling, 12-step support, drug testing, and encouragement for nondrug-related activities, has been shown to be effective in reducing methamphetamine abuse. Contingency management interventions, which provide tangible incentives in exchange for engaging in treatment and maintaining abstinence, have also been shown to be effective. (p. 7)

There are currently no specific medications that counteract the effects of methamphetamine or that prolong abstinence from and reduce the abuse of methamphetamine by an individual addicted to the drug. However, a number of medications that are FDA-approved for other illnesses might also be useful in treating methamphetamine addiction. Recent study findings reveal that bupropion, the antidepressant marketed as Wellbutrin, reduces the methamphetamine-induced high as well as drug cravings elicited by drug-related cues. This medication and others are currently in clinical trials, while new compounds are being developed and studied in preclinical models.

In *Overcoming Crystal Meth Addiction*, Steven Lee (2006) outlined five strategies of overcoming addiction to the drug: (a) learning as much as one can about methamphetamine; (b) examining the role that methamphetamine plays in the life of the user; (c) learning the basic steps to terminating use of methamphetamine; (d) learning how to maintain sobriety; and (e) addressing major "holes" in one's life that methamphetamine may be helping to "fill." These five elements, although broad and generic in their scope, in fact, are characteristics that are evident in many current methamphetamine treatment programs, and thus they provide an overriding framework for considering particular treatment approaches. Moreover, because community-based agencies are often a venue in which methamphetamine users present, either because of the lack of affordability, the stigma associated with the addiction, or the access to such treatment facilities, the translation of treatments models from science to practice is paramount. Cretzmeyer, Sarrazin, Huber, Block, and Hall (2003) suggested multiple modes of communicating research findings to frontline staff and clinicians, as publications in scientific journals are often "too slow to keep with the emerging trends" (p. 267). Empowering clinical staff with tools to engage users in effective treatment, whether it is behavioral, pharmacological, or a combination of both, will almost certainly have the greatest impact on the largest number of methamphetamine users.

Freese, Miotto, and Reback (2002) suggested that little is known about the effectiveness of treatments for use of club drugs, such as methamphetamine. Because data on treatment efficacy for methamphetamine addiction, in particular, are truly limited, and no one approach has proven global efficacy, the chapter has been purposefully titled "Treatment Considerations for Methamphetamine Addiction" rather than "Treatment for Methamphetamine Addiction." While rumors abound about the near impossibility of overcoming methamphetamine addiction, these beliefs are not based on fact, and many individuals can overcome dependence with the correct treatment approach. The following section summarizes current treatment modalities and the scientific evidence for each approach.

## Cognitive–Behavioral Approaches

Cognitive–behavioral therapy (CBT) is a treatment model that is often viewed favorably by community-based practitioners (Morgenstern & McCrady, 1992). CBT is based on social learning theory, which views substance abuse as a learned and maladaptive behavior that is due to distorted beliefs in regard to the power of the abused substance over the individual (Ouimette, Finney, & Moos, 1997). Thus, the goal of treatment is to modify maladaptive learning and help the individual develop coping strategies. A significant element of CBT is functional analysis, which is an iterative process by which therapist and client better understand the function that methamphetamine plays in the life of the user, identifies triggers, including people, places, and things (Irwin, 2006). A key element of the therapy is to develop strategies that address cravings and cognitive distortions when they arise. Through the use of decisional balance exercises, clients challenge distractions while enhancing self-efficacy for abstinence from methamphetamine and delineating the positive and negative outcome expectancies for use of the drug. However, in light of the long-term neural effects of methamphetamine, especially to the frontal lobe, such approaches to address cognitive distortions may prove challenging.

The efficacy of CBT in clinical trials of substance abusers has been validated (Irvin, Bowers, Dunn, & Wang, 1999). CBT has been shown to be an effective treatment for those with cocaine dependence (Huber et al., 1997; Rawson, McCann, et al., 2002) and was found to be even more effective over time (Carroll et al., 1994). Furthermore, within the contexts of a community-based substance-abuse program, Morgenstern, Blanchard, Morgan, Labouvie, and Hayaki (2001) demonstrated the efficacy and impact of CBT with patients who reported abstinence from substances on 90% of the within-treatment days and 85% of the days at 6 months posttreatment. The evidence for CBT in treating cocaine dependence has applicability to methamphetamine users, as Copeland and Sorensen (2001) demonstrated; Irwin (2006) posited that CBT is the most effective treatment for stimulant addiction.

## The Matrix Model

Perhaps the most widely acclaimed treatment approach for methamphetamine dependence is the matrix model, a program based on the principles of CBT (Anglin & Rawson, 2000a; Obert et al., 2000; Rawson, Gonzales, et al., 2002). The program was first developed in the 1980s to address the influx of cocaine addiction in middle-class Americans in response to the belief that traditional inpatient treatment were not medically necessary and that traditional outpatient psychotherapy was neither effective nor relevant to treat the addiction (Obert et al., 2000). Obert et al. (2000) provided an overview of the program, which was developed as part of a NIDA-funded initiative and was first empirically tested in the 1990s through the Methamphetamine Treatment Program, undertaken with seven treatment organizations in the western United States and funded by the Center for Substance Abuse Treatment at SAMHSA (Anglin & Rawson, 2000b; Huber et al., 2000). The study design compared the effectiveness of the program with "treatment as usual" (Galloway et al., 2000).

The matrix program is a 16-week, 48-session, manualized, nonresidential intervention, which is designed on the following tenets: (a) stop using the drug, (b) learn issues critical to addiction and relapse, (c) receive education for family members affected by addiction and relapse, and (d) receive monthly drug monitoring through the use of biologics (Rawson, McCann, et al., 2002). Many of these principles are similar to those described by Lee (2006). However, the matrix model, which is delivered over a fixed period of time, extends beyond simple CBT principles to create a comprehensive approach to drug treatment that includes one-on-one psychotherapy and participation in 12-step programs, creating a more holistic approach to addressing the addiction (Rawson et al., 1995). The approach teaches skills to initiate abstinence and to immediately resume abstinence after relapse per the guidelines articulated by Marlatt and Gordon (1985).

Evidence for effectiveness of the matrix model is given in a study of methamphetamine ($n = 13$) and cocaine ($n = 133$) users provided by Shoptaw, Rawson, McCann, and Obert (1994), who demonstrated both a treatment effect and better outcomes (i.e., abstinence) when treatment dose was greater.

In other words, those who received more of the matrix treatment had better abstinence rates. In a similar type of study, Huber et al. (1997) found that the matrix program helped 19.3% of 500 methamphetamine-abusing individuals to achieve negative drug urinalysis during the 16-week treatment period. In addition, Rawson et al. (2004) compared the effectiveness of the program with a treatment-as-usual comparison in a predominantly heterosexual sample. Although there was no difference between study arms in terms of methamphetamine use at the 6-month follow-up, the participants in the matrix model arm demonstrated more negative urinalyses than those in the control group during the treatment period. Higher levels of success because of treatment with the matrix model are associated with numerous behavioral and intrapsychic characteristics (Hillhouse et al., 2007). Specifically, in their assessment of 420 adults who participated in the program, researchers found that poor posttreatment outcome was associated with use of methamphetamine for 15 or more of the 30 days prior to intake, greater than 2 years of lifetime use of the drug, injection of methamphetamine, higher levels of depression, and use of the drug during treatment. Many of these factors point to a biological and neurological confound to treatment effectiveness, and more recently the intervention has included information about methamphetamine use as a "brain disease" to educate users and their families. According to Obert, London, and Rawson (2002),

> Experience with the Matrix approach suggests that if complex scientific information can be simplified for use with patients, it can reduce patient confusion about their behavior, promote treatment engagement and retention and help family members understand and support patient recovery efforts. (p. 112)

In addition to using imaging as a means of educating users, neural imaging in combination with gene therapy could potentially help clinicians understand the biological vulnerabilities of an individual to methamphetamine abuse (as discussed in chap. 6, this volume) and in turn develop appropriate strategies for early targeted interventions. Chang and Linde (2007) suggested that brain imaging may inform much of our understanding of methamphetamine addiction and future treatment approaches could include image-based diagnosis and treatment planning.

## Motivational Interviewing

Motivational interviewing, developed by W. R. Miller and Rollnick (1991), concentrates on issues of motivation at various points along a continuum of behavior change. Motivational interviewing strategies treat resistance, ambivalence, and diminished capacity for objective self-assessment, which are common among clients in the earlier stages of behavior change. These strategies, which include being empathic, "rolling with resistance," emphasizing client choice and responsibility, and avoiding argumentation, have been found to be particularly effective when compared with more confrontational approaches to addiction treatment. Motivational interviewing has been shown to be effective in addressing a spectrum of drinking problems in both abstinent (Project Match Research Group, 1997a, 1997b) and nonabstinent goal conditions (W. R. Miller, 1995), and it has been shown to be effective with individuals in cocaine detoxification programs (Stotts, Schmitz, Rhoads, & Grabowski, 2001). The approach to treatment is often used to enhance adherence in inpatient or outpatient treatment (Stotts et al., 2001; Swanson, Pantalon, & Cohen, 1999) or in combination with other treatment strategies such as CBT (Baer, Kivlahan, & Donovan, 1999). It should be noted that motivational interviewing has been used in individualized counseling, but the use of techniques in group settings has been operationalized and manualized (Valasquez, Maurer, Crouch, & DiClemente, 2001).

Bux and Irwin (2006) described the elements of motivational interviewing and indicated the four key principles to this approach: (a) expression of empathy to the addicted individual; (b) development of discrepancy in which the addicted individual evaluates fully behaviors in light of consequences; (c) avoidance argumentation with the client and "rolling" with (i.e., working with) his or her resistance to change; and (d) supporting the addict's self-efficacy to not use methamphetamine. It can be suggested that these four elements represent a positive and proactive therapeutic technique and that motivational interviewing is more of an approach to therapy than an actual treatment modality. To date, the empirical support for the use of motivational interviewing in addressing methamphetamine addiction is not available, although numerous funded research endeavors are currently implementing elements of the approach. However, these principles have been applied successfully to safer sex intervention for methamphetamine users (Mausbach, Semple, Strathdee, Zians, & Patterson, 2007), as described later in this chapter.

## Contingency Management

The tenets of contingency management are based on behaviorism and operant reinforcement (Skinner, 1938/1966), whereby individuals are rewarded for their behavior. In some applications with addicted individuals, escalating awards are provided for each time (usually determined by a urinalysis) individuals demonstrate that they have not used the drug. "In brief, CM [contingency management] for the treatment of substance-use disorders is a procedure that decreases the reinforcing efficacy of a drug via delivery contingent on abstinence and/or delivery of punishment contingent on drug use" (Roll, 2007, p. 114). This approach has been applied to treatment for heroin and cocaine addiction (Higgins et al., 1993; Iguchi, Stitzer, Bigelow, & Liebson, 1988), as well as other drug addictions (Higgins et al., 1993; Higgins & Petry, 1999; Higgins & Silverman, 1999). Vouchers are often used to exchange for goods or services to support an addiction-free lifestyle (Shoptaw et al., 2005). Roll (2007) noted that contingency management programs are often delivered in conjunction with pharmaceutical or psychosocial interventions, or both. For the most part, contingency management has been applied in formal treatment settings.

Shoptaw et al. (2005) reported on a large-scale treatment study, which tested the effectiveness of contingency management versus cognitive–behavioral therapy (matrix model) versus contingency management + cognitive–behavioral therapy versus culturally tailored cognitive–behavioral therapy in a sample of 162 gay Black men in Los Angeles. Treatment approaches were delivered for a 16-week period, and methamphetamine use was assessed three times per week during the treatment period and then again at 6 and 12 months postbaseline. Noncash vouchers for the contingency management element were worth $2.50 and escalated by $2.50 for each negative urinalysis, and they were coupled with a $10 bonus for three consecutive urinalyses. The design included testing urine for both methamphetamine and cocaine metabolites to determine whether "stimulant switching" was occurring. Both of the contingency management conditions (i.e., in isolation or in combination with CBT) demonstrated superiority in terms of several markers: (a) consecutive negative methamphetamine urinalyses, (b) retention, and (c) treatment effectiveness assessments. Although these differences were not noted at the 12-month follow-up, all four of the conditions indicated a threefold decrease in methamphetamine use. These findings indicated the more immediate impact of contingency management in addressing methamphetamine addiction, but the success of this approach is equivalent to CBT over the long term. These findings have been corroborated in a study of 171 stimulant abusers (Rawson et al., 2006) and in a parallel study of contingency management in combination with the medication sertraline (Shoptaw et al., 2006). In addition, in a trial involving 113 methamphetamine users who were assigned either to the contingency management or treatment-as-usual condition, those in contingency management demonstrated significantly more stimulant-negative (i.e., methamphetamine and cocaine) urine samples and longer mean periods of abstinence than those in the control condition. In addition, whereas 18% of those in contingency management were abstinent during the entire 12-week trial period, only 6% of those in the control group achieved this state (Petry et al., 2005). Initial indications suggest that contingency management programs may be adapted for use outside of costly traditional treatment settings. The Positive Reinforcement Opportunity Project, based on contingency management but implementing less costly elements than traditional treatment methods, was tested in San Francisco among gay, bisexual, and other men who have sex with men (MSM). Initial data suggest that the program had a 35%

retention rate for the 90-day program period (Strona et al., 2006). Although these studies bolster the efficacy of contingency management in addressing methamphetamine addiction, more replications, which are currently underway including ones enacted in the community, are needed to establish effectiveness across population subgroups (i.e., gender, sexual orientation, developmental stage) over the long term and in nonresearch structures.

## 12-Step Approaches

At the present time, 12-step approaches, primarily in the form of Crystal Meth Anonymous (CMA), are the standard of care for most individuals who are seeking help for this addiction within community settings. Such programs are readily available and accessed for substance-abuse recovery either as formal treatment or in the absence of a formal treatment plan (Humphreys, 1999; Room & Greenfield, 1993).

CMA is based on the models developed first in Alcoholics Anonymous (AA) and later adapted by Narcotics Anonymous (NA) and Cocaine Anonymous (CA). CMA is the latest adaptation of this therapeutic approach. In this paradigm, substance abuse is seen through the disease model of addiction (Ouimette et al., 1997), and individuals in this treatment modality are encouraged to accept their identities as abusers. The 12-step paradigm is nested within the belief that substance abuse is the result of a biological or psychological vulnerability, and thus 12-step programs are centered on the notion that substance abuse is a progressive illness and that the illness affects the body, mind, and spirit. This modality, in particular, embodies the essence of the biopsychosocial paradigm.

Rawson, Anglin, and Ling (2002) suggested that addictions staff trained in traditional 12-step elements feel underprepared to approach methamphetamine addiction. However, the proliferation of CMA groups in the last several years, especially in large metropolitan areas, demonstrates the acceptance of this approach on the part of users who are seeking to address their addictions. For example, in the borough of Manhattan in New York City alone, there are 30 meetings per week (New York Crystal Meth Anonymous, 2007), approximately 20 in Atlanta (Atlanta Crystal Meth Anonymous, 2007), and one every day of the week in Washington, DC (Crystal Meth Anonymous of Washington, DC, 2007). Moreover, the Center for Substance Abuse Treatment recommended participation in 12-step programs to supplement treatments (Donovan & Wells, 2007). Participation in 12-step groups is an important and essential element of the matrix model (Rawson, 1998) and is encouraged in other treatment facilities, such as the Parallax Center in New York City (Parallax Center, 2007), where behavioral therapy in combination with pharmacotherapy and 12-step participation is encouraged among substance users. To date, there are limited available empirical data on the use of

12-step programs by methamphetamine abusers and on the role that 12-step programs may play either as stand-alone treatments or supplemental treatments for treating methamphetamine addiction (Donovan & Wells, 2007).

CMA consists of three core elements: (a) the attendance of 12-step meetings and the development of fellowship with peers in these groups; (b) the utilization of sponsorship by which individuals select others who participate in the group to assist in the achievement and maintenance of sobriety; and (c) service and commitment to the 12-step group such that one plays an active role in the maintenance of the group by, for example, making coffee, assisting with the finance of the group, and/or ensuring that literature is stocked and readily available. Active participation in meetings, rather than simply attending meetings, may be more effective in reducing subsequent drug use, as was shown in a study of cocaine users (Weiss et al., 2005). CMA is based on 12 steps (shown in Exhibit 7.1) through which individuals must navigate their recovery. Although spirituality is central to these 12 steps, CMA groups may vary with regard to the levels that God, spirituality, or both are emphasized. This is true for all 12-step programs but may have particular relevance for CMA in large urban areas where many users are gay men who may feel disenfranchised or ostracized by religion or religious institutions because of their sexuality.

The short- and long-term effectiveness of 12-step programs and interventions that enact elements of 12-step facilitation to treat methamphetamine addiction are rather limited. What little is known is drawn from use of the approach in addressing alcoholism and cocaine addictions, although more recently evidence is amounting for the potential benefit of the approach to address methamphetamine addiction (Fiortentine, 1999). Ouimette et al. (1997) found that the 12-step paradigm yielded more favorable results than CBT in addressing alcoholism. However, in a study of crack cocaine users, CBT was found to be more effective than 12-step facilitation (Maude-Griffin et al., 1998). Twelve-step facilitation was used in a large-scale intervention study of alcohol abuse and dependence known as Project Match (Project Match Research Group, 1997a), which showed that among those who received aftercare from treatment programs, participation in the 12-step facilitation treatment arm supported abstinence (Emrick, Tonigan, Montgomery, & Little, 1993; Tonigan, Toscova, & Miller, 1996). Similarly, T. G. Brown, Seraganian, Tremblay, and Annis (2002a) found that among 70 male and female patients who received initial treatment across three treatment centers for various substance-abuse problems, carefully orchestrated 12-step aftercare yielded process changes and was positively related to improved outcomes. Such success in aftercare provides support for the 12-step paradigm. In fact,

EXHIBIT 7.1
The 12 Steps of Crystal Meth Anonymous

1. We admitted that we were powerless over crystal meth and our lives had become unmanageable.
2. Came to believe that a power greater than ourselves could restore us to sanity.
3. Made a decision to turn our will and our lives over to the care of a God of our understanding.
4. Made a searching and fearless moral inventory of ourselves.
5. Admitted to God, to ourselves and to another human being the exact nature of our wrongs.
6. Were entirely ready to have God remove all these defects of character.
7. Humbly asked God to remove our shortcomings.
8. Made a list of all persons we had harmed and became willing to make amends to them all.
9. Made direct amends to such people wherever possible, except when to do so would injure them or others.
10. Continued to take personal inventory and when we were wrong promptly admitted it.
11. Sought through prayer and meditation to improve our conscious contact with a God of our understanding praying only for the knowledge of God's will for us, and the power to carry that out.
12. Having had a spiritual awakening as a result of these steps, we tried to carry this message to crystal meth addicts, and to practice these principles in all of our affairs.

*Note.* From "The 12 Steps of Crystal Meth Anonymous," Crystal Meth Anonymous. Retrieved July 17, 2008, from http://www.crystalmeth.org. Copyright 2007 by Crystal Meth Anonymous. The Twelve Steps Crystal Meth Anonymous ("CMA"), as adapted by CMA with permission of Alcoholics Anonymous Services World, Inc. ("AAWS"), are reprinted with permission of CMA and AAWS. AAWS' and CMA's permission to reprint the foregoing material does not mean that AAWS or CMA has reviewed or approved the contents of this publication, or that AAWS or CMA necessarily agrees with the views expressed therein. Alcoholics Anonymous is a program of recovery from alcoholism only - use or permissible adaptation of A.A.'s Twelve Steps in connection with programs and activities which are patterned after A.A., but which address other problems, or in any other non-A.A. context, does not imply otherwise.

Morgenstern, Labouvie, McCrady, Kahler, and Frey (1997) indicated that 12-step programs, in the form of Alcoholics Anonymous and so forth are the most prevalent approaches to aftercare for substance abusers after the termination of treatment. Twelve-step experimental aftercare programs result in outcomes as effective as other community-based aftercare programs (T. G. Brown, Sereganian, Tremblay, & Annis, 2002b; Morgenstern et al., 1997; Ouimette et al., 1997).

In direct comparisons with both CBT and motivational enhancement therapy in Project Match (Project Match Research Group, 1997b), aftercare participants who were alcohol dependent at the onset of treatment demonstrated better posttreatment outcomes when they were in the 12-step facilitation condition. Furthermore, patients with low-psychiatric severity had more abstinent days following 12-step than cognitive–behavioral treatments. However, among those with severe mental illness, there were no differences in abstinence rates between those in the 12-step and cognitive–behavioral treatment arms of the study. In the end, although no differences were noted across treatment modalities with regard to the primary outcomes of abstinence in Project Match, the 12-step intervention was associated with better outcomes among outpatients and measures that emphasized continuous abstinence.

Fiorentine (1999) corroborated findings on the effectiveness of 12-step programs among stimulant polydrug users who participated in an outpatient drug-treatment program. Those who attended posttreatment 12-step meetings reported higher levels of abstinence from both drugs and alcohol than those who did not attend such meetings. Greater success toward abstinence was noted among those who attended 12-step meetings once a week or more, and such effects were long term if participation in the 12-step meetings was continuous and active. Those who did not attend 12-step meetings or terminated their participation in such meetings posttreatment demonstrated poorer abstinence rates. The effects of treatment and 12-step aftercare participation had more pronounced effects than either element enacted singly (Fiorentine & Hillhouse, 2000).

## Medication Approaches

The use of pharmacotherapy remains an area of speculation for the treatment of methamphetamine addiction (Vocci & Ling, 2005), and this avenue of study is not as elaborated as it is in reference to either cocaine or heroin dependence (Colfax & Shoptaw, 2005). However, Vocci and Appel (2007) suggested that a rationale exists for developing such treatments to alter the pharmacokinetics, pharmacodynamics, or both, of methamphetamine or its effects on the appetitive systems of the brain. In particular, such treatments might function in treating the addiction by (a) limiting the exposure of methamphetamine to the brain; (b) modulating the effects of methamphetamine at the neural transporter level; or (c) by intervening in the neurotransmitter pathways, which reinforce the effects of methamphetamine use. In the last decade, pilot and Phase II clinical trials initiated by NIDA and the Methamphetamine Clinical Trials Group considered the use of ondansetron (a serotonin receptor antagonist used mainly to treat nausea and vomiting following chemotherapy), bupropion (i.e., Wellbutrin; Zyban, an antidepressant, that inhibits the reuptake of norepinephrine and dopamine) for the treatment of methamphetamine addiction. Imiparmine, another antidepressant, also has been tested for the treatment of the addiction (Galloway, Newmeyer, Knapp, Stalcup, & Smith, 1994). Other safety trials have considered the use of aripiprazole (aka Abilify), a drug used to treat schizophrenia (Newton et al., 2008). Medication treatments for the abuse of methamphetamine seek to address the craving of the drug, inkling cravings due to environmental cues as well as the reduction in physiological symptoms associated with the termination in use.

The short- and long-term effectiveness of pharmacotherapy to treat methamphetamine addiction is only currently being determined. In one of the first medication studies, Galloway et al. (1994) reported on the use of Imipramine in a sample of methamphetamine and cocaine users, who were randomly assigned to either 10 mg or 150 mg of the drug per day to address their addictions. Participants were followed for approximately 6 months, and they also were provided outpatient counseling services, which included several elements of previously noted approaches, including relapse prevention, avoidance of cues, management of cravings, and analysis of drug-using situations. Results indicated that both the methamphetamine and cocaine users remained in treatment longer if they were assigned the larger dose of Imipramine, yet other outcomes did not differ across the dosage groups. In a laboratory study of methamphetamine, Newton et al. (2006) tested the effects of bupropion substance cravings by using videotapes to mirror environmental situations or cues. A total of 20 participants completed the study in which they received an intravenous baseline dose of methamphetamine after admission, and thereafter a similar dosage 6 days after the initiation of either a twice-daily oral placebo or bupropion treatment. Results indicated that treatment with bupropion significantly reduced cue-induced cravings as self-reported by the study participants and suggested that treatments may reduce the abuse liability of methamphetamine.

The development of effective pharmacotherapies, when coupled with behavioral treatments, may provide the most pronounced impact on methamphetamine addiction. If such drugs were to be developed to combat the severe withdrawal symptoms experienced by chronic methamphetamine users and the cravings triggered from social or emotional cues, then the likelihood of long-term engagement in drug counseling would probably be heightened (Vocci, 1996). Moreover, such combined approaches would simultaneously address the psychological and physiological addiction to methamphetamine, thereby enhancing the likelihood of treatment effectiveness. Combination therapies, albeit medication combination therapies, are standard of care in HIV treatment. There is multiple evidence based on the antecedents and effects of methamphetamine use to suggest that the Zeitgeist of this approach presents the best likelihood of engaging and retaining methamphetamine users in treatment on their roads to recovery and abstinence. However, caution must be exercised in the use of medications for the treatment of methamphetamine dependence, given the potential susceptibility that abusers of this substance may have toward any drug dependence. The use of pharmacotherapy has, in fact, recently come into question (Ashton, 2008). In a study utilizing Zoloft to help treat methamphetamine addiction, the drug was found to cause unpleasant side effects that may have interfered with the behavioral intervention that participants were receiving and in effect may have undermined the recovery process. In this multiarm intervention study, those who were on Zoloft alone attended fewer relapse prevention sessions and were more likely to demonstrate attrition from the program. Also, compared with those on placebo, a smaller proportion of those on Zoloft achieved 3 consecutive weeks of drug-free urine samples (34% vs. 47%). These latest findings are based on just one study. However, the results indicate that caution should be used in terms of the type of pharmacotherapy used to treat methamphetamine addiction.

## ADDRESSING THE METH–SEX LINK

The behavioral literature on the use of methamphetamine suggests conclusively that a very strong link does exist between use of the substance and sexual risk-taking behavior, especially in relation to the transmission of HIV and other sexually transmitted pathogens (see chap. 5, this volume). The direct effects of methamphetamine on HIV disease are beginning to be understood (see chaps. 4 and 5, this volume); however, these relations are complex, and the direct effects of the drug on HIV transmission are not fully delineated (Shoptaw & Reback, 2007a, 2007b). Nevertheless, the association between use of methamphetamine and sexual risk taking necessitates the development of treatment approaches that recognize that the use of the drug does not always occur in isolation of sexual behavior. Whether it is the desire for sexual behavior that predisposes users to the drug, or the drug itself, which creates a heightened level of sexuality, the need to consider the role that sex plays in the lives of its users must not be overlooked. Moreover, treatment modalities must delve into the underlying psychological processes that may serve as current and life-long antecedents of sexual risk taking and the role that environmental factors, including specific sexually charged contexts, may serve to strengthen the link between sexual risk taking and methamphetamine use.

In such considerations, emphasis also must be placed on the fact that methamphetamine use in relation to sexual behavior does not occur in a monolithic fashion, nor that risks involved with sexual behavior are equally present in all segments of society. For gay, bisexual, and nonidentified MSM, treatment considerations that engage users with regard to their sexual behavior are likely needed. In this segment of the population, sexual risk taking may be more pronounced, and HIV does affect these men disproportionately. As a result, much attention has been focused on behavioral interventions for methamphetamine and associated sexual risk taking among MSM (Shoptaw & Reback, 2007b) and the use of substance-abuse treatment as HIV prevention for MSM has been articulated (Shoptaw & Frosch, 2000; Shoptaw, Reback, Frosch, & Rawson, 1998). "Drug use treatment can be an efficient tool for leveraging sexual risk reductions . . . a comprehensive prevention strategy should include elements of both [sexual risk taking, drug use]" (Shoptaw & Reback, 2006, p. 1155). High-intensity programs are suggested for those methamphetamine users who present to outpatient or residential treatment, whereas low-intensity programs that address the meth–sex link may be sufficient for recreational or chronic users (Shoptaw & Reback, 2006).

CBT and motivational interviewing can be combined to address the meth–sex link. HIV behavioral researchers have recently combined motivational elements with skill-building approaches to improve on the well-documented success of skills-based, behavior-change interventions. Motivation is a key to treatment success because patients are more likely to be committed to a behavior-change plan they perceive as their own and because ambivalence about change is likewise addressed. Carey and his colleagues (Carey et al., 1997; Carey, Purnine, Maistos, Carey, & Simons, 2000) have published two studies that document the success of an intervention that integrates CBT and motivational interviewing. Other researchers have also found interventions that combine elements of motivational interviewing and CBT to be successful in promoting HIV-behavior change (Kalichman, Cherry, & Browne-Sperling, 1999; Rhodes, Wolitski, & Thornton-Johnson, 1992). Jaffe, Shoptaw, Stein, Reback, and Rotheram-Fuller (2007) recently indicated that through the use of growth-curve modeling, MSM in outpatient treatment for methamphetamine abuse also tended to show improvements in levels of depression and decreases in sexual risk taking over time, and these findings demonstrate the synergies that exist between sexual behaviors, drug use, and mental health factors and that treatments must consider all of these elements as part of a treatment program. Finally, Rawson et al. (2008) showed that treatment for methamphetamine addiction through the matrix model in the Methamphetamine Treatment Project resulted in a decrease in HIV risk behaviors over 26 months of assessment among study participants. Moreover, reduction in methamphetamine use was associated with the decrease in sexual risk behaviors.

Recently at the Center for Health, Identity, Behavior and Prevention Studies, we developed a framework for an intervention that can be delivered on the community-based level. It combines both cognitive–behavioral and motivation enhancement therapies (CBT/MET) to address methamphetamine use and associated sexual risk taking among gay and bisexual men while simultaneously addressing the struggles that gay and bisexual men face in their lives and relationships. It is provided here as a guide for considering how such approaches might be designed. This framework has not been fully enacted but is modeled on our knowledge of the meth–sex link, the needs of the community agencies with whom we work, and the myriad of gay and bisexual methamphetamine-using men who have participated in our behavioral studies. The CBT/MET approach is based in abstinence from methamphetamine, consistent condom use, and strategies for remaining safe (ABC model). The CBT/MET approach consists of 10 weekly sessions rather than a more lengthy intervention, based on providers' needs for easy integration with current standards of care in community-based agencies that serve the lesbian, gay, bisexual, and transgender (LGBT) community (e.g., short-term counseling and short-term services for substance abusers, HIV-positive support groups), and implementation at such sites was central to our development process. In addition, evidence suggests that brief CBT/MET-inspired interventions also may be effective in the treatment of stimulant use (Woolard et al., 1995) when supported by frequent contact with an intervener and a peer network, as our model proposes. Research also indicates that a therapeutic alliance that provides clients with a consistent source of nonjudgmental social support increases treatment efficacy (Jerome, Halkitis, & Siconolfi, 2009; Sorensen et al., 1998). Therapeutic alliance is particularly important to our intervention given the stigma that exists surrounding methamphetamine use and unsafe sexual practices. Compounding this further is the shame and secrecy some gay men continue to live with regarding their sexuality, which further underscores the need for a strong therapeutic alliance (Jerome et al., 2009). Finally, we selected a group rather than an individual modality because the LGBT treatment centers with whom we have worked clearly indicated that group intervention was the standard of care for their LGBT clientele. Furthermore, group interventions allow providers to reach vulnerable clients who might not otherwise be able to afford treatment. In addition, LGBT centers often report they are understaffed and overworked and that an effective group treatment model would afford more productivity. Last, they indicated that the group sessions outlined here could be used easily and effectively in combination with individual sessions that are currently offered.

In the first few sessions of the proposed approach, we emphasize the establishment of group rules, introduce basic theories behind MET, and assess each member's readiness to change. Participants are encouraged to reflect on their motivations to change on the basis of individually established goals elicited from group exercises (see Exhibit 7.2). MET-informed strategies are used to elicit reflections on abstaining from methamphetamine and engaging in sex under the influence. Because MET is, in principle, a series of techniques used by the provider to elicit client-centered change, MET is used throughout the 10 sessions by raising concerns, working with ambivalence, constructing decisional balances, as well as helping the client choose from a "menu of options." The tenets of CBT are introduced in Session 2, and in the remaining sessions we use a CBT/MET theoretical integration. We apply group tools and exercises to first introduce important concepts, explain them, and then therapeutically work on the individual session topic. During the subsequent homework exercise,

EXHIBIT 7.2
Outline for a Proposed Cognitive–Behavioral Therapy/Motivational
Enhancement Therapy Meth-Sex Intervention

1  Stopping Crystal Sex: Getting Ready to Work on Change:
   *Goals:* Welcome/prep talk, Overview of session structure. Introduce group. Set
   ground rules, specifically surrounding issues of confidentiality, and commitment
   to safety among group members. Participants are introduced to tenets of ABC
   model & readiness to change is assessed.
   *Tools:* Stages of Change Wheel and definitions of stages of change
   *Homework:* Set goals for treatment

2  Exploring the Internal Cravings ("What's going on inside me before I do crystal
   and have sex?"):
   *Goals:* Check in, exploration of ambivalence regarding change (in particular to
   sex on crystal), discussion about "trigger, thought,
   *Tools:* Motivational directives, challenges within discussions, cravings, crystal
   use/sex scheme
   *Homework:* Exploring internal cravings

3  Situations that Lead to Using Crystal and Having Sex on Crystal (People,
   Places, and Things):
   *Goals:* Check in, participants to discuss the situations in which they feel like
   using crystal
   *Tools:* Motivational directives, challenges within discussions
   *Homework:* Situations leading to crystal use and sex on crystal

4  Negotiating Consistent Condom Use (Raising Self-Efficacy in Condom Use):
   *Goals:* Check in, for participants to identify important and necessary aspects of
   negotiating safe condom use.
   *Tools:* Motivational directives, challenges within discussions
   *Homework:* Negotiating safe and consistent condom use

5  What Can You Do to Avoid Crystal and Sex on Crystal? ("Saying 'no' to something
   negative and 'yes' to something positive"):
   *Goals:* Check in, For participants to enhance their self-efficacy and chances for
   success for future goals regarding ability to avoid or refuse situations involving
   crystal and sex
   *Tools:* Motivational directives, challenges within discussions
   *Homework:* constructing a plan to avoid/refuse crystal and sex on crystal

6  Building A Crystal-Free Support System ("My New Address Book"):
   *Goals:* Check-in, for participants to explore their understanding of systems that
   support their ABC recovery, for participants to identify their own social support
   networks and to rate their effectiveness.
   *Tools:* Motivational directives, challenges within discussions
   *Homework:* Building a crystal-free support system

7  Men Who Have Sex with Men ("Rediscovering ourselves"):
   *Goals:* Check-in, for participants to be able to categorize their own beliefs sur-
   rounding sexual identity, for participants to be able to categorize community
   norms/beliefs surrounding crystal use.
   *Tools:* Motivational directives, challenges within discussions
   *Homework:* Identity as gay, bisexual, or MSM, and community

(*continues*)

---

8  Intimacy (Thinking about faithful monogamy):
   *Goals:* Check-in, for participants to re-evaluate their struggles and successes around sexual intimacy and safer sex.
   *Tools:* Motivational directives, challenges within discussions, develop counters for negative beliefs
   *Homework:* Intimacy and faithful monogamy

9  Relapse Prevention Strategies ("Game Plan, Part I"):
   *Goals:* Check-in, for participants to voice their feelings regarding their future successes and potential set-backs, and to devise a workable plan for themselves that encourages relapse preventions using the ABC model.
   *Tools:* Motivational directives, challenges within discussions
   *Homework:* Constructing a high-risk situation and a plan of action for abstinence, faithful monogamy, and consistent condom use

10  Preparing for Treatment Termination and Working for More Recovery ("Game Plan, Part II"):
   *Goals:* Check-in, to review the participants' plan for maintaining the gains they made in treatment. To obtain feedback on the program from the participants, to provide the opportunity for closure, to provide comprehensive referrals for further treatment.
   *Tools:* Motivational directives, challenges within discussions, Referral list; Goodbye

---

clients work individually on understanding sequences of internal and external triggers related to the use of methamphetamine and sex under the influence. By promoting self-efficacy throughout the sessions, clients obtain the skills necessary for increasing confidence in interrupting maladaptive affect, behavior, and cognition sequences in order to resist and negotiate problematic situations and behaviors. Methamphetamine-related sex motivations and behaviors that are salient in the lives of gay men are infused into every session of the ABC treatment model. Particularly important is the need for family and peer social support to cope with cravings and put into practice adaptive behaviors learned during group. This is addressed in Sessions 5 and 6 together with issues most often and uniquely related to use in the gay community. In Session 7, we continue to explore issues central to the experiences of MSM and the gay community, such as self-concept, community, and the role these play in methamphetamine use and sexual behaviors. In Sessions 8 to 10, we prepare clients for continuing the work posttherapy by learning to manage negative beliefs and cravings through individualized plans created through group exercises and informed by their new cognitive skills. Clients have an opportunity to provide feedback about the process and are given comprehensive referrals for further treatment. In this model, we have envisioned two peer group leaders who are facilitating the sessions.

Others have implemented and tested various behavioral treatments to address the use of methamphetamine and associated sexual risk-taking behaviors. Shoptaw et al. (2005) compared the efficacy of CBT (in the form of the matrix model) to contingency management. The effects of both CBT and contingency management have previously been described. In addition, both approaches enacted a behavioral change with regard to sexual behavior among users. Specifically, within the 1-year period of assessment, rates of unprotected anal intercourse with nonprimary partners were reduced from three instances to one instance in the 30 days prior to assessment. In an intervention study of the matrix model among methamphetamine abusers (58 of whom abused methamphetamine) that incorporated both males and females as well as heterosexual and gay users, the number of sexual partners reported by the study participants 6 months postadmission was significantly less than the number of partners reported 6 months prior to treatment. The use of this approach has been associated with pronounced reduction in sexual risk among heterosexual men and women, as well as gay and bisexual men and women (Shoptaw et al., 1998, 2005). Safer sex was also indicated by those with longer treatment episodes and who participated in a higher frequency of treatment activities.

The issue of safer sex and methamphetamine use was considered in a slightly different manner by Patterson and Semple (2003), who have worked effectively with regard to methamphetamine treatment among HIV-positive men. Building upon these ideas, Mausbach et al. (2007) reported on the efficacy for increasing safer sex among HIV-positive, methamphetamine-using MSM. A sample of 341 active methamphetamine users in San Diego, California, were assigned to a safer sex intervention (known locally as "EDGE") or a time-equivalent, diet–exercise condition. EDGE is based on the principles of motivational interviewing and is informed by social–cognitive theoretical paradigms. In the intervention, participants receive four individual counseling sessions focused on unsafe sex within the context of methamphetamine use. Analyses indicated that those in EDGE reported more protected sexual acts and greater self-efficacy for safer sex over time than those in the control condition. Even though the men were continuing to engage in methamphetamine use and reducing or eliminating methamphetamine use was not the target of the intervention, those in the safe-sex intervention implemented behaviors that were less likely to transmit HIV. These findings suggest the possibility of addressing HIV-related, sexual-risk behaviors even among those who continue to engage in active use of methamphetamine and posit a model to address one risk behavior at a time.

## CONCLUSION

An article in *TIME* magazine (Lemonick, 2007) posited how individuals become addicted. Central to the argument in this article was the idea that addictions such as methamphetamine dependence have a key biological basis and that a tension exists between traditional treatment approaches, such as a

12-step program, which view addiction as a lifelong struggle and condition, and the more biomedical approach currently espoused by NIDA, that addiction is a medical condition that can be cured. A similar tension exists on the community level, where individuals who support harm-reduction approaches to addiction are often at odds with those who believe that abstinence is the only manner acceptable to address drug addiction. However, both sets of dichotomies are rather artificial in nature given the complexity of treating addictions, especially dependence on a drug such as methamphetamine. With regard to the former, it is unlikely that even the most staunch advocates of a curable disease model do not recognize that biological, psychological, and social elements are at play when considering methamphetamine dependence. In that regard, 12-step programs do recognize the disease element of addiction, and programs such as the matrix model have begun to incorporate magnetic resonance imaging-based findings to help the users understand and overcome their addictions. Even though the harm reductionist and abstinence-only modalities are often perceived as antipodes, many harm-reductionists espouse abstinence as the ultimate goal of treatment. Similarly, many care providers in abstinence-only programs acknowledge the value of gradual decrease in use, as a means toward the ultimate goal of abstinence. In fact, Kellogg (2003) used the term *gradualism* and defined it as the belief that abstinence can be built into harm reduction approaches, with abstinence being the desired end point. Bidirectional linkages between harm reduction and abstinence-based treatments would provide a continuum of care for users and allow these individuals to take the transformational path to control their addiction (Kellogg & Kreek, 2005).

The ultimate treatment for methamphetamine dependence will rest on healing both the mind and the body while considering the connectedness that exists between the two spheres, which are intersecting and synergistic. As the review of treatment approaches in this chapter has shown, there are rich ideas that have resulted in some success in addressing methamphetamine dependence, yet not one approach in and of itself has proven fully efficacious in addressing what might be considered the most difficult of addictions to treat because of the enormous physiological and psychological impacts. These ideas are confounded by the fact that some individuals undertake a "natural recovery" without attendance in a structured treatment program (Stall & Biernacki, 1986). Such ideas are supported by naturalistic studies in which no interventions are being tested but methamphetamine use decreases over time (Colfax et al., 2005; Halkitis, Pandey, & Palamar, 2007). It is possible that such individuals possess a level of resilience, and thus future studies should seek to illuminate these robust processes and inform the development of treatment approaches.

Four more considerations are given with regard to treating methamphetamine addiction. First, our nature as behavioral scientists is to study problems, maladaptive behaviors, such as methamphetamine dependence; yet the majority of the population engage in adaptive behaviors, and studying such individuals may inform our understandings of the development and treatment of addictions. Second, methamphetamine addiction does not develop overnight, in a vacuum, or in a monolithic manner. Addiction to this drug is a lifelong process, and adolescence and especially emergent adulthood represent developmental stages in which entrée into the world of drugs is highly pronounced. Understanding how some individuals emerge from these periods dependent on drugs such as methamphetamine while others do not will allow us to further examine the trajectories of drug use and, moreover, to consider the differences that exist between the two sets of individuals. Third, all work regarding the treatment of methamphetamine addiction must and should happen on the hyphen of theory–practice, a partnership between researchers and those who confront methamphetamine users on a daily basis in settings such as clinics, hospitals, community-based organizations, shelters, and schools. More often than not, individuals along the entire spectrum of methamphetamine addiction, but especially those who believe their use is recreational, will more likely present at such venues than at a drug-addiction facility. Such partnerships are possible and desired, and they are based on building open communication and trust between researchers and practitioners (Marinelli-Casey, Domier, & Rawson, 2002). Our own collaboration with the LGBT Community Center of New York City is one such example of a successful venture in infrastructure development between theory and practice (Halkitis & Warren, 2005). Although federal entities have indicated clearly that the gap between theory and practice be closed (Institute of Medicine, 1998), the reality is that this gap still exists in part because this matter requires funding and community-centered research is a difficult sell when true randomized control trials are set as the hallmark of the best science. Finally, what remains central is the understanding and treatment of methamphetamine from a biopsychosocial perspective and treating the "whole of the person":

> While there is a great deal of merit and empirical support for the efficacy of current manualized treatment protocols in transforming maladaptive behaviors, including methamphetamine use, specific drug using behaviors do not exist in a vacuum, and contribute and interact within a larger landscape that makes up the individual personality. This has been demonstrated by the comorbid psychological conditions, traumatized developmental histories and anti-social behaviors so often associated with methamphetamine abuse. Other factors such as sexual identity, cultural identity, adolescent identity, HIV serostatus and gender interact with the psychological motivations to use methamphetamine and can also be overlooked when therapists are encouraged to

adhere to rigid and inflexible treatment protocols. (Shrem & Halkitis, 2008, p. 676)

This understanding of the biopsychosocial elements of addiction is evident in ideas in regard to the prevention, intervention, and treatment of substance-use disorder put forth by the Institute for Research, Education, and Training in Addictions, which included 50 diverse experts working in the substance-abuse field (Flaherty & Langer for the Institute for Research, Education, and Training in Addictions, 2006). Viewing addiction as a chronic illness, these experts concluded that care should focus on treating the addiction while simultaneously preventing the onset of other potentially related conditions, and the emphasis of treatment was shifted in view from one of pathology to one of wellness and recovery. In the model proposed, the person is at the center of the treatment (see Figure 7.1), and the needs of the individual are viewed in a culturally relevant manner. In addition, addiction is viewed in relation to prevention, intervention, and treatment, which are

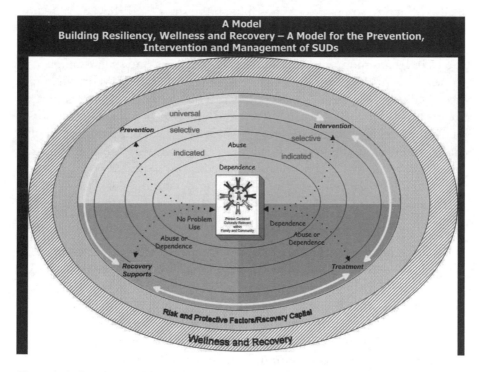

*Figure 7.1.* Drug wellness and recovery conceptual model. From "A Unified Vision for the Prevention and Management of Substance Use Disorders Building Resiliency, Wellness, and Recovery: A Shift From Acute Care to a Sustained Recovery Management Model," by M. T. Flaherty. Copyright 2006 by the Institute for Research, Education and Training in Addictions. Reprinted with permission.

associated with recovery supports and systems and are directed by the needs of individuals nested within the context of their communities (Flaherty, 2006). In the end,

> recovery occurs on the world of the client, in his/her space and life amidst numerous forms of support and intervention, one of which is psychological intervention. . . . It is our role to provide open intervention amongst many and work with the client to understand his/her needs and his/her outside life so we can offer the best opportunity to achieve wellness and recovery. (Flaherty & Langer for the Institute for Research, Education, and Training in Addictions, 2006, pp. 12–13)

Given the state of methamphetamine addiction in the United States, the approach formulated by this group resounds loudly and clearly.

As we seek to treat those with methamphetamine addiction, we must also consider and enact prevention strategies to deter the onset of this drug use. In chapter 8, consideration is given to local and national U.S. prevention strategies as well as school-based efforts to address the onset of methamphetamine use in children and adolescents.

# 8

## PREVENTION EFFORTS TO ADDRESS METHAMPHETAMINE

Throughout this volume, consideration has been given to grassroots and educational efforts to address methamphetamine addiction. There have been abundant undertakings focused on the development and dissemination of educational poster campaigns to warn against the dangers of methamphetamine. These campaigns are highly reminiscent of the HIV-educational posters that appeared on the international landscape during the 1st decade of the disease. (In the United States, such HIV posters have been highly sanitized in recent years because of limitations placed by conservative legislators and other politicians on agencies receiving public funding with regard to the provocative nature of the images and messages that are portrayed.) Although there are a multitude of educational posters addressing methamphetamine, some common themes have emerged: (a) fear tactics are abundantly used; (b) warnings about the damaging effects of methamphetamine are visibly depicted; and (c) the link between methamphetamine use and HIV seroconversion is often described (especially in posters targeting gay, bisexual, and other men who have sex with men). Conversely, these campaigns do not provide information on (a) how to avoid using the drug, (b) a healthier alternative through which an individual can experience the perceived benefits bestowed by the use of methamphetamine, and (c) how to begin a process of termination if one is already using the drug. To date, there has also been limited research on the effectiveness of such campaigns.

This chapter offers an overview of such prevention effort. It is impossible to review all such efforts, but the work of two prominent groups is particularly worth discussion. The Montana Meth Project works with the methamphetamine problem in rural America, as the name implies. The Crystal Meth Working Group has its origins in New York City and considers the methamphetamine problem among urban gay men. This chapter also outlines federal initiatives and drug education curricula in schools. A consideration of the role of scare tactics in these efforts concludes the chapter.

## MONTANA METH PROJECT

The Montana Meth Project is a large-scale prevention program aimed at significantly reducing first-time meth use through public service messaging, public policy, and community outreach" (http://www.montanameth.org). This prevention group, which is the state affiliate of the Meth Project, approaches methamphetamine use, abuse, and addiction as a consumer problem. In other words, methamphetamine is viewed as any other consumer product.

Thomas Siebel, a rancher in Montana, originally conceived of the concept of the Meth Project. It is the goal of this initiative to educate and inform youth and emergent adults about the dangers and costs associated with methamphetamine use, to deter them from using the drug. The organization uses television, radio, and print media (see Figure 8.1) to disseminate messages that are formulated on the basis of data collection. Most recently, an episode of the HBO documentary *Addiction* focused on "Montana Meth."

The organization also undertakes multidisciplinary and innovative ideas to address the methamphetamine problem. For example, the Montana Meth Project initiated a competition named Paint the State 2006. This effort asked teens to paint images with "strong" antimethamphetamine images in public spaces, such as on garage doors, barns, abandoned vehicles, billboards, and road signs, such that the message was highly visible. This educational initiative garnered over 660 public displays from 56 state counties. While using a fear-based approach similar to many other prevention campaigns, the Paint the State 2006 nonetheless functioned to some extent to dually educate the artists and also the individuals viewing the art, while using a multidisciplinary educational approach.

The effectiveness of the Montana Meth prevention efforts has been considered through a series of survey studies. The first survey (The Benchmark Survey) was conducted in 2004, and two follow-up surveys, the 2005 Survey (8 months post initial messaging) and the 2007 Survey (18-months post initial messaging), were undertaken to determine the effectiveness of the prevention

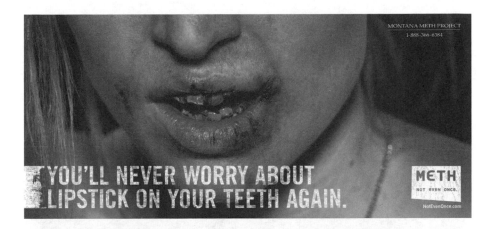

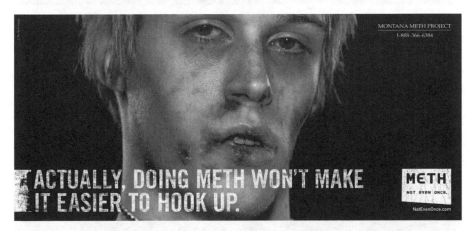

*Figure 8.1.* Prevention images from the Montana Meth Project. Copyright 2008 by the Meth Project Foundation, Inc. Reprinted with permission.

(*continues*)

*Figure 8.1.* (*Continued*)

campaigns in shifting attitudes and behaviors toward methamphetamine. These surveys and results are shown at http://www.montanameth.org/News_ Events/survey.php.

> Findings from the 2007 Meth Use & Attitudes Survey indicate that there have been dramatic shifts in attitudes toward Meth in past two years. Compared to the 2005 Benchmark survey, Montana teens, young adults, and parents are more aware of the dangers of taking Meth, more likely to disapprove of taking the drug, and more likely to have had parent-child discussions about the subject. (¶ 4)

# THE CRYSTAL METH WORKING GROUP

The Crystal Meth Working Group's origin can be found in the well-publicized campaign of activist Peter Staley, whose posters appeared in New York City bus stops in January 2004 and warned, "Buy Crystal, Get HIV Free" (see Figure 8.2). It has been argued that this message was oversimplified; however, the campaign was extremely effective in capturing the attention of health professionals, local politicians, and the press. Within a year, the New York City Council started granting $150,000 awards to leading community-based agencies and organizations to address the methamphetamine problem. Many of these funds were used to develop educational print campaigns. Currently, there is no indication of how effectively these tax dollars were spent, and my own recommendations to evaluate the poster campaigns have fallen on deaf ears, despite the need for sound scientifically driven evaluation.

Since its original inception, the Crystal Meth Working Group has launched numerous print campaigns to address the danger of methamphetamine, including *Crystal Methamphetamine: Nothing to be Proud* (June 2004), *Crystal Free and Sexy* (December 2004), and *Crystal Meth Makes Me Sexy* (June 2005). The *Grow Up* campaign is shown in Figure 8.3, and examples of the other campaigns have been shown throughout this volume. This organization has recently become affiliated with service organization Lifenet and is also responsible for the Crystal Meth Manifesto shown in chapter 1.

Unlike Montana Meth, which undertook a rigorous evaluation research effort, the Crystal Meth Working Group has yet to produce empirical evidence in regard to the effectiveness of these campaigns. My own research team at the Center for Health, Identity, Behavior, and Prevention Studies (Halkitis, 2008) have hypothesized that the campaigns have effectively deterred the onset of methamphetamine use. However, through the stigmatizing and criticizing nature of Meth Working Group this organization's effort, it is unclear whether those who are in most need of help have gone underground with their addiction, hence silencing methamphetamine use. Without definitive data, however, such hypotheses are nothing more than beliefs and assumptions.

The approaches of these two organizations are typical of those taken by local health and community-based organizations throughout the United States and Western Europe to educate the populace about methamphetamine. Such measures consistently use scare tactics and often portray the dangerous physical damage engendered by use of the drug. Figure 8.4 shows a variety of efforts, depicting the images and messages transmitted in San Francisco (Department of Health); Tennessee (Meth FreeTN, The District Attorney's Office of Tennessee); and London, England (Community for Action Against Methamphetamine, which is affiliated with Life Or Meth and the Community for Action Against Methamphetamine, Sydney, Australia).

*Figure 8.2.* Methamphetamine prevention campaign developed and distributed by Peter Staley. Copyright 2008 by the Crystal Meth Working Group. Reprinted with permission.

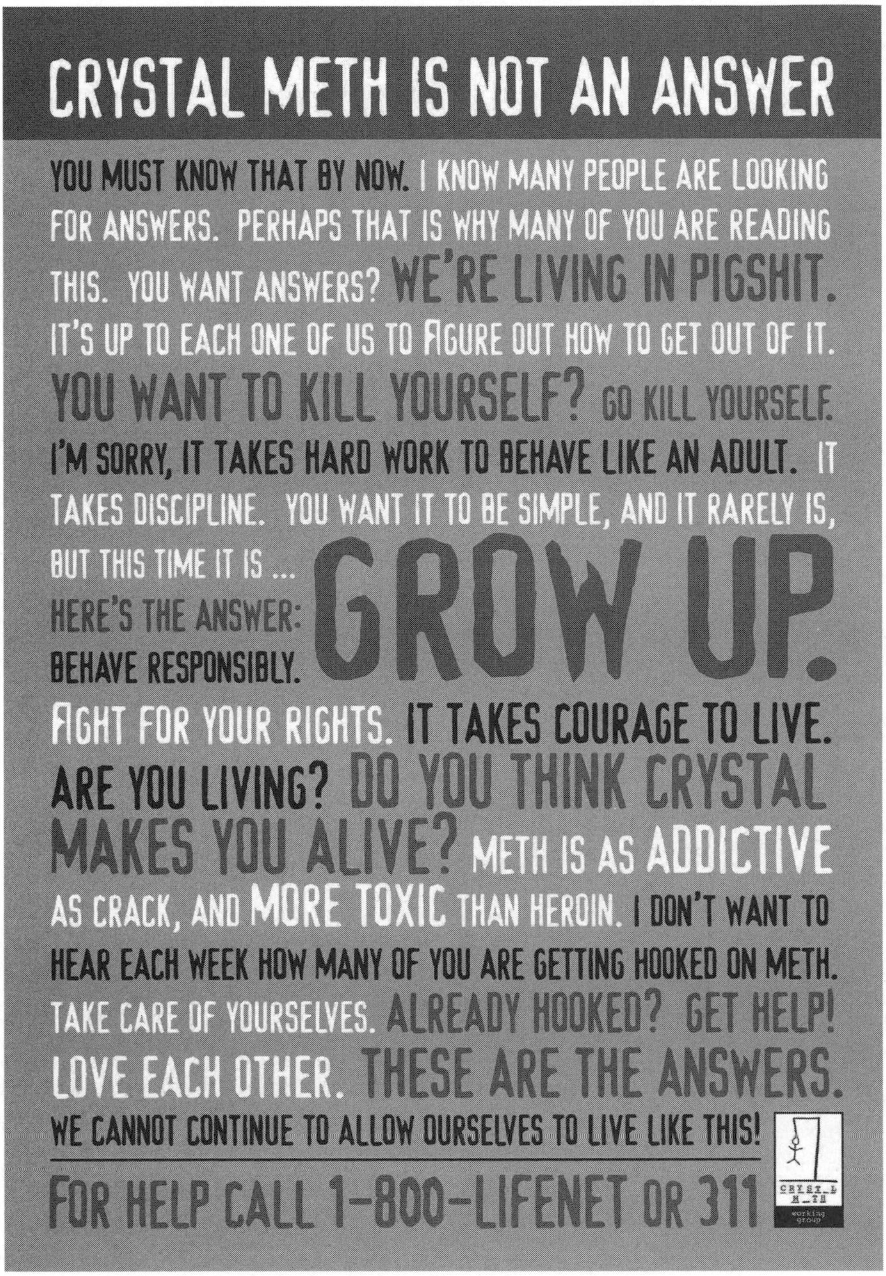

Figure 8.3. The grow up campaign from Lifenet. Copyright 2006 by The Crystal Meth Working Group. Reprinted with permission.

*Figure 8.4.* Prevention campaigns from San Francisco Department of Health, MethFreeTN, Life or Meth and Community for Action Against Methamphetamine.

# NATIONAL INITIATIVES

In chapter 3, consideration was given to the laws enacted to curtail the production of methamphetamine in the United States. Although there is some evidence that such legislation has impacted methamphetamine use, the long-term effects of these laws have yet to be discovered. However, some preliminary evidence further supports the enactment of these laws. As a result of such regulations, which have resulted in a restriction of sales of decongestants containing pseudoephedrine, there has been an associated reduction in the production of methamphetamine in the U.S. and an increase in importation from Mexico. As noted in *The Economist* (May 3, 2008), in an article reporting on the survey work of the University of Michigan, the proportion of 18-year-olds who indicated the onset of methamphetamine use declined by two thirds between 1999 and 2007. It is suggested that the greater restriction of the drug's predecessors, the need for importation, and the escalation in prices associated with these factors have been in part responsible for this decrease.

Of course, the attention focused on methamphetamine has also resulted in the proliferation of numerous educational and prevention efforts targeting various segments of the population. On the national level, such undertakings have been led by the work of the Partnership for a Drug-Free America, which coordinates the efforts of scientists and families to help prevent the onset of substance use in children, adolescents, and emergent adults. Among the numerous programs that have been developed by the organization, one specifically targets methamphetamine. The program is described as follows:

> Our Methamphetamine Program educates families and community members about the dangers meth abuse and manufacturing poses to children, the environment, communities and our society. It also warns potential users of the rapid addictive quality of meth as well as the severe physiological and psychological damage it causes to those using it. This program provides prevention and educational messages as well [as] resources for taking action and getting help. (Partnership for a Drug-Free America, 2006, ¶ 1)

The approach to education in the Methamphetamine Program is multimodal; it includes information dissemination, testimonials, and strategies for working with youth. *Meth Stories* provides firsthand accounts of former users of the drug, and *Faces of Meth* depicts the effects of the drug on the appearance and physiological well-being of the user. In addition, Partnership for a Drug-Free America provides information on how methamphetamine labs can be identified within one's residential community. As with the efforts described earlier in the chapter, the approach to addressing the drug is rooted primarily in sharing information and instilling fear.

More recently, the Partnership for a Drug-Free America has developed targeted prevention strategies on the national level that address the addiction of methamphetamine in the Native American community (see Figure 8.5).

> The Bureau of Indian Affairs Office of Law Enforcement Services surveyed Tribes with whom they work closely on law enforcement (surveys were sent to 150 Tribal law enforcement agencies, 96 responded) [the "BIA Law Enforcement Study"]. Seventy-four percent of Tribes indicated that meth is the drug that poses the greatest threat to their community. (National Congress of American Indians, 2007, p. 5)

In addition, the report suggested that 40% of violent crimes in this population are attributable to methamphetamine.

Finally, in conjunction with the Academy of Pediatrics and the Consumer Health Products Association, in 2003, the Partnership for a Drug-Free America initiated the Methamphetamine Demand Reduction Campaign (Advertising Educational Foundation, 2006). This media-campaign template was aimed at reducing substance abuse among adolescents by speaking about health consequences for both adolescents and their parents; the program was implemented in St. Louis, Missouri, and Phoenix, Arizona. Its goals were to help reduce use of methamphetamine and other club-drugs (e.g., Ecstasy) among teens by encouraging antidrug attitudes and increasing parent–youth dialogue. Preliminary results of this endeavor, as reported by the Advertising Educational Foundation (2006) suggested a successful undertaking. Within a 1-year period, positive changes in behaviors were noted. Specifically, the proportion of parents who indicated that methamphetamine is a health risk increased from 48% to 56%. The proportion of adolescents who reported a risk associated with use of the drug increased from 81% to 88%. Approximately 60% of the parents surveyed indicated that they had spoken with their children about methamphetamine in the year prior to assessment and indicated that television news stories, newspaper articles, and television commercials prompted these discussions with their children. Although these data are usually not readily available for such efforts, it is evident that a strong support for the campaign is provided.

In 2007, the White House Office on National Drug Control Policy (ONDCP) adopted the advertising campaign of the Meth Project for use on a national level (PRNewswire-USNewswire, 2007). The advertisements targeted areas where methamphetamine treatment admissions were noted to be relatively high, including Alaska, California, Illinois, Indiana, Iowa, Kentucky, Oregon, and Washington. In addition to these advertisements, the efforts of the ONDCP through the Anti-Meth Campaign are widespread, including print, radio, and television advertisements, as well as photograph exhibits. They are guided by the following mission: "Through various advertising and communication vehicles, the purpose of The Anti-Meth

*Figure 8.5.* Partnership for a Drug-Free America prevention campaign targeting Native Americans. Copyright 2008 by the Partnership for a Drug-Free America, National Congress of American Indians. Reprinted with permission.

Campaign is to prevent meth use, dispel the myth that meth treatment does not work and get people who need help for meth use into treatment" (ONDCP, 2007, ¶ 1).

The ONDCP's efforts using the Anti-Meth Campaign are drawn from the experiences of substance-abuse experts, law enforcement, and former users of the drug, using testimonials as primary means for conveying information about methamphetamine. Furthermore, in conjunction with the Department of Health and Humans Services and the Department of Justice, the ONDCP sponsors the Web site http://www.methresources.gov, which provides information about treatment sites, research, current programs, funding, technical assistance, and policies and legislation. All of this information is readily available to users of the Internet, although very little information is provided about these various initiatives and their effects on methamphetamine use in the United States.

## SCHOOL-BASED CURRICULA

Systematic reviews of the literature on the effectiveness of drug education programs indicate mixed results in ultimately changing drug-using behaviors in youth and adolescents. In a seminal study of drug education programs disseminated in schools, Bangert-Drowns (1988) suggested two major conclusions: (a) that evaluations of these drug education programs are poorly designed, and (b) that the evaluations do not provide evidence that the programs reduce the onset of drug use. In a meta-analysis of 33 studies, Bangert-Drowns showed that the programs had their greatest impact on knowledge and attitudes but had little effect on behaviors and moreover that peer-led interventions were most effective in shifting the students' attitudes. In addition, as noted by McBride (2003), there are programs being implemented and endorsed in schools that have not been designed by researchers, hence they are lacking empirical data and formal evaluation. These limited findings may be due in part to the "just say no" attitude, which shapes the program development and the measurement plans in the evaluation. As J. Beck (1998) suggested, a more appropriate evaluation model would be one that considers drug use in form of "informed choice" and "harm reduction" (i.e., not whether a student uses drugs but rather the choices that students makes about drug use).

These ideas concur with the results of a 6-year analysis of the Drug Abuse Resistance Education (D.A.R.E.) program (Rosenbaum & Hanson, 1998). Drawing from a sample of 1,798 students followed from Grades 6 through 12 in a set of urban, suburban, and rural schools, the study indicated that D.A.R.E. had no long-term effects on drug use. In addition, the short-term positive effects of the program had been eradicated by the conclusion of the study, and suburban students actually experienced harm, with an increase in drug use after engagement with the D.A.R.E. program.

Orme and Starkey (1999) examined the attitudes of 575 students, ages 11 to 16, in the United Kingdom, with regard to drug education in schools. It is interesting to note that most had received education pertaining to tobacco and alcohol specifically, and other illegal drugs generally. A conclusive finding from this survey was that drug education programs should be developed in coordination with the target audience (e.g., with youth if the program is school based). This idea is consistent with previous work suggesting that, to be valuable, drug education efforts must be relevant to the program's intended audience (Tobler & Stratton, 1997; White & Pitts, 1998). As with the treatment approaches reviewed in chapter 7, the notion of importance to the target population is significant when addressing prevention. Culturally tailored prevention efforts enhance the relevance to the target populations. The programs enacted must be developmentally appropriate for the various stages of a child or adolescent's life and, to be meaningful, must be contextually nested (Midford, Munro, McBride, Snow, & Ladzinki, 2002).

Drug education curricula that specifically address addiction to methamphetamine have been limited. It is likely this drug is included under the umbrella of drug education in schools. However, one program worth mentioning is the curriculum created by Life or Meth and titled, "Life or Meth: What's the Cost?" With a facilitator's guide, the program is presented by the Midwest High Intensity Drug Trafficking Area (HIDTA) and the Iowa Governor's Office of Drug Control Policy (2008; available at http://www.lifeormeth.org) and is intended for children in Grades 5 through 8. Consisting of five lessons, the program is interactive in nature and can be implemented in approximately 45 minutes, and it is intended to supplement existing drug education programs in schools. The program is appropriate for whole group, small group, or individual instruction because the lessons are delivered electronically. Although the first part of the curriculum is didactic, as it provides the students much information on the effects of drugs in general and methamphetamine in particular, the last two lessons are psychoeducational in nature. Students have an opportunity to practice decision making and assertiveness, and they are also given an opportunity to explore how they make healthy choices. These latter elements provide a level of innovation and sophistication to the curriculum and help to build on the informative, somewhat cautionary, and fear-based elements incorporated in the first three lessons of the series. Rigorous evaluation data are not available about the program, due in part to lack of funding for such endeavors (B. Swift, Office of Drug Control Policy, personal communication, August 4, 2008).

Southeast Missouri State University has also developed a school-based program to prevent methamphetamine use. Named Meth Education for

Elementary Schools (MEDFELS; Southeast Missouri State University's Office of Continuing Education, 2007), and funded by the Midwest HIDTA, Southeast Missouri State University, the Missouri State Government, and the Missouri Department of Public Safety, it is designed for use with students in Grades 3 and 4. Although intended primarily for inclusion in the curricula of this cohort, the program is suggested for use by teachers of other grades, parents, and members of the community. The foundation encompasses five main themes: (a) the effects of methamphetamine, (b) methamphetamine and health, (c) methamphetamine and the law, (d) prevention and treatment, and (e) the costs of methamphetamine to society and individually. The numerous activities detailed on the Web site include "fill in the blank," interactive images such as maps designating the methamphetamine laws in states, and game-style quizzes. Unlike the Life or Meth curriculum, this project, which is still a work in progress, is purely knowledge based. A fear-based approach is present in this program, as exemplified by the "Danger Teller," an origami fortune teller game in which the central message is, "Danger! Meth Can Kill You. Talk to Family & Friends. Get Treatment. Call 1-800-HELP" (see Figure 8.6). To date, no evaluation data are available about the MEDFELS program:

> As far as we know, there have not been empirical evaluations conducted on the program. We continually receive email messages from across the country where different groups have accessed the program. A number of elementary schools have utilized the program and have sent comments in reference to the success of the program. All we have is anecdotal evidence of the program's value. (L. Keena, personal communication, July 16, 2008)

A third set of school-based materials addressing methamphetamine addiction has been developed by the Phoenix, Arizona, government (titled "METH: Don't Even Start", Jones, 2007; see also http://www.phoenix.gov/meth). Designed for both junior high and high school students, the curriculum guide encourages the use of selected activities based on the needs of the students to facilitate cooperative learning. The curriculum incorporates both didactic elements and skill building. Students can be introduced to the effects of methamphetamine use, the factors that might drive adolescents and young adults to use the drug, and the link between methamphetamine use and sex. Skill building and decision-making activities encourage students to think about numerous elements related to methamphetamine use. In one activity, specifically, students are encouraged to consider why they would or would not use the drug. Videos, pretests, posttests, and vocabulary and crossword activities are provided as part of the program. There are no published evaluation data on this program.

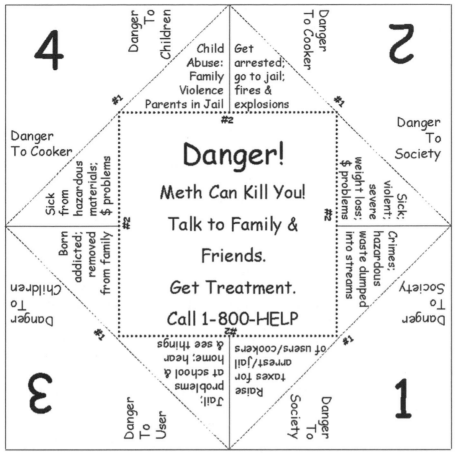

DIRECTIONS: 1. Cut along on the solid bottom line. 2. Fold toward the non-printed side on all four #1 dashed lines. 3. Fold toward the printing on all four #2 heavily dotted lines. 4. Crease in halves toward the "Danger to..." side. 5. Flip up each of the four numbered flaps. Insert a thumb or index finger in each flap.

TO PLAY: For two or more. One person picks a number between 1 and 4. Another person opens and closes the Danger Teller the chosen number of times. The first person picks a flap (for example "Danger to Children ) and the the Danger Teller operator lifts the flap and reads the "fortune." COM-1

*Figure 8.6.* Origami meth danger teller from the Meth Education for Elementary Schools curriculum. Copyright 2008 by Midwest High Intensity Drug Trafficking Areas. Reprinted with permission.

## FEAR TACTICS IN METHAMPHETAMINE PREVENTION AND EDUCATION

This chapter has considered the methamphetamine prevention efforts within communities and school settings. During the last decade, community-based prevention efforts have become increasingly popular. For instance, in 2008, California political and drug enforcement officials launched an

$11 million campaign consisting of billboards, bus wraps, and cable TV ads to supplement a Web site geared to deter gay men from using methamphetamine (M. Engel, 2008). The popularity of the drug is further verified in an analysis of Google and Yahoo searches on the term *crystal meth* yielding over 1,000,000 and 3,000,000 hits, respectively, pertaining to media stories, informational Web sites, testimonials, and scholarly publications relating to methamphetamine.

Although broad and extensive in their portrayal of the drug, one element seems consistent in most educational campaigns. Embedded in fear tactics, the campaigns seek to warn the American public about the dangers of methamphetamine in relation to their loved ones, their children, their communities, their financial well-being, and their lives. Such approaches to the antidrug efforts should not be surprising given the outpouring of frightening stories one can witness on the local news, for example, the spread of staph infections, collapsing bridges, drive-by shootings—all of which function to instill fear. As one would expect, the results of these fear-based approaches have been mixed in terms of effecting change, especially with health behaviors, whether the message concerns the consistency of condom use for safer sex or the use of illicit substances (e.g., methamphetamine). Furthermore, most primary prevention efforts which are fear based, rely primarily on the dissemination of information without fully addressing the complex biopsychosocial realities that predispose individuals to use illicit substances. In addition, Bergeret (1983) noted that the combination of fear tactics with simplistic informational messages may contribute to the overexaggeration of a drug problem.

The ONDCP was established during the Reagan era under the Anti-Drug Abuse Act of 1988. Social marketing efforts to address methamphetamine addiction across all subgroups in the United States through educational and informational print campaigns parallel many efforts by the organization. These initiatives have focused primarily on dissemination and have used fear as a tool to discourage and prevent the use of illicit substances. However, these seemingly well-intentioned motives likely raise awareness of a drug problem, but they have debatable impacts on changing behaviors (DeJong & Wallack, 1999). In addition, although intimidation approaches have been argued to be effective by some, Hastings, Stead, and Webb (2004) clearly articulated, "Laboratory studies, which have been the basis for most research on fear appeals and which generally suggest that fear works, have limitations that include forced exposure, short-term measurement, and over-dependence on students' samples" (p. 961). Montana Meth has revealed some positive effects of their multifaceted approach to education; however, the fear-based educational efforts of other organizations remain untested and are potentially causing harm. In fact, Witte and Allen (2000) mentioned that one outcome of approaches intended to encourage panic is the development of maladaptive fear controls (e.g., avoidance, reactance) that can potentially worsen the drug problems in our society. For almost a decade, my research center at New York University has conducted work concerning methamphetamine use and gay men in New York City. This team of researchers has long speculated that the ill-informed and nonscientifically rooted print campaigns, fixed with tainted speeches from community leaders, may have caused many men, specifically those in most need of help, to take their behavior underground, perpetuating a culture of stigma and risk.

To effectively prevent and terminate methamphetamine use, educational efforts need to use a biopsychosocial perspective. Such approaches must consider individuals along the entire spectrum of use (i.e., not all users are addicted to the drug) and recognize that there are social, emotional, and biological bases that fuel attraction to the drug. Put simply, messages and information must be tailored to meet people "where they are" and to respect "why they are there." To date, most prevention efforts, including those delineated in this chapter, have failed in their efforts. Part of this could be due to how they have assumed that methamphetamine use occurs within subpopulations in a monolithic, simplistic, and linear manner. These ideas correspond with those of Bass and Kane-Williams (1993), who pointed out in their examination of substance use among African American children and adolescents, an expanded framework must be used that acknowledges the various dimensions of substance use and the dimensions of involvement, exposure, and victimization. Only through such an extensive outline will effective understanding key into the role that the drugs play in individuals and in communities and, more important, how educational interventions can be tailored to these realities. Sensitivity to the diversity across and within methamphetamine-using subpopulations seems all but absent in current educational efforts. Even those well versed in the nuances of their own cultural groups (e.g., Crystal Meth Working Group) occasionally fail to recognize the diversity that exists even with population subgroups (i.e., not all gay men are alike).

## CONCLUSION

It is important to note educational efforts that address methamphetamine in the United States occur within the sociopolitical realities of our time. In some ways, these efforts are shaped by the media and draw attention to the problem of the moment. When considering the coverage of methamphetamine in the popular press, this following opening sentence is from an article that appeared in *The New York Daily News* (Gesslein, 2007): "Valerie, a transgender dominatrix, couldn't control her crystal meth addiction, which fueled day-long binges of club hopping and sex" (¶ 1). Stories like this one in regard to methamphetamine have become increasingly present in the popular press in the last several years. These stories have ranged from investigative reports and general science articles to entertainment and gossip-based stories of industry idols, such as popular singer, Fergie. These stories in the media all seem to take a sensationalist approach, emphasizing the cost and destruction of the drugs and neglecting to mention how to help the addict other than through policing efforts. In some respects, these news accounts at their core are not vastly different from the methamphetamine education and prevention efforts enacted in the last decade.

Ultimately, educational efforts and media portrayals with regard to methamphetamine addiction must be informed by science. The Entertainment Industries Counsel (http://www.eiconline.org) is a prime example of an entity whose goal is to link seemingly disparate fields by having scientists and artists collaborate for the purposes of awareness, education, and abolishing the negative social stigma of drug addiction. As a researcher who has an investment in this realm, I take an optimistic view of the well-intentioned efforts of community leaders, educators, and politicians who are trying to address the methamphetamine problem in the United States. I hope that scientists, practitioners, and those who are most affected by the harsh realities of addiction can find similar common ground and cohesively and effectively achieve the goal of educating the public about the methamphetamine menace. If the various constituents can establish a foundation on the hyphen of theory–practice, then it is anticipated that these educational efforts will succeed.

As crucial as these methamphetamine education initiatives are, they are limited in the absence of rigorous evaluations. Thus, there is a dire need for funding to undertake the necessary evaluations to scrutinize the programs that have been described in this chapter. Both sets of school-based curricula are currently enacted without such evidence, and there is no clear indication of the effectiveness of most prevention campaigns. In the absence of such data, these efforts may be causing more harm than good. As noted by Betsy Smith (personal communication, August 4, 2008) of the Iowa Office of Drug Policy, which created the Life or Meth curriculum, "We've never had the funding to conduct such an evaluation, though if the opportunity arose we would like to do so in the future."

In the subsequent chapters, Antonio E. Urbina, a medical practitioner, and J. Daniel Carragher, a mental health practitioner, each share their direct and personal experiences of working within the realm of methamphetamine addiction. Their anecdotes can be used as tools to further exemplify the concepts and views present in this volume.

# 9

# WORKING WITH THE METHAMPHETAMINE-ADDICTED CLIENT IN MEDICAL SETTINGS

Medical settings play an essential role in the management of those addicted to methamphetamine. As described in previous chapters, the detrimental effects of methamphetamine are protean and place the user at increased risk for medical and psychiatric complications. Medical settings can provide methamphetamine-addicted patients with medical and social services to prevent chronic illnesses and to help patients recover from their addiction. The medical provider's role in the rehabilitation of addicts is crucial and should involve a multidisciplinary and integrative approach. This chapter describes how medical settings and individual providers can implement best practices for patients struggling with methamphetamine addiction.

This chapter was authored by Antonio E. Urbina, MD, a physician who specializes in HIV care and is the medical director of the HIV/AIDS Education and Training at St. Vincent's Comprehensive HIV Center, New York.

# THE EXPERIENCE OF THE MEDICAL CARE PROVIDER

The first patient with methamphetamine addiction I encountered was a young African American man from the Midwest who had a promising career as a violinist. Prior to his addiction, he was articulate, bright, and exuded confidence beyond his years. On moving to New York City he experimented with methamphetamine. At first he would use the drug only recreationally, but this escalated, and in less than 3 years he was homeless, severely depressed, isolated, and seeking treatment for his newly contracted HIV infection. At the time, I had little understanding of how this drug could so rapidly deteriorate the life of this once-promising individual. Despite my efforts, which included referring him to substance-abuse counselors, detox and rehab centers, psychiatrists and addiction support groups, this talented individual succumbed to his addiction and was found dead on a New York City rooftop. The cause of death was hypothermia. In addition to this patient, there were others with whom I came in contact and whose lives had been greatly altered by their methamphetamine addictions—the Wall Street banker who lost his job, the physician whose license was suspended, and the college graduate who spiraled into a world of prostitution to support her habit. In her case, methamphetamine addiction also led to infection with HIV and hepatitis C.

For all of these tragedies, there have also been success stories—individuals who have been able to pull themselves out of addiction and into productive and enriched lives. Their journeys have not been easy nor have they been left unscathed. As described in previous chapters, methamphetamine use of any duration is associated with substantial health risks, some of which are irreversible. Abusers must be informed of these risks early in an attempt to circumvent chronic illnesses.

Working with the methamphetamine-addicted client in medical settings is challenging, and many health care practitioners and institutions are not equipped to deal with the interdisciplinary approach that is required for patients to succeed in obtaining sobriety. Moreover, medical settings play a vital role in integrating recovery from methamphetamine addiction.

# PATIENT ASSESSMENT

It is important to screen all patients for substance abuse. Medical providers should include this as part of their initial assessment. In particular, young patients (<50 years old) who present with acute cardiovascular or psychiatric events should be routinely tested for methamphetamine (Gray, Fatovich, McCoubrie, & Daly, 2007; Wako, LeDoux, Mitsumori, & Aldea, 2007). Of course, certain demographic groups (e.g., men who have sex with men [MSM]) are at higher risk of methamphetamine addiction (Mansergh et al., 2001), but selective screening of only these groups will exclude others from being identified and adequately treated (Centers for Disease Control and Prevention, 2006; Molitor, Truax, Ruiz, & Sun, 1998; Zule, Costenbader, Meyer, & Wechsberg, 2007). The best way to screen for substance abuse is with an open-ended question that has the effect of normalizing the behavior. For example, instead of "Do you use any drugs, such as methamphetamine?" the medical provider should rephrase the question to "Do you find it difficult to not use drugs when you go out?" or "Have you relied on drugs to help you cope with work or a relationship or to finish job assignments or chores around the house?" By normalizing the behavior, individuals are more likely to feel comfortable about disclosing substance-abuse related issues. If screening is positive, providers should then ask about route of use (i.e., ingestion, rectal douching, intranasal, smoking, or intravenous) and frequency and duration of use. As described in previous chapters, route of drug administration affects risk of drug dependence and medical harm (Cunningham, Liu, & Muramoto, 2008).

If methamphetamine addiction is identified, health care providers should respond in a manner that is compassionate but that also demonstrates appropriate concern and need for medical intervention. I cannot emphasize this point enough. A health care provider's initial reaction and comportment will lay the foundation of trust between the provider and the patient. Importantly, as the patient's primary caregiver, the health care provider is responsible for oversight of the patient's medical management and treatment of his or her addiction.

After assessing the patient's readiness to seek treatment, an integrated and collaborative treatment plan that involves other trained health professionals with experience in methamphetamine addiction is essential. This may involve coordinating referrals to addiction specialists, psychiatrists, substance-abuse counselors and support groups, and managing any health-related complications that arise from methamphetamine addiction. Communication with these consultative services should be ongoing and reciprocal. Moreover, the primary care provider should set up frequent and structured medical follow-ups with the patient to assess progress and adherence to the treatment plan. The following case highlights the importance of establishing trust and coordinating services for patients who are addicted to methamphetamine. Cindy first came to my office in 2004 for treatment of her HIV infection. It turned out that she was also 12 weeks pregnant and addicted to methamphetamine. Cindy came to my office because she had decided not to terminate her pregnancy and wanted help with her addiction.

Among other abnormalities, abuse of methamphetamine during pregnancy can lead to infant clefting, cardiac and liver anomalies, and fetal growth reduction deficits (Chomchai, Na Manorom, Watanarungsan, Yossuck, & Chomchai, 2004; Dahshan, 2008; Plessinger, 1998; Smith et al., 2003, 2006;

Thaithumayanon, Limpongsanurak, Praisuwanna, & Punnahitanon, 2005). Cindy knew she had to stop using in order to protect and keep her child and that she needed medical intervention to prevent transmitting HIV to her baby. On this first visit, I could tell that Cindy was not only scared but extremely ashamed of her predicament. I picked up on this and spoke to her frankly, explaining that her situation was not hopeless and that she could take steps to improve not only her life but the life of her unborn child. My challenge was to first establish a trusting relationship with Cindy and then to devise a treatment strategy that would help her with her addiction. I referred Cindy to an outpatient medical detox program that also provided specialty HIV and obstetrical care. I consulted frequently with the faculty at the detox program and became an integral part or her medical care. Cindy was promptly started on her HIV medications and initiated group and cognitive–behavioral therapy. As a result of directly observed therapy, Cindy's adherence to her HIV medication was excellent, and she delivered a healthy, HIV-negative baby boy.

Part of my success in treating methamphetamine-addicted patients is that I have never operated alone, always relying on the expertise and input from my colleagues in the field. Also, after consent from the patient, I also try to enlist the support of spouses and partners, family members and friends. Finally, providers must be patient, consistent, and accessible to patients during their illness.

## HEALTH RISKS OF ACUTE AND CHRONIC METHAMPHETAMINE INGESTION

As described in chapter 4 of this volume, methamphetamine abuse leads to substantial health risks, even in the casual user. It is important to note that users need to understand that ingestion of methamphetamine causes profound increases in blood pressure and heart rate (Lynch & House, 1992). Because of the long half life of methamphetamine (approximately 12 hours), these effects can persist for hours even after drug ingestion has stopped (Oyler, Cone, Joseph, Moolchan, & Huestis, 2002). These effects contribute to the increased risks of heart attacks, strokes, heart and kidney failure (M. A. Miller & Coon, 2006; Richards, Johnson, Stark, & Derlet, 1999; Westover, Nakonezny, & Haley, 2008; Yeo et al., 2007). Patients with underlying cardiovascular disease (e.g., history of prior heart attacks or strokes) may be at even greater risk for these complications (Kaye, McKetin, Duflou, & Darke, 2007). The neuropsychiatric effects are well described in this book. Chronic abusers are at risk of major depression and cognitive deterioration that may persist even after discontinuation of use (Kalechstein et al., 2000).

# DRUG INTERACTIONS

Fatal interactions between amphetamine analogues and the protease inhibitor (PI) ritonavir, used to treat HIV infection, have been reported (Baker & Bowers, 1997; Hales, Roth, & Smith, 2000; Henry & Hill, 1998). Ritonavir is metabolized primarily by the CYP3A4 and CYP2D6 isoforms and also inhibits these enzymes. Because amphetamines are also substrates for the CYP2D6 isoform, concomitant administration may result in three- to tenfold increases in the levels of methamphetamine (Pritzker, Kanungo, Kilicarslan, Tyndale, & Sellers, 2002). Because of this interaction, patients should be made aware that combining methamphetamine with ritonavir could lead to dangerously high levels of methamphetamine. Such increases can predispose individuals to cardiovascular events such as heart attacks and strokes as well as to acute psychotic episodes. In patients who are methamphetamine abusers and on ritonavir, I would consider changing to a non ritonavir-containing regimen or discontinuing their medications altogether if their immune function is stable and the risk of HIV-disease progression is low.

Additionally, commonly used medications with anticholinergic properties such as antihistamines (commonly found in over-the-counter cold remedies), antipsychotics, antispasmodics, and tricyclic antidepressants may exacerbate methamphetamine's neurotoxic effects, resulting in mental status changes, including delirium (Okuda et al., 2004). It is essential that health care professionals educate methamphetamine abusers about these risks.

# LABORATORY AND OFFICE TESTING

All persons with a history of methamphetamine use should be regularly tested for HIV infection. I recommend testing twice annually and more frequently in persons who engage in ongoing high-risk behavior. Because methamphetamine use increases the risk of acquiring HIV infection (Carey et al., 2008; Liang et al., 2008; Nair, Mahajan, Sykes, Bapardekar, & Reynolds, 2006; Potula & Persidsky, 2008), persons who present with signs and symptoms of acute HIV infection should be properly screened with both antigen (viral load) and antibody testing. These flu-like symptoms include fever, headache, sore throat, swollen lymph glands, body aches, diarrhea, and rash (Quinn, 1997). Although 10% to 40% will not experience these symptoms (Zetola & Pilcher, 2007), every person who becomes infected with HIV goes through acute HIV infection. This phase of infection presents an enormous risk both to the person who has become infected and to his or her sexual and needle-sharing partners. During the peak stage of early HIV infection, the amount of virus circulating in the newly infected person can make him or her up to 1,000 times more likely to transmit HIV than during the chronic stage of the infection

(Jacquez, Koopman, Simon, & Longini, 1994), which is typically 8 years or more after infection and before the onset of AIDS. The viral load test detects HIV itself unlike the more standard antibody test, which detects only the antibodies that develop weeks or, more rarely, months after infection. Most people will get negative results on an HIV antibody test for 3 to 6 weeks after infection (Zetola & Pilcher, 2007). The viral load test, however, can detect HIV 5 to 7 days after infection. Therefore, it is important to include HIV viral load testing in those persons you suspect to be in acute HIV infection and counsel them about the risk of enhanced transmission. Because treatment with HIV antiretrovirals during this early phase may have a beneficial effect on disease progression (Blankson, 2005; Hecht et al., 2006; Kassutto et al., 2006; Rosenberg et al., 2000), I recommend referring patients to academic centers with experience in treating patients in acute HIV infection.

In addition to HIV testing, persons abusing methamphetamine should undergo serologic testing for hepatitis A, B, and C. Those who are not immune to hepatitis A and B should be vaccinated. As with HIV, those infected with hepatitis C will go through an acute phase. Although injection drug use and receipt of infected blood or blood products are the most common routes of hepatitis C infection, the virus may be sexually transmitted. Vaginal penetrative sex is believed to have a lower risk of transmission than sexual practices that involve higher levels of trauma to the anogential area (e.g., anal penetrative sex, fisting, use of sex toys; Marincovich et al., 2003; Turner et al., 2006). Between 60% and 70% of people infected develop no symptoms during the acute phase. In those that do, they are generally mild and nonspecific and include decreased appetite, fatigue, abdominal pain, jaundice, itching, and flu-like symptoms (Maheshwari, Ray, & Thuluvath, 2008). Blood tests during this time will typically show elevation of liver enzymes. Approximately 20% to 30% of persons infected with hepatitis C clear the virus from their bodies during the acute phase. The remaining 70% to 80% develop chronic hepatitis C. Once chronic, hepatitis C infection increases the person's risk of developing cirrhosis and liver cancer (Perz, Armstrong, Farrington, Hutin, & Bell, 2006). In those persons you suspect may be in acute hepatitis C infection, testing should include hepatitis C viral load, liver enzymes, and hepatitis C antibody. Because treatment during the acute phase of infection has a much higher success rate of clearing the virus then treatment during the chronic phase (Jaeckel et al., 2001) health care providers should be vigilant in screening.

As previously mentioned, persons abusing methamphetamine are at increased risk of acquiring sexually transmitted infections. Health care providers should routinely test for gonorrhea, chlamydia, and syphilis. Both women and men should undergo testing for human papillomavirus (HPV), and health care providers should consider offering the HPV vaccine.

Finally, because the chronic use of even low doses of methamphetamine increases the risk of cardiovascular events (Kaye et al., 2007) health care providers should monitor patients closely for signs of heart and peripheral vascular diseases. This should include a thorough cardiovascular and neurological examination, monitoring of vital signs including heart rate and blood pressure, baseline electrocardiogram and referral for more specific testing such as echocardiography and stress testing if the patient is symptomatic or has positive clinical findings. It is important to note that referral to a cardiologist or a neurologist is indicated if the patient has worsening symptoms or any positive clinical or laboratory findings.

## HARM REDUCTION

For those who inject methamphetamine, information on how to reduce the harms associated with injection may be lacking. Providing information and referrals for services such as syringe exchange programs (SEPs) can help those who inject methamphetamine reduce the risk associated with injection practices. In addition to providing sterile syringes, SEPs can provide other harm reduction techniques. This is important because sharing of injection equipment other than syringes (e.g., water, bottle caps used to mix drugs, cotton used to filter the mixture) also carries risk of acquiring viral hepatitis and HIV infection (Hagan et al., 2001; Mandell, Vlahov, Latkin, Oziemkowska, & Cohn, 1994).

The following case illustrates why it is important for health care providers to understand the health literacy of their patients. Mike had been my patient for several years. In his early 30s, he had a good job, a good network of friends, and a steady boyfriend for the last 3 years. Although he had used methamphetamine intranasally in his 20s, stating, "It was very common in the San Francisco scene at the time," Mike had not used since he moved to New York City 5 years ago. Mike was in excellent medical condition, adhered to safe-sex guidelines, and would always come to see me for his annual physical exam. One day I received a message from him stating that he was not feeling well. Specifically, he complained of abdominal pain, fever, extreme fatigue, discoloration of his urine, and yellowing of his eyes. Because I was certain that I had immunized him against hepatitis A and B, I was a little perplexed by his symptoms and asked him to come in and see me. On exam, Mike clearly had signs of liver disease; he was jaundiced and icteric (both his skin and his eyes were yellow). On questioning Mike about any potential causes for his symptoms, I asked him about any use of new medications, including herbs or anabolic steroids. After he said no, I probed further and asked him about any other symptoms, including weight loss, exposure to toxic chemicals, or recent drug use. Mike said that he had gone online and hooked up with a group of guys that were shooting ("slamming") methamphetamine. He said that this was the first time that he had done this, and despite this he had protected sex. On further questioning, I asked him whether he shared any of the injection equipment. He said, "I don't think so. I used a capped needle that was lying on the table. I assumed it was clean." I also asked him whether he had shared any other injection equipment, like water or cotton swabs. It was then that Mike told me that everyone at this party was withdrawing their syringes from the same bowl. When I explained to Mike that pathogens like HIV and hepatitis C can be transmitted this way, he seemed stunned and really had no idea that equipment other than needles could transmit these infections. Subsequent testing confirmed that Mike had been acutely infected with hepatitis C. HIV testing was negative. I promptly referred Mike to a liver specialist for treatment. Despite adhering to the difficult treatment regimen, Mike's hepatitis C was not cured.

Because persons who abuse methamphetamine are at increased risk of acquiring HIV infection, information about nonoccupational post exposure prophylaxis (PEP) against HIV should be given to patients as part of harm reduction counseling (New York State Department of Health AIDS Institute, 2004). PEP consists of administering antiretrovirals for 4 weeks to persons exposed to HIV either through high-risk sexual behavior or through needle sharing. For PEP to be effective, the patient must have ready access to antiretrovirals within 72 hours but ideally within 2 hours, because PEP is more likely effective when given earlier (Tsai et al., 1998). Medical settings that are dealing with methamphetamine clients should have protocols for providing PEP. Because PEP is only indicated for isolated high-risk exposures, persons presenting for PEP should also undergo counseling to further reduce ongoing high-risk behavior.

As described elsewhere in this volume (see chap. 4), dental decay is accelerated in those who abuse methamphetamine. Health care providers need to educate patients about this health effect and encourage them to maintain good dental hygiene as well as refer them for regular dental care, preferably with dentists that have experience in treating methamphetamine-abusing populations.

Last, protracted use of methamphetamine can lead to decreased caloric intake, impaired digestion, and nutritional deficiencies. All these factors increase the abuser's risk of developing the metabolic syndrome (Virmani, Binienda, Ali, & Gaetani, 2006, 2007) and increase the user's susceptibility to infections.

## MANAGEMENT OF ACUTE INTOXICATION

The short-term effects of methamphetamine are mediated through the release of large amounts of dopamine and to a lesser extent norephinephrine. As previously described, these effects lead to increased heart rate, elevated blood pressure, increased rate of breathing, and increases in core body temperature (Numachi et al., 2007). Because patients in acute intoxication are at increased risk for cardiovascular, renal, and hyperthermic events, hospitalization should be considered for those patients who are medically unstable. Oftentimes, just hydrating these patients with intravenous fluids and administering sedatives, such as diazepam or lorazepam will prevent serious medical complications.

The psychiatric effects of acute methamphetamine ingestion are well described in this book and include personality changes, restlessness, tension, irritability, insomnia, and psychosis. Verbally threatening behavior and physical aggression have also been observed (Milne, 2003). Patients who present to medical settings in acute psychosis should be immediately referred for psychiatric evaluation and considered for neuroleptic medication and hospitalization.

## CONCLUSION

Medical settings play a central role in the care of the methamphetamine-addicted patient. Methamphetamine's unique pharmacologic properties and neuropsychiatric complications require that health care settings incorporate an interdisciplinary approach to the treatment and care of persons who use or are addicted to methamphetamine. It is important to note that social and psychiatric services must be included in the management of the methamphetamine-using patient. Providers involved in the care of patients who are using methamphetamine should be alert to the heightened risks of acute HIV and hepatitis infections, as well as cardiovascular and neuropsychiatric events. Last, providers should explain to their patients ways that they can reduce the harms associated with methamphetamine use, including counseling on safer injecting practices and information on postexposure prophylaxis for HIV in the event of a high-risk exposure.

# 10

# WORKING WITH THE METHAMPHETAMINE-ADDICTED CLIENT IN MENTAL HEALTH SETTINGS

To understand the impact that methamphetamine has on a community, it is important to consider the individual psychological reasons behind the needs to seek, use, and abstain from the drug. Research provides trends and averages, but it is only through one-on-one work with clients who are struggling to understand how they came to be so intimately associated with methamphetamine that one truly appreciates just how many personal paths an individual can take along this communal journey. Researchers talk of "variables" and therapists talk of "individual differences," as if these are completely separate phenomenon when in fact it is the nexus of empirical and clinical thinking that best serves our clients. This chapter tells the story of my own discovery of that connection and the people whose individual stories create the bigger picture. It is meant to shed some light on the ways we conduct both our surveys and our sessions and to acknowledge that the reasons why someone struggles with methamphetamine form a story and not just a statistic.

This chapter was authored by Daniel J. Carragher, a licensed psychologist with a PhD in clinical and school psychology, and a former project director at New York University's Center for Health, Identity, Behavior and Research Studies. He teaches adjunct in the field of educational psychology, provides diversity training surrounding gay and lesbian issues, and maintains a private practice the in Metro New York area.

# UNDERSTANDING METHAMPHETAMINE ADDICTION

Mental health workers often wear many hats, which proves useful in our clinical work (Morrow, 2000). With degrees in counseling and clinical psychology, I have worked as a clinician, a researcher, and a diversity trainer and educator in the metropolitan New York area for the last 10 years. The clinician within me knows that to provide effective substance-abuse treatment (or any treatment for that matter) it is essential that I understand the cultural realities of the community that I am serving. For the most part my work has been nested within the gay population of New York City. Thus, my approach to and understanding of methamphetamine addiction are rooted within the realities of the lives of gay people, although the lessons I have learned can be broadly applied, as we are all social, cognitive beings.

As a researcher, I am empowered to identify the most effective information to help me do the best clinical work I can. I do this in part because I have access to data sets, but anyone interested in good interventions should take it on themselves to do the same. Furthermore, the data have helped me to dispel mythologies. For instance, not all gay men use illicit drugs (let alone crystal meth)—a fact that as a diversity trainer I find myself saying over and over again (Cochran & Mays, 2006). I also know full well how challenging, if not impossible, it is to even estimate how many gay people there are in any given location, let alone how many of them are doing a particular drug (or combination of drugs) at any particular time (Savin-Williams, 2006). These statements would seem to muddle my work as a clinician, but I argue instead that what we do know, and also what we do not know, from research in this field is invaluable to informing our therapeutic practices.

My own first foray into the world of gay men and substance abuse was as a researcher and as the project director for Project BUMPS (described in "Clinician as Researcher" section below). Although I considered myself learned in the general issues surrounding the gay community, the nuances of the subcultures of this population were still relatively new to me.

The intersection between methamphetamine use and the gay community has been called the "perfect storm." In methamphetamine, we have a drug that increases libido, causes insomnia, and renders one potentially unable to maintain an erection. My clients, who were either using the drug or were familiar with men who had been using, began using terms like "instant bottom" and "crystal dick," referring to the fact that men who used crystal were more likely to be the receptive partner in anal sex because they could not maintain an erection to be the insertive partner. As the drug emerged, the overall club scene environment also changed. Within the subculture of the gay community who were using the drug, the world was vastly different "pre-Tina" (Klitzman, 2006). The mood "post-Tina" was reported as "darker," more "aggressive." In lieu of stories about meeting men at clubs and bars and spending an evening touching and fondling (i.e., the Ecstasy phenomenon), now men who had never before engaged in such behavior were reporting weekend binges involving sex parties, bathhouses, and public sex environments (Halkitis, Parsons, & Wilton, 2003b). And if they were not doing the drug themselves, they knew someone who was using it.

In addition, as methamphetamine use continued to escalate, the needs of the men who were seeking substance-abuse treatment began to change. But were we, as professionals, ready to address this addiction (Lee, 2006)? Every mental health worker knows how potentially formidable a task substance-abuse treatment can be. Few, however, were prepared for the onslaught of these new challenges posed by the methamphetamine crisis. For those of us on the front lines, and in my case both as researcher and clinician, the methamphetamine epidemic made us think long and hard about ourselves as a community—particularly in terms of our health and mental health issues. Surely these clients knew the risks they were taking? What made crystal different?

True, some men reported how scared they were of "that bitch, Tina," and how they did not like they way it made them feel or what it made them do, but many benefits of this drug were also being noted. Over and over I heard clients refer to having "the best sex I ever had." User after user, from various walks of life, of varying ages and races, talked about how finally they were able to be the sexual person on the outside that they felt they were on the inside. Some said they no longer worried about the sex that they were having—at least while they were having it. Subcultures (or the rumors thereof) formed within the methamphetamine-using community. Men already diagnosed with HIV reported using methamphetamine only with other HIV-positive men. Those just coming out wondered whether this is what they "had" to do to fit in (even though it was not really "their thing"). Others did not like all this talk about a dirty little secret of what some gay men were doing, for fear that it fueled the perceptions of society of the deviant gay life. The time was right for a more formalized investigation of the substance and the meaning it held in men's lives.

## CLINICIAN AS RESEARCHER

My first true experience understanding methamphetamine addiction came in my role as researcher. The lessons I would learn here would have both short- and long-term effects on my thinking about substance-abuse treatment as it allowed me reside on the hyphen between theory–practice.

Right out of my doctoral work, I was hired to direct Project BUMPS, a longitudinal investigation of club drug use among gay and bisexual men in New York City, funded by the National Institute on Drug Abuse. For the purposes of the study, "club drugs" were defined as cocaine, Ecstasy, gamma-hydroxybutyrate, ketamine, and methamphetamine. One aim of the study was to examine the developmental trajectories of club drug use in this segment of the population. The study is further described in Halkitis, Green, and Carragher (2006). Because of the excellent recruitment and screening procedures (targeted recruitment occurred at various gay-identified venues throughout New York City, and nearly 1,500 men were screened), the final pool of participants included a wide range of drug-using men, including those men just beginning to dabble (who had maybe used it once or twice at a party); the "weekend warriors" (who might take a bump of Tina on a Friday so that by Monday they would be sober enough to drag themselves to work); and the more frequent, sometimes daily users (though a person could not be interviewed for the project while under the influence).

Project BUMPS used a mixed-methods approach to data collection to help us realize our study aims. The quantitative data gave us the answers to how much methamphetamine (and other drugs) these men were using and how often. It also enabled us to empirically establish patterns and psychological correlates of drug use and sexual behaviors. We said we knew but now began to see statistically that it was not as simple as "drugs = unsafe sex" (or any sex at all). Some men used drugs and were sexually safe. Some men really did try methamphetamine only once or twice and never again (dispelling the myth that once you tried it you were somehow hooked for life). What did become apparent, however, was that the men who scored differently on our mental health variables—those with more depression, less social support, with differing outcome expectancies for drug use (Carragher, 2006)—did engage in riskier behavior. This gave the clinician in me valuable insight as I sat back and listened to the participants' stories that emerged from the interviews in this study.

From the qualitative data we established more intimate connections: When did men start using? Why? What did they like about it? How did it make them think? feel? As every interview was tape recorded and eventually transcribed, this meant that with 450 men assessed four times over the course of a year, I had a plethora of rich clinical data that helped me establish the foundation for my future private practice interventions. I was able to understand firsthand how this one drug not only changed individuals but also the community.

Project BUMPS was not an intervention study. The research protocol was very clear in that we were not to intervene (save for a health or mental health crisis). In addition, after so many years of master's and doctoral-level graduate training in counseling–therapy in addition to occupational experience in the field of substance abuse, it was fascinating to me how this experience of sitting, sometimes for hours, and listening to the participants simply tell their stories— without (the opportunity for) judging or advice giving—proved to be an invaluable clinical experience in and of itself (for both the interviewer and the interviewee). It taught me how, when given a referral in outpatient or private setting or a chart during my inpatient experiences, I may have jumped too quickly into the diagnosis and treatment plan and not spent enough time really listening to what the drug use meant for my client. Although I knew it was not as simple as "just say no," perhaps I never fully appreciated the complexities of "why say yes?"

From these rich narratives, I began to understand what it was specifically about methamphetamine that made it such a draw for these men. The interventions the clinician in me would have liked to have made (but could not) became not just about behavioral modifications for environmental triggers and challenging beliefs about drug use in general but focused more heavily on exploring and challenging the reasons why. In story after story that I heard first-hand or while reviewing audio tapes, the participants repeated how with methamphetamine they were finally able to not worry, be calm, feel okay about gay sex, and not think about their diagnosis. It is important to note that most of them were convinced that while sober they would never be able to think or feel that freely again.

Certain protocol questions intrigued and fascinated me. For example, when I asked "What do you like about using methamphetamine?", I could clearly see how much those who used it enjoyed how it altered them cognitively. Here, at last, was a way for a lot of these men to think differently or not think at all. Some examples follow:

> [I liked] the way it would shut down my critical thinking capacity. That way I didn't have to think. I didn't have to decide. (27 years old, HIV-negative, African American)

> [I liked the] heightened social confidence . . . [the] complete reduction of anxiety, um, complete, um, [the] complete removal of different voices in your head or different like . . . different lines of thinking. (32 years old, HIV-negative, White)

Sitting and listening to these stories, the therapist in me wanted to ask follow-up questions. "What sort of thoughts were you hoping to stop having?" and "What was the source of the anxiety that crystal helped assuage?" because often the answers to such questions went hand in hand with a true pleasure in the behaviors the drug gave them permission to do or feelings that it was okay to be gay. It was frustrating to me that I could not provide such challenges, not even when the participants did report the source of their anxiety or that only with crystal could they feel so good:

> It makes me smile. It doesn't make me think bad things. . . . when I'm sober and I'm not on drugs, I can't feel the same feeling. Only when I'm stoned. (43 years old, HIV-positive, Latino)

> It made me so confident and made me think that being gay was the most wonderful thing in the world and just having sex, just as much sex as was humanly possible to escape from self-hatred and self-doubt and feelings that the world was an evil place. Growing up in Winston-Salem included

going to the Southern Baptist church every Sunday [which] left its scars. Crystal was my "get out [of] hell free card" because the Southern Baptists say "you faggots are going to get AIDS and die!" . . . crystal takes that away, no doubts, no fear. (28 years old, HIV-negative, White)

It was extremely difficult for me not to challenge the notion that these men were incapable of thinking or feeling certain things without methamphetamine, as if crystal had given them powers they were incapable of accessing alone.

It was also clear that sex was often a motivation for methamphetamine use—not just in terms of quantity and quality of sex (although these areas both, clearly, were reportedly increasing as well) but also how the participants felt about this sex. It was the sex they always wanted in their heads but had never dared to ask or the sex they used to have back in the "good old days," before silence was not the only thing that equaled death. It was sex without the immediate cognitive baggage.

> The best part about crystal for me was the fact that it helped me get out of my head . . . it allowed me to just go with it, go with the flow, lessen my inhibitions. (39 years old, HIV-positive, White)

> I think mainly that it releases inhibitions for me sexually . . . so I do things and explore things I probably wouldn't otherwise. It also gives me permission to be sexual in a way that I probably wouldn't be otherwise. (33 years old, HIV-positive, White)

> I feel totally uninhibited sexually . . . I'm relaxed, y'know? I really don't give a shit about anything . . . Because in normal circumstances I would be shy . . . or, you know, be all stressed out. (37 years old, HIV-positive, Latino)

But for the majority of the participants, the baggage would follow their methamphetamine use. By the end of my tenure as project director of BUMPS, we began to meet men who had first lauded crystal but had now begun to demonize it. For some, not only did their use stop, but (more important to the cognitive psychologist in me) so their attitude toward the drug changed. They called it the "new crack," which implied that it had negative social connotations and that its use had begun to be looked down upon by members of the community. Some told us that simply having to come in for their next BUMPS appointment to sit and talk about how much they used and why they kept using was enough to make them think twice about picking it up. And all we did was listen. When we asked these men to describe intervention ideas for addressing methamphetamine addiction, the clinician in me was more than ready to take note. For many of the men, it was important to have an environment like the one provided by BUMPS—nonjudgmental. The men wanted to talk about the reality of crystal use in their language with someone who knew of or would be willing to listen to stories about that world and who would not necessarily be shocked.

Not so much information as much as allowing each individual to know that they are OK. (43 years old, HIV-positive, White)

I trust my brain more than I trust my dick and my brain is like, "You know you shouldn't be using drugs this much (at least as much as you want to), and you know you shouldn't be barebacking, and you shouldn't be topping, and you shouldn't be all these things!" I would go somewhere [for treatment] where there is full acknowledgement of what's going on out there and supporting those sorts of things that I think are basically good for the health of our community. (28 years old, HIV-positive, White)

The fact that the information would be presented non-judgmentally . . . it needs to be as objective as possible because the "just say no!" doesn't work and it actually makes it more difficult because then whenever you end up not being able to say "no," [you feel] even more guilty. (28 years old, HIV-negative, White)

The men with whom we spoke also wanted treatment from "folks" who could appreciate the lure of crystal and help them deal with life without it. For a lot of the men, using methamphetamine opened a Pandora's box. They knew using the drug was not a healthy behavior, but it did give them a taste of physical and cognitive pleasures they had never thought possible. For a lot of the participants, "saying no to methamphetamine" meant saying goodbye to a sexual and cognitive freedom they were not sure they could now live without.

I know all of the scare tactics . . . I'm not going to attend [treatment] if I feel it's just a lecture about "don't do it!" Because it's like, "Yeah I know don't do it." But it's [got] to be informational and acknowledge that people do drugs because on some level it feels good . . . you can feel good for a short period of time and have this effect on your body and take the risk of causing irreparable damage but we can't deny that it feels good. It's like people say smoking is terrible. Well, it's terrible, but a lot of people like doing it. You have to address why they like doing it and deal with it in a non-judgmental way. (39 years old, HIV-positive, White)

Some of the men saw hope (and I saw their insight) by stating that in order to terminate use of methamphetamine, they would have to relearn certain behaviors and patterns. With that type of statement, many of them were telling me that all was not lost. Termination of use would not be easy, but perhaps in new social circles, they could still feel good without methamphetamine. It became difficult, at times, for the clinician in me to weed out wherein lays the addiction—with methamphetamine or with the life?

I would like to be in a group that's more focused on where are you today . . . how are you doing [with] re-socialization, because I have to de-socialize myself [from methamphetamine]. I [just] dumped this guy I had great sex with [because] he was still socializing in that realm. (27 years old, HIV-negative, African American)

I would like to learn how to have hot interesting safer sex without the drug. (40 years old, HIV-positive, White)

Over the course of this study, I felt that I had received some of the best substance-abuse treatment education of my career. The study participants were extremely honest about why they used methamphetamine and what (they thought) not using methamphetamine would mean to them. By listening to their stories, I was able to formulate the broadest of clinical pictures. The 24-year-old man, disowned by his parents for being gay, would still be disowned by them when he was sober. The 45-year-old Black, HIV-positive man would still live in a racist world every morning when he took his handful of medication without crystal. If I wanted to help a methamphetamine user, I needed to focus on the user and not just on the drug. And the therapist within me was ready to help.

## THE NONINTERVENTION INTERVENTION: CLINICAL CASE STUDIES

Shortly after the conclusion of the study in 2005, I opened up my private practice in the Manhattan section of New York City. On inception of this practice, I undertook targeted outreach and advertisement of my services in the gay community. Although it not an exclusively gay practice or one solely focused on substance abuse, because of the timing I certainly saw my share of gay and bisexual men affected by methamphetamine. I of course took all of my training with me as a cognitive–behavioral therapist, but I also took my experiences from Project BUMPS and my diversity work and knowledge of the gay community.

From BUMPS, I learned that my treatment plan for methamphetamine addiction (or even for the casual user, though with crystal these men seemed few and far between) needed to be truly rooted in a biopsychosocial approach. Biologically, the men I treated had questions about what crystal was doing to their bodies, and I needed to have (or be prepared to find) the answers. We talked about dopamine. We talked about paranoia and aggression. In addition, with some, we talked about what we think we know about how methamphetamine and HIV medications interact. I was always prepared with referrals to general medical practitioners, psychiatrists, or both, as needed. Depending on the level of addiction, some men needed inpatient referrals. Psychologically, the majority of my clients who used methamphetamine were clearly dealing with other mental health issues. Like the rest of my caseload (in spite of whether or not substances played a significant role in their lives), these men presented with histories of anxiety, depression, and trauma. Trained as a cognitive–behavioral therapist, I sought the connections between my clients' realities and how they themselves perceived it. No one came into my office saying "Everything else in my life is just fine, I only wish I could stop using crystal." Socially, I wanted to hear about my client's life before crystal, why they started, and why they thought they could not stop. For a lot of the men with whom I worked, methamphetamine was their social world—online or face to face, much of their day revolved around those with whom they used or wanted to use. The challenge here, then, involved helping the men to not only to create a new social circle but also to accept that they could.

The following case illustrations are summaries of some of the therapeutic cases on which I have worked over these few years. Obviously, names have been changed. These specific cases have been chosen to illustrate some of the points raised in the discussions earlier in this chapter; in particular, how working with clients who use, abuse, and are addicted to methamphetamine is never as simple as building skills in only one area of their lives.

The treatment plans remained true to my cognitive training. For the majority of the cases, the needs of the men in my private practice exactly mirrored those, who as a researcher, with whom I worked while directing Project BUMPS—What role did crystal play in their day-to-day lives and why? and How could one learn to live without what the drug was giving them? What did they think crystal provided for them that they thought they could not provide for themselves? In addition, an honest discussion of how, yes, things might seem better with crystal, but they might be just as good without.

### Andy

In this first case, we see how both socialization and perceived support affected one young gay man's first true intimate relationship with another man, and how, in turn, these same psychosocial factors played a significant role in this man's relationship with crystal. Like some of the participants in Project BUMPS who intimated that for them to stop using crystal their social scene needed an upheaval, so too in this case my client would have to sacrifice what he knew to become who he really wanted to be.

Andy was a 22-year-old, White, HIV-negative, (recently) openly gay male from rural Ohio who had moved to New York City after graduating college just over a year before starting therapy. Andy presented as rather anxious and reported that he had come into therapy because he was having "relationship problems." He currently lived with his boyfriend in a gay-identified neighborhood in Manhattan.

He reported that he met his boyfriend just after moving to New York, and that he had not really had much of a chance to socialize or make any friends of his own. He also reported that he moved in with the boyfriend (at the boyfriend's request) almost "immediately." Andy had only told himself and a few other close friends that he was gay while he was in college, and aside from joining a gay support group in his last semester at his suburban college campus, Andy had never really been exposed to any kind of gay community; certainly nothing like the one he in which he was currently living in Manhattan.

Unbeknownst to Andy at the time, his boyfriend was using methamphetamine on the occasional weekend before they met. Shortly after they began living together, the boyfriend introduced Andy to crystal one night before heading out to a dance club. Before that night, Andy reported that he had only drank alcohol socially and tried cocaine "once at a party." He also reported that the sex he and his boyfriend had that night was "amazing," and that he was finally able to have an orgasm while receiving anal sex (something that he had never experienced before and which became a rather significant, intimate moment for Andy and his boyfriend).

A day or two after their taking crystal, Andy reported that his boyfriend would consistently become upset about their use, particularly that Andy had used (even though it had been the boyfriend who initiated it). This confused Andy and made him feel extremely guilty. He would reportedly try hard to "make it up to his boyfriend," acting in ways he knew pleased him, for example, submitting to his request not to socialize with anyone but him (even when the boyfriend was away on business).

Eventually, however, the boyfriend would buy more crystal and insist they use it. Even though Andy began to protest, he would concede. Again, they would have "great sex," and, again, the boyfriend would become angry, sometimes violent the next day. After a particularly vicious argument, the boyfriend actually kicked Andy out of their apartment (making him stay with a female friend who lived in their same building). When we first began therapy, Andy had just moved back in with his boyfriend after this incident. He was extremely self-deprecating, stating that he wanted to figure out why he was making his boyfriend so unhappy (when he himself seemed miserable). He "wanted to learn to be a better boyfriend."

Although Andy's therapy focused on challenging his beliefs about the balance of responsibility toward his methamphetamine use, it obviously focused rather heavily on the role he played within his relationship. It became clear that Andy actually had very little information about what it meant to be in a relationship (he often brought up the fact that his parents' relationship had ended in a rather bitter divorce). In fact, he had not really ever explored his own admitted confusion regarding the dynamics of dating another man. Through time, he was able to admit that he was very unhappy about not being "allowed" to make other friends and that perhaps it was he who was being treated unfairly. As the discussions surrounding Andy's social life and relationships continued, there was a marked change in Andy. He was no longer as self-deprecating. He even began to (rightfully) challenge suggestions brought up in therapy!

There was also a noted change in his crystal use. While Andy's boyfriend continued to ask Andy to use, Andy began to refuse. Furthermore, Andy now attempted to get his boyfriend to admit that he was the one responsible for initiating their use and it was unfair to place all the blame and guilt on Andy. Andy also started to hang out with other gay people in different social situations in which he gained additional perspectives about the gay community, his own relationship, and what he wanted out of life.

Eventually, Andy realized that the relationship was not healthy for him and that he needed to get out, which, over time, he did. He also reported that whereas he continued to think about using crystal, particularly in relation to sex, he felt confident that if he could continue to be open with his partners and have better communication from the beginning, then the better (sober) sex would follow. Indeed, as we discussed in a follow-up, it did.

## Kevin

Unlike the previous case, in which the client remained fairly unaware of the role methamphetamine was playing in his relationship, here we see how methamphetamine can sometimes be used as the conscious "excuse" people need to engage in behaviors of which they would rather not be conscious.

Kevin, a then 32-year-old, self-reported "sexually compulsive," White bisexual man whose HIV status was reportedly "unknown," stated when he came into therapy that he was there because of his sexual "acting out." He went on to explain how he had been, over the previous 2 years, going into bathhouses and sex clubs or hooking up with men he met online at first completely sober but eventually always high on crystal, to seek out other men "fucked up" on methamphetamine.

Kevin reported that he had a very difficult time having sex with sober men, that sex, for him, was best when he did not have to care about anyone else's pleasure other than his own. Methamphetamine helped him achieve that goal. The fun, however, only lasted so long, for after a while Kevin was no longer content staying sober. He reported initially that he started to use more crystal to simply join in the fun; later he was able to talk about how he needed the crystal to assuage his guilt. Where at first he could perform anal sex on someone high on crystal (sometimes without condoms, sometimes in a very aggressive, "uncaring" way) and not think about it, he now needed crystal to engage in the same act.

Kevin wanted to be cognitively disconnected from sex. He could convince himself that men high on crystal "got what they deserved." Sober Kevin, and Kevin with sober sexual partners, was not so sure. The addiction for Kevin was an addiction to what he was convinced was the only sexual outlet he had.

Kevin's individual therapy, in combination with his attendance at a sexual compulsivity anonymous group, helped him realize that he harbored much information about his sexuality. In his own words, Kevin stated that he was able to "disassociate" from his sexual experiences, and nearly always had. Even when he masturbated he tried not to think about himself having sex with other men because that was too "scary." Most of our sessions revolved more around his sexual comfort level and the thoughts he currently held as true in terms of gay men and gay sex, rather than a direct confrontation of his use. When the methamphetamine use was broached, Kevin at first insisted that we work on stopping his attendance at the bathhouses and public sex environments but not on stopping his crystal use. Eventually, he admitted that he thought too highly of sex on crystal to consider letting it go, and we were able to talk about how, perhaps, he could have sober sex in which he took pleasure. Rather than be repulsed by a connection with his partner, we challenged the misinformation he had about how "bad" his fantasies were and that it was okay to be connected and feel good. Through visualization and a constant challenge and redirection of his steadfast beliefs about intimacy between two men, Kevin was eventually able to begin a dialogue about sex that did not involve methamphetamine and explore a whole new world of connected sobriety.

## Richard

In this last case, we can see how methamphetamine provides, for some, a false sense of a renewed energy that could be attained by other means. We also see how it can provide a false hope of actually battling one's depression rather than facing that challenge.

Richard was a 55-year-old gay, HIV-positive, Latino man. He stated that he had been positive "before there were tests." He admitted that he enjoyed and actively sought out bareback sex as the insertive partner, and he always had. Before using crystal, Richard was an active cocaine user but felt that he had that "under control." Methamphetamine, he admitted, had "kicked his ass." Before crystal, Richard said he only barebacked with other HIV-positive guys; that a few "buddies" would get together. One of the things that brought Richard into therapy was that he was now barebacking (both as a top and a bottom) without knowing anyone's status (or revealing his own) and that he just "didn't give a shit anymore."

When Richard came into therapy, he reported that he was depressed. "As depressed as I was when I first found out I had AIDS." When asked what he meant by "depressed," Richard reported that he was isolating himself, not eating, not sleeping, and had missed a few doctor's appointments. He was also continuing to use crystal and struggling to stop. The content of his speech was filled with phrases like "hopeless case," "I've had it," and "too much." For Richard, the Internet was his sexual (and sole) social connection.

Richard's therapy involved working on ways for him to reduce and eliminate the methamphetamine. He eventually began to attend Crystal Meth

Anonymous groups in addition to his individual therapy, which not only gave him useful information and support for his addiction but also provided him a much-needed reason to get out of his apartment. Richard's therapy also addressed the larger issue of his depression. Richard had not just had it with drugs, he'd also had it with many of the issues in his life. The drugs were an addictive Band-Aid, and the wound needed to heal. He was put in touch with a psychiatrist who was familiar with the HIV medication Richard needed to take. Over the course of our time together, Richard was able to explore the feelings of loss he had experienced because of his illness. This loss included not only the actual loss of lovers and friends but also the loss of what he viewed as his "right" to sexual freedom. Even though Richard continued to bareback, he now felt guilty. What if he caught something else? What if he gave something else to someone? Methamphetamine took all of that away.

Richard described being high on crystal as being like "the 70s," a time that, for him, was carefree and for the most part guilt-free. Our therapy helped end his avoidance of the negatives (yes, he was HIV-positive), rework his negative thinking (he could still feel carefree in many ways), and, in turn, helped to decrease his need for crystal. Richard needed to learn that sex without crystal is not sex without thinking; it was sex thinking differently. It was sex, thinking. And that could be okay.

## CONCLUSION

To understand how to best provide mental health treatment for those who use crystal, one has to be ready, able, and willing to listen to the users' stories. Addictions have many layers, as do our clients, and we never know what will be at their core. People do not live in vacuums. Drug epidemics, therefore, do not exist in one either.

What has the methamphetamine epidemic taught me? I have been given a unique perspective to help me answer that question. During my years of formal training, I spent a lot of my time getting to clinically understand the gay community before I began to do research in this area. As previously stated, however, "classroom" knowledge only goes so far (in particular given a major shift within a culture unknown and unheard of when I received my education).

The research that I started shortly after receiving my doctorate gave me firsthand knowledge about methamphetamine and the psychosocial needs of the men who used it. Project BUMPS forced me to wait before intervening— to listen before I acted. As a cognitive psychologist, I believe that therapy is a relationship, a chance to lay down theories and see whether they ring true. Perhaps, before, I had been too quick to conclude.

By the time I had my own private therapy practice I could combine all of my knowledge in an attempt to provide the most effective intervention.

However, was it just as simple as "let the clients talk"? I am a realist. In these days of managed care, we do not always have the luxury of unstructured time. Neither, too, do many of the people most in need of help have the resources to afford lengthy care. I, of course, am jaded by the type of research that I do. I believe it's not just about quantity, but quality. In other words, in therapy, doing what you can with the time you have is important. For me, that means providing my clients with that nonjudgmental environment, and that my assessment does not end as soon as I know substance use is involved. It also means appreciating the reasons why our clients do drugs—all of the reasons, whatever they may be.

I also understand that agencies, both big and small, are desperately trying to come up with effective formulaic interventions, and I applaud those efforts. It is encouraging to see new treatment advances that specifically target the unique challenges of quitting methamphetamine (Roll et al., 2006), particularly those that use community, biopsychosocial methodologies, or both (Homer et al., 2008; Hser, Evans, & Huang, 2005). I just hope that part of the equation involves the "unknowns." Every person I have worked with who used methamphetamine was, at the core, more different than alike. There are generalizations we, as mental health workers, are forced to make, but the most successful treatments, in my opinion, come when we tap into the idiosyncratic.

Methamphetamine makes a lot of people feel good. For most people, this is only temporary, but we have to understand just how good some people say it feels in order to really appreciate what we are up against. What tools do we have at our disposal against great sex, increased productivity, and cognitive freedom? We have them, for sure, but we need to come to the battle armed. I have never met a client who would rather do crystal to be happy than to be happy on his own. However, I have met lot of clients who were unhappy without it. Somehow, we need to convince our clients that sobriety is a risk worth taking and that how they think they can feel only when on crystal, all the ways they are "finally" able to feel, could be theirs for the taking: sober, with help, and little understanding.

# 11
## METHAMPHETAMINE:
## FUTURE DIRECTIONS FOR
## RESEARCH AND PRACTICE

The first time I encountered methamphetamine was when I was 32 years old. At the time I was concluding my doctorate, and, after weeks of work and studies, I spent my Saturday nights navigating between my two favorite bars in New York City, The Spike and The Eagle, in what was once considered an undesirable and perhaps dangerous part of New York City across the road from the piers on 12th Avenue. (Shortly thereafter, land developers and Rudolph Giuliani, with a little help from the creators of *Sex and the City*, changed all that.)

The local drug dealer whispered his offerings as men strolled back and forth between the two bars, which were located on two corners of adjacent city blocks. The offerings remained consistent from week to week and year to year. Then, on one memorable night, the menu was appended to include "crystal." I had heard friends in Los Angeles and San Francisco discuss this drug, but most of my social circle had no familiarity with it. The year was 1995, and 13 years later I find myself writing this volume after many years of research and consideration of the meaning that methamphetamine holds in the lives of many Americans. Like many others, my own life has been touched by this powerful drug through my personal transactions with loved ones and acquaintances who have, in some cases, succumbed to the devastation of the substance.

In the preceding pages, I have attempted to provide an all-encompassing view of the drug, which has simply come to be known as "meth." Antonio E. Urbina and Daniel J. Carragher have also provided meaningful insights into their own practices and interactions with methamphetamine users, which demonstrate the struggle presented on a clinical level. In the last decade, much has been learned about how the drug is used, the impact it has on the lives of its users, and the potential devastation it can cause if use is allowed to spin out of control. Much research has focused on the intimate link between the drug and sex for the gay subpopulation, despite methamphetamine's pervasiveness in all segments of the population. This emphasis in the science is likely due to the concentration of HIV among gay men, which creates a more dangerous synergy within this group than others. What has also become clear is that despite our attempts to curtail use of the drug, including education, law enforcement, and legislation, its use continues in various and diverse segments of the population and across all geographic regions. Moreover, attempts to treat the addiction have been limited and met with circumscribed success, indicating, in part, the power that methamphetamine has over the biological, psychological, and social person. This is not to say that all primary and secondary prevention efforts have been fruitless nor that attempts at treatment have been misguided; on the contrary, a wealth of knowledge has been generated to help us more fully understand the manifestation of this drug addiction in our population.

It has been my intention in the preceding pages to present and synthesize some of the most seminal ideas and knowledge in regard to methamphetamine—to take the reader on a journey and to tell story of this drug (which at times has felt Scheherazadian to me), in the hope of arriving at some "truth" that could inform processes to curtail the presence of this drug in our society. The truth is we have made strides in our understanding of methamphetamine and its associated addiction, and these strides, in turn, have informed the broader arena of addiction research. However, we are still "not there" in truly and successfully confronting this drug and its associated addiction, which begs the question "What's next?" How do we proceed to understand, curtail, and treat dependence on methamphetamine? The answers to these questions are as complex as the humans who are drawn to methamphetamine.

In this chapter, it is not at all my intention to provide answers. What I hope instead to do is to macromodel some thoughts that will inspire the many who are working on the frontlines in both research and practice, those whose lives are affected by this addiction, and moreover, our political leaders to make decisions and take actions that will effectively address the methamphetamine phenomenon in the United States.

In the end, any impact on the proliferation of methamphetamine addiction will be most successfully realized if researchers work with practitioners to address the methamphetamine problem. Change will come about if all of us, researchers and practitioners, move outside of our silos, our own comfort zones, and build on the common ground at the intersection of research and practice. Each of the themes detailed below is described in relation to the interplay that must exist between these areas; although to some, these areas are seemingly antipodal, I believe they are ultimately synergistic domains. The themes to be discussed are based on those concepts that were introduced in the Preface, articulated in the Foreword by Cathy J. Reback, as well as the findings presented throughout this volume. In addition to those in the academy and those on the front lines, it is my hope that the media—the news media in particular—will take note of the themes that are presented in this volume, as their role in helping to address the methamphetamine problem is in many ways dependent on their dissemination of accurate and nonsensationalistic information to the public. In the next sections, I outline the three main areas of consideration with regard to methamphetamine abuse and addiction: (a) embracing a biopsychosocial model to our understanding of this drug, (b) implementing a model of "total health" for addressing methamphetamine addiction, and (c) emphasizing the importance of understanding the period of development known as emergent adulthood in preventing the onset of methamphetamine use. In addition to these three main directions, a set of circumscribed suggestions is provided.

## EMBRACE A BIOPSYCHOSOCIAL PARADIGM TO UNDERSTAND METHAMPHETAMINE USE

The tenets of a biopsychosocial paradigm are the foundation on which this volume has been based, and one that has consistently been considered throughout these pages. In this perspective, methamphetamine use and methamphetamine addiction must be more than just a biomedical condition. Rather, they represent the interplay between the cellular–neural–physiological domain with the emotional–psychological domain and in turn with the social–contextual domain. The abuse of this drug affects cells, organs, systems behaviors, emotions, cognitions, families, relationships, and societies, and the totality of this disease must be viewed in the context of the interplay of these elements. For a more complete understanding of the applications of this model, see Frankel, Quill, and McDaniel (2003). At its core, a biopsychosocial understanding of health empowers all of us to consider not only the biological and medical manifestation of diseases and well-being but also the role of societal influences and intrapsychic factors in maintaining the health of our population. Biomedical approaches to health have too long dictated the manner in which practitioners have transacted and worked with their patients, as if any disease could be understood simply in terms of the pathogens that cause it.

For methamphetamine addiction (as for all diseases), there is no doubt that there are biological factors that both predispose individuals to the addiction as well as numerous biological and medical consequences of using the drug.

In addition, from the perspective of the health care provider, addressing these factors, especially the medical sequelae, is of utmost importance in ensuring the homeostasis of the organism. But for all diseases, especially for addictive disorders, the role of psychosocial and societal factors cannot and must not be overlooked. Methamphetamine users are not simply biological organisms but are instead complex human beings who hold numerous identities, roles, and places within the contexts in which they navigate. If we are to help these individuals effectively control their addictions, then we must consider the meanings that methamphetamine holds in their lives; the societal and personal factors that led to the trajectory of methamphetamine addiction; and the manner in which use of the drug has influenced roles and positions in social circles, families, and other relationships.

The disease of methamphetamine addiction not only creates damage in the numerous bodily systems but also the emotional and social systems of persons' lives, and thus the totality of the human experience must be considered in understanding both methamphetamine addiction and the physical, social, and emotional manifestations of the disease. These elements work in synchronicity and cannot be addressed in isolation. It is for this reason that pharmaceutical treatments for methamphetamine must be viewed with great caution. The same is true for simple psychoeducational approaches. Each of these seemingly disparate and opposed approaches for addressing methamphetamine addiction encompasses its own biases—the first bias is that the addiction is purely a medical condition that can be treated with chemicals; another bias holds that addiction is a social and learned disease that can be considered and treated solely though education and support. The lack of strong evidence with regard to the efficacy of one treatment for methamphetamine addiction provides ample support to suggest that any approach that will work must attack the addiction on all fronts and consider the interplay that exists among the biological, the psychological, and the social domains. In my view, the knowledge is already there. What remains to be done is a "repackaging" of current treatment approaches in such a way that the best of each is brought to the user.

In recent years, there has been a movement in the health sciences to consider the interplay between mind and body. Such a mind–body paradigm has informed my own work as I have considered how frontal lobe activity in relation to social cognition can help us to better understand both drug addiction and other risk-taking behavior. In this view, the manners in which individuals enact behaviors cannot simply be viewed through a behavioral system but requires one that also considers the neural process associated with the motivations for behavior, the enactment of the behavior, and the outcomes of the behavior. A mind–body understanding of health is, in effect, a formulation for considering health behavior that is based on the synergies that exist within the biological, psychological, and social person. It is imperative that both social and medical scientists draw on the tenets and theories that inform their work and recognize that human behavior cannot be considered in a purely psychological or purely biomedical context.

## WORK WITHIN A MODEL OF TOTAL HEALTH TO TREAT METHAMPHETAMINE ADDICTION

A second recommendation for our work with methamphetamine addiction follows naturally from the ideas posited by a biopsychosocial paradigm and indicates that models for health delivery should focus on the total health of the person rather than on a dissected, condition-specific understanding. In chapter 5, the link between methamphetamine use and sexual risk-taking behavior was presented and was shown to cross lines of gender and sexual orientation. From the onset, behavioral researchers have recognized that any attempt to reduce methamphetamine use also needed to consider the role of sex, sexuality, sexual behavior, and sexual risk taking because these domains are not only intimately linked but also fuel and exacerbate each other—they represent *syndemics*, a framework developed in relation to the AIDS crisis (Singer, 1994, 1996; Stall, Friedman, & Catania, 2007)—but which has high applicability to the present discussion. Prevention efforts in regard to methamphetamine have used the tenets of this paradigm, linking use of the drug to HIV seroconversion in the gay male subpopulation. Such understandings are embedded in the belief that these two behaviors often are enacted in synchronicity by many individuals, and thus to fully address one health condition, it is essential to consider, and possibly address, the other. This simple dyadic intersection, which must seem obvious to anyone who has even a basic understanding of methamphetamine addiction, provides a foundational basis for a movement to an approach of total health.

For example, consider a client who consistently presents in a clinic with a sexually transmitted infection (STI). Year after year, the health care provider treats the condition with the most effective antibacterial or antiviral medications, and the client is almost always relieved of the disease or its symptoms. Although such a treatment plan may seem appropriate, it is also in many ways short-sighted. The client is surely enacting behaviors (i.e., unprotected sexual behavior) on an ongoing basis that place the client at risk of acquiring STIs. In a total health approach, an understanding and delineation of the factors that predispose the client to these physical problems would be considered as important as treating the actual symptoms caused by the pathogens. Helping to delineate the emotional, social, or biological factors that place the client at risk of contracting STIs would be part of the diagnosis, which in turn would be accompanied by a plan to "treat" the factors (e.g., depression) that predispose the client to sexual risk-taking behavior. This idea makes logical sense, and from the perspective of policy holds potential for cost saving in health care delivery if proactive and preventive efforts are taken in medical care. We ask older adults to eat well and exercise to maintain their health. My suggestion is that we also must be empowering individuals to care for their social and emotional health, which may affect overall well-being.

Inherent in a total health approach is the realization that for many Americans, acquiring diseases such as HIV or developing addictions to drugs such as methamphetamine is not the primary presenting concern or problem. Rather, many face a multitude of other presenting problems, which might include (a) economic burdens and disparities in access to health care; (b) educational disadvantages; and (c) social realities of stigmatization, prejudice, and victimization, all of which compromise well-being. A holistic approach to health would not neglect these very real conditions but rather appreciate how such socioemotional conditions can fuel disease and undermine well-being. Moreover, an effective prescription for care would attempt to address these elements in manner that reduces the probabilities that physical health problems would develop. In other words, an approach to total health must consider not only the physical health of the individual but also the socioemotional integrity and well-being of the whole person.

Applying such an understanding to both the prevention and treatment of methamphetamine addiction suggests that strategies must move beyond the addiction itself and consider the totality of the human experience in relation to the numerous vulnerabilities that predispose an individual to use and, in some instances, become addicted to the drug. The manifestation of the drug in segments of the population that face struggles in U.S. society (e.g., the economically poor, gay men, racial and ethnic minorities) is not a matter of coincidence. Individuals from these segments of the population are drawn to the drug because many do not benefit from the same privileges of those in White, heterosexual, middle-class America. It is not because they are gay, poor, or individuals of color. It is because they are members of victimized, stigmatized, and marginalized groups whose voices are often muted in the discussion of the American landscape. Use of the drug is for many of them, and for many of us, a reaction to the realities of our lives and the prejudices that we face—even those of us who navigate the often revered halls of the academy are not free of such social conditions. Although much of the research has focused on the manifestation of methamphetamine use in these subpopulations, future research and political efforts should not only consider the manifestation of this addiction in these segments of our society but also ask why, in a larger societal context, these subpopulations are disproportionately present in this drug "epidemic." The answer is simple: because these subpopulations suffer from enormously varying health disparities because of the place they hold in our society. Thus, shifting the conversation in the research, practice, and the media along this line will also help to stop the finger-pointing to methamphetamine as a "gay drug" or a "redneck drug" and allow us to ask what is structurally wrong in our social system that individuals from these segments of the population are drawn to the drug in the first place.

In the end, it is certainly not my contention that those of us working within the arena of methamphetamine addiction or in health care provision, in general, are required to or equipped to combat these social ills. However, where we can enact a change is in the manner in which we consider the issue of health and well-being in its totality and in working with lawmakers, policymakers, and educators to enact change.

## FOCUS ON EMERGENT ADULTHOOD IN METHAMPHETAMINE PREVENTION

In the last decade, the period of emergent adulthood has garnered much attention in the behavioral sciences. This developmental period, which is hypothesized to span ages 18 to 25 and is viewed as a transition from childhood–adolescence to adulthood, is beginning to be understood as a period of great vulnerability in which lifelong patterns and behaviors may be shaped. This transition stage, which was first defined by Arnett (1992, 1997, 2000), may be one in which exposure to the use of drugs such as methamphetamine and the development of addictions is greatly heightened. As adolescents begin to try to find their places in the world, the demands of adult life may create levels of stress that predispose these young adults to the use of drugs as a means of coping with the expectations in their life.

Given the vast diversity in race, ethnicity, culture, sexual orientation, and social class in our population and among emergent adults specifically, there is no longer one pattern for transition into adulthood in our society. The demarcation of these years as a developmentally significant period emerged from such demographic trends as an increase in the median age at marriage–partnership, lengthier periods of formal schooling, and later ages for having a first child. The fact that there is no longer a lock-step pattern for transition from age 18 into adult activities, especially for the half of the population that does not go on to college, makes this a challenging period of exploration and self-discovery. Black and Latino emergent adults are especially challenged during this developmental period because of societal stereotypes about the competencies of minority youth (Eccles, Templeton, Barber, & Stone, 2003) and the decline in employment opportunities for those with only a high school education (Wilson, 1987). Still, those who successfully negotiate more of the tasks of this period (e.g., education, citizenship, peer involvement) experience greater well-being than those who falter and stall (Schulenberg, Sameroff, & Cicchetti, 2004). Finally, the risk bases encountered during childhood and adolescence, including but not limited to parental psychopathology, victimization, and mental health burden, may fuel the development of methamphetamine and other drug use during this developmental stage.

This behavioral and sociological understanding is complemented by recent neurological findings indicating that during the period of emergent adulthood, the brain continues to form and some plasticity is still present. During this stage of development, the brain undergoes important changes, including myelination and pruning in the frontal lobe, which leads to greater efficiency and higher levels of cognitive functioning (Rubia et al., 2000). However, these changes also mean that the frontal lobes of emergent adults may be particularly susceptible to neurological damage induced by drug use and chronic stress. The neurological damage caused by drug use and chronic stress may in turn impair cognitive functioning, particularly for those functions associated with the frontal lobes, such as executive functions (i.e., planning, monitoring, and evaluating behaviors) and social cognitions. This is particularly true for methamphetamine, which has been related to structural and functional changes in the prefrontal cortex. In the presence of illicit drug use, such as methamphetamine, addictions in emergent adulthood may have long-term implications for cognitive and social–emotional development, and thus the well-being of the individuals as they transition into adulthood may be compromised.

These ideas in regard to emergent adulthood indicate this period of human development as one in which lifelong maladaptive behaviors may first surface. For this reason, intervention and prevention strategies targeting drug use, including methamphetamine use, should not neglect this segment of the population, and in fact should target this age group, perhaps, at higher rates than others. This is not to say that prevention efforts should be eradicated for children and adolescents. In fact, these are also crucially important. However, efforts designed and enacted for young adults may have been underrepresented, perhaps directed by a false belief that by some magical process, an 18-year-old is equipped with all the wisdom and convictions of any adult. The fact remains that these young adults, as a whole, are perhaps more vulnerable than those who are both younger and older than they are, as they seek to find their places in the world. It is my hope that future research efforts will consider this crucially important development period and delineate the risk and protective bases that increase the vulnerability of emergent adults to methamphetamine and other illicit drug use. Such work, if conducted correctly and in collaboration with educators and social service agencies, may help to delineate the not only paths to addiction but also paths of resilience. The latter can generate further understandings of how some remain healthy in body and mind, and in turn, psychological, social, and educational strategies may be developed to work with those who may lack these resiliencies. It is likely that providing support on all fronts during this developmental period, in which emergent adults are struggling with endless demands, questions, and fears, will empower these future leaders of our society to make decisions that consider their own well-being as well as that of their friends, larger social networks, and society. I strongly believe that investment in such strategies will yield benefits in the long run.

# CONCLUDING THOUGHTS

In 2003, I took part in a community forum regarding methamphetamine addiction in the gay community, titled "An Evening with Tina," sponsored by the LGBT Community Center of New York City. What should have been a conversation on how to best address the problem many of us were encountering in our work and seeing in our social circles morphed instead into an exchange of overexpressed opinions—a hostile debate on the merits of harm reduction versus abstinence-based approaches in treating methamphetamine addiction. In chapter 7, I considered these seemingly opposed paradigms and indicated that, in fact, both harm-reductionist and abstinence-based practitioners use tenets of each orientation in their work. Moreover, the distinction between these manners of thinking is an artificial one. This debate is a fruitless one and is based more on political aspirations and self-aggrandizing than on caregiving to those who are affected by this addiction. In their purest forms, harm reduction and abstinence philosophies attempt to achieve the same end point. The problem arises when individuals manipulate the philosophical tenets of the paradigm.

The fact remains that we are far from the ideal in combating methamphetamine or any other drug addiction. In the interim, as we try to arrive at what may be in the long run an allusive end point, all approaches that help individuals control the use of methamphetamine in their lives should be considered viable. Along these lines, I return to the notion that the best knowledge exists on and emanates from the hyphen of theory–practice. Through this transaction, the day-to-day realities encountered by practitioners can be informed by and can, in turn, inform the scientific studies that we design and undertake. Too often those working on the front lines of the methamphetamine war are not equipped to engage in scientific inquiry; also, scientists often work in isolation from the realities encountered and experienced by practitioners. In my view, the best work will be done when these two groups come together and talk with each other, learn from each other, and respect each other. These ideas extend to all aspects of health care delivery, including the prevention and intervention strategies we used with methamphetamine addiction, and require the cultivation of a dialogue between those working within the community structure and those researchers who are truly dedicated to improving the health of the communities they study. (Years in academia have shown me that the latter is hardly the norm.) However, for those of us who do enact such approaches to research "with and for the community," there is a recognition that continuous open and honest dialogue with our community partners will help to create excellent science (Halkitis, 2006a). Such ideas were eloquently expressed by Reback, Cohen, Freese, and Shoptaw (2002), who stated, "Building partnerships takes time and a good amount of planning and negotiation . . . However these collaborations can result in more effective efforts to solve common problems and reach common goals" (p. 837).

Just as scientists need to navigate toward this hyphen of theory–practice, so do those working in community settings, with a recognition that the scientific knowledge that is generated cannot be discarded simply because it does not adhere to one's belief system or because it challenges the efforts one has made. In New York City, I had such an unfortunate encounter when I publicly stated that there was limited evidence for the effectiveness of the methamphetamine prevention posters that the New York City Department of Health was funding with thousands of taxpayer dollars. I further hypothesized that by stigmatizing the behavior, those in most need of help would be less likely to seek it in a hostile environment. One of those who had developed these campaigns confronted me and stated, "I thought we were all in this together." My response to this individual was that "being in it together" suggests that we, as scientists work with practitioners, engage in dialogue, and occasionally debate, such discussions may at times lead to disagreement but ultimately will lead to a place where better knowledge is generated and where better strategies and approaches are developed. It is through these transactions, which may at times be difficult, that we can move the discussion forward.

In 2008, both a United States national summit and a global conference on methamphetamine were organized. The attention being placed on this particular substance both on a local and international level is an indicator of the pervasiveness of the drug in our world as well as the concern that the drug holds potential for creating even greater damage in the lives of its users and their loved ones. In the preceding pages, insights have been provided into why methamphetamine is the drug of the moment and why we as researchers and practitioners must continue to be on guard with regard to this drug. Methamphetamine is in many ways like no other drug problem we have experienced in the United States. The damages that the drug creates to the physical, emotional, and social person are compounded by its impact on society and the environment. Hazards on both the micro and macro level have been recounted in this volume. Moreover, the intimate link between methamphetamine and sexual risk taking creates the reality of a "dual epidemic" (Halkitis, Parsons, & Stirratt, 2001).

Although laws have been enacted to curtail the production of methamphetamine within U.S. borders, the fact remains that this drug is still one that is being abused. Compounding this problem is that no one intervention modality has been shown to be foolproof in treating the addiction, and no one prevention strategy provides the deterrent needed to stop the growth in the number of new users and addicts. In reality, we are far from the ideal in combating methamphetamine or any other drug addiction. There is no one ideal method to date to treat methamphetamine addiction in all people, and until one such approach is found, it is our responsibility to develop and consider methods that may help those who are struggling with the disease. In this view, funding should be provided to any and all treatment approaches for addressing this addiction that demonstrate promise, be it the goal a total eradication of methamphetamine use, a reduction in use, or some other behavioral outcome (e.g., engaging in safer sex strategies while using the drug). And such decisions must be separate from lawmakers' political ideologies and be driven by scientific knowledge and the knowledge that stems from practice. In this view, it is my hope that I never have to encounter a debate regarding abstinence versus harm-reductionism again.

In the end, the thought that most permeates my mind is whether the numerous ideas presented in this volume could have been written about any illicit drug or about alcohol. Some themes may be transferable, but methamphetamine addiction is a problem unlike that created by other drugs of use and dependence. It is, in the end, not only the addiction of the moment but also perhaps the most insidious drug problem we have faced. The themes with which I have chosen to conclude this volume—applying a biopsychosocial paradigm, implementing a focus on total health, and understanding the importance of emergent adulthood—are of paramount importance as we continue to struggle with methamphetamine addiction within our own borders and globally. These notions provide the basis for a Zeitgeist that moves beyond demonizing the methamphetamine user and rather aims to enhance understanding and compassion as we seek to prevent and treat methamphetamine addiction.

# REFERENCES

Advertising Educational Foundation. (2006). *Methamphetamine demand reduction campaign 2006*. Retrieved November 23, 2008, from http://www.aef.com/exhibits/social_responsibility/pda/6000

Ahmad, K. (2002). Addictive drug increases HIV replication and mutation. *Lancet Infectious Diseases, 2*, 456.

American Dental Association. (2005a). *ADA warns of methamphetamine's effect on oral health*. Retrieved June 14, 2007, from http://www.ada.org/public/media/releases/0508_release01.asp

American Dental Association. (2005b). For the dental patient: Methamphetamine use and oral health. *Journal of the American Dental Association, 136*, 149.

American Psychiatric Association. (2000). *Diagnostic and statistical manual of mental disorders* (4th ed., text rev.). Washington, DC: Author.

Anglin, D., & Rawson, R. (2000a). The CSAT methamphetamine treatment project: What are we trying to accomplish? *Journal of Psychoactive Drugs, 32*, 209–210.

Anglin, D., & Rawson, R. (Eds.). (2000b). The CSAT methamphetamine treatment project: Moving research into the "real world." *Journal of Psychoactive Drugs, 32*, 135–136.

Anglin, M. D., Burke, C., Perrochet, B., Stamper, E., & Dawd-Noursi, S. (2000). History of the methamphetamine problem. *Journal of Psychoactive Drugs, 32*, 137–141.

Arnett, J. J. (1992). Reckless behavior in adolescence: A developmental perspective. *Developmental Review, 12*, 339–373.

Arnett, J. J. (1997). Young people's conceptions of the transition to adulthood. *Youth & Society, 29*, 3–23.

Arnett, J. J. (2000). Emerging adulthood: A theory of development from the late teens through the twenties. *American Psychologist, 55*, 469–480.

Ashton, E. (2008). Setraline does not help methamphetamine abusers quit. *NIDA Notes, 21*, 4–5.

Atlanta Crystal Meth Anonymous. (2007). *Atlanta Meetings*. Retrieved July 27, 2008, from http://atlantacma.org/meeting.html

Baer, J. S., Kivlahan, D. R., & Donovan, D. M. (1999). Integrating skills training and motivational therapies: Implications for the treatment of substance dependence. *Journal of Substance Abuse Treatment, 17*, 15–23.

Baker, R., & Bowers, M. (1997, March 5). Ritonavir and ecstasy. *Bulletin of Experimental Treatments for AIDS*. San Francisco: AIDS Foundation.

Banerjee, N. (2006, November 3). Accused of gay liaison, head of Evangelical group resigns. *New York Times*. Retrieved March 3, 2007, from http://www.nytimes.com

Bangert-Drowns, R. L. (1988). The effects of school-based substance abuse education—meta-analysis. *Journal of Drug Education, 18*, 243–264.

Barr, A. M., Panenka, W. J., MacEwan, G. W., Thornton, A. E., Lang, D. J., Honer, W. G., et al. (2006). The need for speed: An update on methamphetamine addiction. *Journal of Psychiatry & Neuroscience, 31*, 301–313.

Barrett, D. C., Bolan, G., Joy, D., Counts, K., Doll, L., & Harrison, J. (1995). Coping strategies, substance use, sexual activity, and HIV sexual risks in a sample of gay male STD patients. *Journal of Applied Social Psychology, 25*, 1058–1072.

Bass, L. E., & Kane-Williams, E. (1993). Stereotype or reality: Another look at alcohol and drug use among African American children. *Public Health Reports, 108*(Suppl. 1), 78–84.

Beck, A. T., Steer, R. A., & Brown, G. K. (1996). *Manual for Beck Depression Inventory II (BDI-II)*. San Antonio, TX: Psychology Corporation.

Beck, J. (1998). 100 years of "just say no" versus "just say know." *Evaluation Review, 22*, 15–45.

Beebe, D. K., & Walley, E. (1995). Smokable methamphetamine ("ice"): An old drug in a different form. *American Family Physician, 25*, 213–214.

Bergeret, J. (1983). Primary prevention in the area of drug addiction: Perspectives, errors, and falacies. *Drug and Alcohol Dependence, 11*, 71–75.

Blankson, J. N. (2005, May). Primary HIV-1 infection: To treat or not to treat? *The AIDS Reader, 15*, 250–251.

Bolding, G., Hart, G., Sherr, L., & Elford, J. (2006). Use of crystal methamphetamine among gay men in London. *Addiction, 101*, 1622–1630.

Brady, K. T., Dansky, B. S., Sonne, S. C., & Saladin, M. E. (1998). Post traumatic stress disorder and cocaine dependence: Order of onset. *American Journal of Addiction, 7*(2), 128–135.

Brannan, T. A., Soundararajan, S., & Houghton, B. L. (2004). Methamphetamine-associated shock with intestinal infarction. *Medscape General Medicine, 6*, 6.

Brecht, M. L., O'Brien, A., von Mayrhauser, C., & Anglin, M. D. (2004). Methamphetamine use behaviors and gender differences. *Addictive Behaviors, 29*, 89–106.

Bremner, J. D., Southwick, S. M., Darnell, A., & Charney, D. S. (1996). Chronic PTSD in Vietnam combat veterans: Course of illness and substance abuse. *American Journal of Psychiatry, 153*, 369–375.

Bridges, S. (2007). No more sunsets: The last days of a meth addict [Video file]. Video retrieved December 12, 2007, from http://www.aheartylife.com/2007/03/27/meth-addict-shawn-bridges-dies-of-heart-failure

Brook, J. S., Brook, D. W., Gordon, A. S., Whiteman, M., & Cohen, P. (1990). The psychosocial etiology of adolescent drug use: A family international approach. *Genetic, Social, and General Psychology Monographs, 116*, 111–267.

Brown, A. H., Domier, C. P., & Rawson, R. A. (2005). Stimulants, sex, and gender. *Sexual Addiction & Compulsivity, 12*(2–3), 169–180.

Brown, L. S. (2003). Sexuality, lies, and loss: Lesbian, gay, and bisexual perspectives on trauma. *Journal of Trauma Practice, 2*, 55–68.

Brown, T. G., Seraganian, P., Tremblay, J., & Annis, H. (2002a). Process and outcome changes with relapse prevention versus 12-step aftercare programs for substance abusers. *Addiction, 97*, 677–689.

Brown, T. G., Seraganian, P., Tremblay, J., & Annis, H. (2002b). A randomized trial of aftercare regimes for the substance abuser. *Addictive Behaviors, 27*, 132–142.

Buchanan, J., & Brown, C. (1988). Designer drugs: A problem in clinical toxicology. *Medical Toxicology and Adverse Drug Experience, 3*, 1–17.

Buffenstein, A., Heaster, J., & Ko, P. (1999). Chronic psychotic illness from methamphetamine. *American Journal of Psychiatry, 156*, 662.

Bull, S. S., Piper, P., & Rietmeijer, C. (2002). Men who have sex with men and also inject drugs-Profiles of risk related to the synergy of sex and drug injection behaviors. *Journal of Homosexuality, 42*(3), 31–51.

Burke, K., & Marzulli, J. (2006, December 1). Meth lab in 'high' rise: Feds say it was 1 of 9 drug setups. *Daily News*. Retrieved April 3, 2007, from http://www.nydailynews.com

Burton, B. (1991). Heavy metal and organ contaminants associated with illicit methamphetamine production. In M. Miller & N. Kozel (Eds.), *Methamphetamine abuse: Epidemiologic issues and implications* (pp. 47–58). Rockville, MD: National Institute on Drug Abuse.

Butterfield, F. (2004, February 23). Home drug-making laboratories expose children to toxic fallout. *New York Times*. Retrieved April 2, 2007, from http://www.nytimes.com

Bux, D. A., & Irwin, T. W. (2006). Combining motivational interviewing and cognitive–behavioral skills training for the treatment of crystal methamphetamine abuse/dependence. In M. Wainberg, A. Kolodny, & J. Drescher (Eds.), *Crystal meth and men who have sex with men: What mental health professionals need to know* (pp. 131–141). New York: Hawthorn Press.

Callaghan, R. C., Brands, B., Taylor, L., & Lentz, T. (2007). The clinical characteristics of adolescents reporting methamphetamine as their primary drug of choice: An examination of youth admitted to inpatient substance-abuse treatment in Northern British Columbia, Canada, 2001–2005. *Journal of Adolescent Health, 40*, 286–289.

Canon, W. B. (1936). The role of emotions in disease. *Annals of Internal Medicine, 11*, 1453–1465.

Cantwell, B., & McBride, A. J. (1998). Self detoxication by amphetamine dependent patients: A pilot study. *Drug and Alcohol Dependence, 49*, 157–163.

Carey, J. W., Mejia, R., Bingham, T., Ciesielski, C., Gelaude, D., Herbst, J. H., et al. (2008). Drug use, high-risk sex behaviors, and increased risk for recent HIV infection among men who have sex with men in Chicago and Los Angeles. *AIDS and Behavior*. Advance online publication. Retrieved February 17, 2009. doi: 10.1007/s10461-008-9403-3

Carey, K. B., Purnine, D. M., Maistos, S. A., Carey, M. P., & Simons, J. S. (2000). Treating substance abuse in the context of severe and persistent mental illness: Clinicians' perspective. *Journal of Substance Abuse Treatment, 19*, 189–198.

Carey, M. P., Maisto, S. A., Kalichman, S. C., Forsyth, A. D., Wright, E. M., & Johnson, B. T. (1997). Enhancing motivation to reduce the risk of HIV infection for economically disadvantaged urban women. *Journal of Consulting and Clinical Psychology, 65*, 531–541.

Carragher, D. J. (2006, August). *Who's next? HIV seroconversion amongst gay and bisexual club drug users*. Paper presented at the International AIDS Conference, Toronto, Ontario, Canada.

Carrico, A. W., Johnson, M. O., Moskowitz, J. T., Neilands, T. B., Morin, S. F., Charlebois, E. D., et al. (2007). Affect regulation, stimulant use, and viral load among HIV-positive persons on anti-retroviral therapy. *Psychosomatic Medicine, 69*, 785–792.

Carroll, K. M., Rounsaville, B. J., Gordon, L. T., Nich, C., Jatlow, P., Bisighini, R. M., et al. (1994). Psychotherapy and pharmacotherapy for ambulatory cocaine abusers. *Archives of General Psychiatry, 51*, 177–187.

Cartier, J., Farabee, D., & Prendergast, M. L. (2006). Methamphetamine use, self-reported violent crime, and recidivism among offenders in California who abuse substances. *Journal of Interpersonal Violence, 21*, 435–445.

Centers for Disease Control and Prevention. (1989, December 8). Epidemiologic notes and reports: Lead poisoning associated with intravenous methamphetamine use—Oregon, 1988. *Morbidity and Mortality Weekly Report, 38*, 830–831.

Centers for Disease Control and Prevention. (2005). *HIV/AIDS Surveillance Report* (Vol. 17). Atlanta, GA: Author.

Centers for Disease Control and Prevention. (2006, June). *Youth risk behavior surveillance—United States, 2005*. Atlanta, GA: Author.

Centers for Disease Control and Prevention. (2006, March 17). Methamphetamine use and HIV risk behaviors among heterosexual men—preliminary results from five Northern California counties, December 2001–November 2002. *Morbidity and Mortality Weekly Report, 55*(1), 273–277.

Centers for Disease Control and Prevention. (2007, January). *Methamphetamine use and risk for HIV/AIDS*. Retrieved June 14, 2007, from http://www.cdc.gov/hiv/resources/factsheets/meth.htm

Chang, L., Ernst, T., Speck, O., Patel, H., DeSilva, M., Leonido-Yee, M., et al. (2002). Perfusion MRI and computerized cognitive test abnormalities in abstinent methamphetamine users. *Psychiatry Research Neuroimaging, 114*, 65–79.

Chang, L., & Linde, P. (2007). Response: Images and interventions. *Science and Practice Perspectives, 3*, 17–19.

Chen, J. (2007). Methamphetamine-associated acute myocardial infarction and cardiogenic shock with normal coronary arteries: Refractory global coronary microvascular spasm. *Journal of Invasive Cardiology, 19*, 89–92.

Chen, C., Lin, S., Sham, P., Ball, D., Loh, E., & Murray, R. (2005). Morbid risk for psychiatric disorder among the relatives of methamphetamine users with and without psychosis. *American Journal of Medical Genetics Part B: Neuropsychiatric Genetics*, 136B, 87–91.

Chilcoat, H. D., & Breslau, N. (1998). Posttraumatic stress disorder and drug disorders: Testing causal pathways. *Archives of General Psychiatry*, 55, 913–917.

Chin, K. M., Channick, R. N., & Rubin, K. J. (2006). Is methamphetamine use associated with idiopathic pulmonary arterial hypertension. *Chest*, 130, 1657–1663.

Cho, A. K. (1990, August 10). Ice: A new dosage form of an old drug. *Science*, 249, 631–634.

Cho, A. K., & Melega, W. P. (2002). Patterns of methamphetamine abuse and their consequences. *Journal of Addictive Diseases: The Official Journal of the American Society of Addiction Medicine*, 21, 21–34.

Choi, K., Operario, D., Gregorich, S. E., McFarland, W., MacKellar, D., & Valleroy, L. (2005). Substance use, substance choice, and unprotected anal intercourse among young Asian American and Pacific Islander men who have sex with men. *AIDS Education and Prevention Special Issue: HIV/AIDS among Asians and Pacific Islanders in the United States*, 17, 418–429.

Chomchai, C., Na Manorom, N., Watanarungsan, P., Yossuck, P., & Chomchai, S. (2004). Methamphetamine abuse during pregnancy and its health impact on neonates born at Siriraj Hospital, Bangkok, Thailand. *Southeast Asian Journal of Tropical Medicine and Public Health*, 35, 228–231.

Chrousos, G. P. (1998). Stressors, stress and neuroendocrine integration of the adaptive response. *Annals of the New York Academy of Science*, 851, 311–335.

City of White Rock, The. (2006). *Crystal methamphetamine*. Retrieved August 30, 2007, from http://ww.city.whiterock.bc.ca/2005Fire-and-Police/Crystal-Meth.html

Cimino, K. (2005). *The politics of crystal meth: Gay men share stories of addiction and recovery*. Boca Raton, FL: Universal Publishers.

Clemens, K., Van Nieuwenhuyzen, P., Li, K., Cornish, J., Hunt, G., & McGregor, I. (2006). MDMA ("ecstasy"), methamphetamine and their combination: Long-term changes in social interaction and neurochemistry in the rat. *Psychopharmacology*, 173, 318–325.

Clinard, R., & Von Holtum, J. (2005). Safety precautions in methamphetamine lab sites for child protection workers. *Minnesota Department of Human Services Bulletin* (Publication No. 05-68-02).

Cochran, S. D., & Mays, V. M. (2006). Estimating prevalence of mental and substance-using disorders among lesbians an gay men from existing national data. In A. M. Omoto & H. S. Kurtzman (Eds.), *Sexual orientation and mental health: Examining identity and development in lesbian, gay and bisexual people* (pp. 143–165). Washington, DC: American Psychological Association.

Cohen, H. (1972). Multiple drug use considered in the light of the stepping stone hypothesis. *International Journal on Addictions*, 7, 27–55.

Cohen, J. B., Dickow, A., Horner, K., Zweben, J. E., Balabis, J., Vandersloot, D., et al. (2003). Abuse and violence history of men and women in treatment for methamphetamine dependence. *The American Journal on Addiction, 12*, 377–385.

Coleman, E. (2004, September). *FDA regulation of obesity drugs, 1938–1999.* Paper presented at the FDA Endocrinology and Metabolic Drug Advisory Committee, Rockville, MD.

Colfax, G., Coates, T. J., Husnik, M. J., Huang, Y., Buchbinder S., Koblin, B., et al. (2005). Longitudinal patterns of methamphetamine, popper (amyl nitrate), and cocaine use and high-risk sexual behavior among a cohort of San Francisco men who have sex with men. *Journal of Urban Health, 82*(Suppl. 1), i62–i70.

Colfax, G., & Shoptaw, S. (2005). The methamphetamine epidemic: Implications for HIV prevention and treatment. *Current HIV/AIDS Reports, 2*, 194–199.

Colliver, J. D., & Gfroerer, J. C. (2006, May). *Methamphetamine use, abuse and treatment: Survey findings, 2002–2004.* Paper presented at the meeting of the American Psychiatric Association, Toronto, Ontario, Canada.

Copeland, A. L., & Sorensen, J. L. (2001). Differences between methamphetamine users and cocaine users in treatment. *Drug and Alcohol Dependence, 62*, 91–95.

Cottler, L. B., Compton, W., Mager, D., Spitznagel, E. L., & Janca, A. (1992). Posttraumatic stress disorder among substance users from the general population. *American Journal of Psychiatry, 149*, 664–670.

Cretzmeyer, M., Sarrazin, M. V., Huber, D. L., Block, R. I., & Hall, J. A. (2003). Treatment of methamphetamine abuse: Research findings and clinical directions. *Journal of Substance Abuse Treatment, 24*, 267–277.

Crystal Meth Anonymous. (2007a). *What is Crystal Meth Anonymous?* Retrieved July 27, 2008, from http://www.crystalmeth.org

Crystal Meth Anonymous. (2007b). *The 12 steps of Crystal Meth Anonymous.* Retrieved July 27, 2008, from http://www.crystalmeth.org

Crystal Meth Anonymous of Washington, DC. (2007). *Problem with crystal meth. We can help you.* Retrieved July 12, 2007, from: http://www.dccma.com

*Crystal meth use falls.* (2007, February 5). POZ. Retrieved February 24, 2007, from http://www.poz.com/articles/1_11229.shtml

Cunningham, J., & Liu, J. (2003). Impacts of federal ephedrine and pseudoephedrine regulations on methamphetamine-related hospital admissions. *Addiction, 98*, 1229–1237.

Cunningham, J. K., Liu, L. M., & Muramoto, M. (2008). Methamphetamine suppression and route of administration: Precursor regulation impacts on snorting, smoking, swallowing and injecting. *Addiction, 103*, 1174–1186.

D'Augelli, A. R., Grossman, A. H., & Starks, M. T. (2006). Childhood gender atypicality, victimization, and PTSD among lesbian, gay, and bisexual youth. *Journal of Interpersonal Violence, 21*, 1462–1482.

Dahshan, A. (2008). Prenatal exposure to methamphetamine presenting as neonatal cholestasis. *Journal of Clinical Gastroenterology, 43*, 88–90.

Dansky, B. S., Roitzsch, J. C., Brady, K. T., & Saladin, M. E. (1997). Posttraumatic stress disorder and substance abuse: Use of research in a clinical setting. *Journal of Traumatic Stress, 10,* 141–148.

Darrow, W. W., Echenberg, D. F., Jaffe, H. W., O'Malley, P. M., Byers, R. H., Getchell, J. P., et al. (1987). Risk factors for human immunodeficiency virus (HIV) infections in homosexual men. *American Journal of Public Health, 77,* 479–483.

Davidson, C., Gow, A. J., Lee, T. H., & Ellinwood, E. H. (2001). Methamphetamine neurotoxicity: Necrotic and apoptotic mechanisms and relevance to human abuse and treatment. *Brain Research, 36,* 1–22.

Dawes, M. A., Antelman, S. M., Vanyukov, M. M., Giancola, P., Tarter, R. E., Susman, E. J., et al. (2000). Developmental sources of variation in liability to adolescent substance use disorders. *Drug and Alcohol Dependence, 61,* 3–14.

De Bellis, M. D. (2002). Developmental traumatology: A contributory mechanism for alcohol and substance use disorder. *Psychoneuroendocrinology, 27,* 155–170.

Degenhardt, L. (2005). Drug use and risk behaviour among regular ecstasy users: Does sexuality make a difference? *Culture, Health & Sexuality, 7,* 599–614.

Degenhardt, L., & Topp, L. (2003). 'Crystal meth' use among polydrug users in Sydney's dance party subculture: Characteristics use patterns and associated harms. *International Journal of Drug Policy, 14,* 17–24.

DeJong, W., & Wallack, L. (1999). A critical perspective on the drug czar's antidrug media campaign. *Journal of Health Communication, 4,* 155–160.

Derogatis, L. R., Lipman, R. S., Rickels, K., Uhlenhuth, E. H., & Covi, L. (1974). The Hopkins symptom checklist. *Behavioral Science, 19,* 1–15.

Derogatis, L. R., & Melisaratos, N. (1983). The brief symptom inventory: An introductory report. *Psychological Medicine, 13,* 595–605.

DeSandre, P. (2006). Methamphetamine emergencies. In M. Wainberg, A. Kolodny, & J. Drescher (Eds.), *Crystal meth and men who have sex with men* (pp. 57–65). Binghamton, NY: Haworth Medical Press.

De Vito, M. J., & Wagner, G. C. (1989). Methamphetamine-induced neuronal damage: A possible role for free radicals. *Neuropharmacology, 28,* 1145–1150.

Diaz, R. M. (1998). *Latino gay men and HIV.* London: Routledge.

Dielman, T. E., Campanelli, P. C., Shope, J. T., & Butchart, A. T. (1987). Susceptibility to peer pressure, self-esteem, and health locus of control as correlates of adolescent substance abuse. *Health Education Quarterly, 14,* 207–221.

Disney, E. R. (2007, September). *A few words about treatment for methamphetamine addiction.* Paper presented at the LGBT Health Coalition Meeting, Washington, DC.

Donovan, D. M., & Wells, E. A. (2007). 'Tweaking 12-step': The potential role of 12-step self-help group involvement in methamphetamine recovery. *Addiction, 102*(Supp 1), 121–129.

Dore, G., & Sweeting, M. (2006). Drug-induced psychosis associated with crystalline methamphetamine. *Australasian Psychiatry, 14,* 86–89.

Drug-rehabs.org. (2005). *Hawaii: Crystal meth deaths soaring in 2005*. Retrieved May 3, 2007, from http://www.drug-rehabs.org/content.php?cid=1552&state=Hawaii

Duncan, R. D., Saunders, B. E., Kilpatrick, D. G., Hanson, R. F., & Resnick, H. S. (1996). Childhood physical assault as a risk factor for PTSD, depression, and substance abuse: Findings from a national survey. *American Journal of Orthopsychiatry, 66*, 437–448.

Eccles, J., Templeton, J., Barber, B., & Stone, M. (2003). Adolescence and emerging adulthood: The critical passage ways to adulthood. In M. H. Bornstein, L. Davidson, C. L. M. Keyes, & K. A. Moore (Eds.), *Well-being: Positive development across the life course* (pp. 383–406). New York: Erlbaum.

Eichenthal, G. (2001, October 7). Preview of a tragedy: Crystal meth is more and more a drug of choice for young gay men. Its use is contributing to an increase in unsafe sex-and that likely is pushing HIV infection rates higher. *Los Angeles Times*. Retrieved March 8, 2004, from http://www.latimes.com

Ellenhorn, M. J., Schonwald, S., Ordog, G., & Wasserberger, J. (1997). *Ellenhorn's medical toxicology: Diagnosis and treatment of human poisoning* (2nd ed.). Baltimore: Williams & Wilkins.

Ellis, R. J., Childers, M. E., Cherner, M., Lazzaretto, D., Letendre, S., Grant, I., et al. (2003). Increased human immunodeficiency virus loads in active methamphetamine users are explained by reduced effectiveness of antiretroviral therapy. *Journal of Infectious Diseases, 188*, 1820–1826.

Emrick, C. D., Tonigan, J. S., Montgomery, H., & Little, J. (1993). Alcoholics Anonymous: What is currently known? In B. S. McCrady & W. R. Miller (Eds.), *Research on Alcoholics Anonymous: Opportunities and alternatives* (pp. 41–76). New Brunswick, NJ: Alcohol Research Documentation, Center of Alcohol Studies, Rutgers—The State University of New Jersey.

Engel, G. L. (1977, April 8). The need for a new medical model: A challenge for biomedicine. *Science, 196*, 129–136.

Engel, M. (2008, May 14). Anti-meth campaign aimed at gay men. *Los Angeles Times*. Retrieved March 17, 2008, from http://www.latimes.com

Epel, E. S., Blackburn, E. H., Lin, J., Dhabhar, F. S., Adler, N. E., Morrow, J. D., & Cawthon, R. M. (2004). Accelerated telomere shortening in response to life stress. *Proceedings of the National Academy of Sciences, 101*, 17312–17315.

Ernst, T., Chang, L., Leonido-Yee, M., & Speck, O. (2000). Evidence for long-term neurotoxicity associated with methamphetamine abuse: A 1H MRS study. *Neurology, 54*, 1344–1349.

Evans, D. L., Charney, D. S., Lewis, L., Golden, R. N., Gorman, J. M., Krishnan, K. R. R., et al. (2005). Mood disorders in the medically ill: Scientific review and recommendations. *Biological Psychiatry, 58*, 175–189.

Fernández, M. I., Bowen, G. S., Varga, L. M., Collazo, J. B., Hernandez, N., Perrino, T., et al. (2005). High rates of club drug use and risky sexual practices among Hispanic men who have sex with men in Miami, Florida. *Substance Use & Misuse Special Issue: Club Drug Epidemiology, 40*, 1347–1362.

Fierstein, H., Carlson, D., Kellerhouse, B., Staley, P., Trevor, P., Tierney, S., et al. (2006). A public forum—challenging the culture of disease: The crystal meth-HIV connection. In M. L. Wainberg, A. J. Kolodny, & J. Drescher (Eds.), *Crystal meth and men who have sex with men: What mental health care professionals need to know* (pp. 49–55). Binghamton, NY: The Haworth Press.

Fiorentine, R. (1999). After drug treatment: Are 12-step programs effective in maintaining abstinence? *American Journal of Drug and Alcohol Abuse, 25,* 93–116.

Fiorentine, R., & Hillhouse, M. P. (2000). Drug treatment and 12-step program participation: The addictive effects of integrated recovery activities. *Journal of Substance Abuse Treatment, 18,* 65–74.

Flaherty, M. T. (2006). *A unified vision for the prevention of management of substance use disorder building resiliency, wellness and recovery: A shift from acute care to a sustained recovery management model.* Pittsburgh, PA: Institute for Research, Education and Training in Addictions.

Flaherty, M. T., & Langer D., for the Institute for Research, Education and Training in Addictions. (2006, Fall/Winter). A model to improve resiliency, wellness, and recovery from addiction. *The Addictions Newsletter, 13,* 12–14.

Fleckenstein, A. E., Metzger, R. R., Gibb, J. W., & Hanson, G. R. (1997). A rapid and reversible change in dopamine transporters induced by methamphetamine. *European Journal of Pharmacology, 323,* R9–R10.

Fowler, J. S., Volkow, N. D., Kassed, C. A., & Chang, L. (2007). Imaging the addicted human brain. *Science and Practice Perspectives, 3,* 4–16.

France, D. (2008, April 7). Another AIDS casualty. *New York Magazine.* Retrieved February 2, 2009, from http://www.nymg.com/news/features/45785/

Frankel, R. M., Quill, E., & McDaniel, S. H. (2003). *The biopsychosocial approach: Past, present, future.* New York: The University of Rochester Press.

Freese, T., Miotto, K., & Reback, C. (2002). The effects and consequences of selected club drugs. *Journal of Substance Abuse Treatment, 23,* 151–156.

Freese, T. E., Obert, J., Dickow, A., Cohen, J., & Lord, R. H. (2000). Methamphetamine abuse: Issues for special populations. *Journal of Psychoactive Drugs, 32,* 177–182.

Frosch, D., Shoptaw, S., Huber, A., Rawson, R. A., & Ling, W. (1996). Sexual HIV risk and gay and bisexual methamphetamine abusers. *Journal of Substance Abuse Treatment, 13,* 483–486.

Fullilove, M. T., Fullilove, R. E., Smith, M., Winkler, K., Michael, C. P., & Wallace, P. G. (1993). Violence, trauma, and post-traumatic stress disorder among women drug users. *Journal of Traumatic Stress, 6,* 533–543.

Furst, S., Fallon, S., Reznik, G., & Shah, P. (1990). Myocardial infarction after inhalation of methamphetamine. *New England Journal of Medicine, 323,* 1147–1148.

Gahlinger, P. M. (2001). *Illegal drugs: A complete guide to their history, chemistry, use and abuse.* Las Vegas, NV: Sagebrush Press.

Galea, S., Vlahov, D., Resnick, H., Ahern, J., Susser, E., Gold, J., et al. (2003). Trends of probable post-traumatic stress disorder in New York City after the September 11 terrorist attacks. *American Journal of Epidemiology, 158,* 514–524.

Galloway, G., Marinelli-Casey, P., Stalcup, J., Lord, R., Christian, D., Cohen, J., et al. (2000). Treatment-as-usual in the methamphetamine treatment project. *Journal of Psychoactive Drugs, 32,* 165–175.

Galloway, G., Newmeyer, J., Knapp, T., Stalcup, S., & Smith, D. (1994). Imipramine for the treatment of cocaine and methamphetamine dependence. *Journal of Addictive Diseases, 13,* 201–216.

Gambrell, J. (2007). Candy flavored meth targets new users. *CBS News.* Retrieved May 6, 2007, from http://www.cbsnews.com/stories/2007/05/02/health/main2752266. shtml?source=RSSattr=HOME_2752266

Gavrilin, M. A., Mathes, L. E., & Podell, M. (2002). Methamphetamine enhances cell-associated feline immunodeficiency virus replication in astrocytes. *Journal of Neurovirology, 8,* 240–249.

Gay Men's Health Crisis. (2004). *Confront crystal methamphetamine use in New York City: Public policy recommendations.* New York: Author.

Gay Men's Health Crisis. (2007). *Hurricane Tina* [Brochure]. New York: Laura Horwitz and Francisco Roque.

Gesslein, D. (2007, October 9). Study lifts lid on rampant meth use. *The New York Daily News.* Retrieved February 2, 2009, from http://www.nydailynews.com/ ny_local/bronx/2007/10/09/2007-10-09_study_lifts_lid_on_rampant_meth_ abuse.html

Gibson, D. R., Leamon, M. H., & Flynn, N. (2002). Epidemiology and public health consequences of methamphetamine use in California's Central Valley. *Journal of Psychoactive Drugs, 34,* 313–319.

Giros, B., Jaber, M., Jones, S. R., Wightman, R. M., & Caron, M. G. (1996, February 15). Hyperlocomotion and indifference to cocaine and amphetamine in mice lacking the dopamine transporter. *Nature, 379,* 606–612.

Gold, S. D., Marx, B. P., & Lexington, J. M. (2007). Gay male sexual assault survivors: The relations among internalized homophobia, experiential avoidance, and psychological symptom severity. *Behavior Research and Therapy, 45,* 549–562.

Gorman, E. M., Nelson, K. R., Applegate, T., & Scrol, A. (2004). Club drug and polysubstance abuse and HIV among gay/bisexual men: Lessons gleaned from a community study. *Journal of Gay Lesbian Social Services, 16,* 1–17.

Gorman, M. (1998). A tale of two epidemics: HIV and stimulant use. *Focus, 13*(4), 1–3.

Gossop, M., Griffiths, P., Powis, B., & Strang, J. (1994). Cocaine: Patterns of use, route of administration, and severity of dependence. *British Journal of Psychiatry, 164,* 660–664.

Gray, S. D., Fatovich, D. M., McCoubrie, D. L., & Daly, F. F. (2007). Amphetamine-related presentations to an inner-city tertiary emergency department: A prospective evaluation. *The Medical Journal of Australia, 186,* 336–339.

Green, A. I. (2003). "Chem friendly": The institutional basis of "club drug" use in a sample of urban gay men. *Deviant Behavior, 24,* 427–447.

Green, A. I., & Halkitis, P. N. (2006). Crystal methamphetamine and sexual sociality in an urban gay subculture: An elective affinity. *Culture, Health & Sexuality, 8,* 317–333.

Grinspoon, L., & Bakalar, J. B. (1985). *Cocaine: A drug and its social evolution.* New York: Basic Books.

Guss, J. R. (2000). Sex like you can't even imagine: "Crystal," crack, and gay men. *Journal of Gay and Lesbian Psychotherapy, 13*(3/4), 105–122.

Hagan, H., Thiede, H., Weiss, N. S., Hopkins, S. G., Duchin, J. S., & Alexander, E. R. (2001). Sharing of drug preparation equipment as a risk factor for hepatitis C. *American Journal of Public Health, 91,* 42–46.

Hales, G., Roth, N., & Smith, D. (2000). Possible fatal interaction between protease inhibitors and methamphetamine. *Antiviral Therapy, 5,* 19.

Halkitis, P. N. (2006a, August). *How theory and practice inform each other in community-based research.* Paper presented at the 114th Annual Conference of the American Psychological Association, New Orleans, LA.

Halkitis, P. N. (2006b, November). *The emergence of methamphetamine: Issues in research and practice.* Plenary presented at the South Carolina Drugs of Abuse Conference, Myrtle Beach, SC.

Halkitis, P. N. (2007). Behavioral patterns, identity, and health characteristics of self-identified barebackers: Implications for HIV prevention and intervention. *Journal of LGBT Health Research, 3,* 37–48.

Halkitis, P. N. (2008, November). *Intersections between public health and safety challenges in critical populations affected by methamphetamine-gay and bisexual men.* Plenary presentation at the National Methamphetamine Summit, Washington, DC.

Halkitis, P. N., Fischgrund, B. N., & Parsons, J. T. (2005). Explanations for methamphetamine use among gay and bisexual men in New York City. *Substance Use & Misuse, 40,* 1–15.

Halkitis, P. N., & Green, K. (2007). Sidenafil (Viagra) and club drug use among gay and bisexual men: The role of drug combinations and context. *American Journal of Men's Health, 1,* 139–147.

Halkitis, P. N., Green, K. A., & Carragher, D. J. (2006). Methamphetamine use, sexual behavior, and HIV seroconversion. *Journal of Gay & Lesbian Psychotherapy, 10,* 95–109.

Halkitis, P. N., Green, K., & Mourgues, P. (2005). Longitudinal investigation of methamphetamine use among gay and bisexual men in New York City: Findings from Project BUMPS. *Journal of Urban Health, 82*(Suppl. 1), i18–i25.

Halkitis, P. N., Homer, B. D., Moeller, R. W., & Solomon, T. M. (2007, March). *Methamphetamine and social cognition: Findings from project MASC.* Paper presented at the New York University Developmental Psychology Colloquium.

Halkitis, P. N., & Jerome, R. (2008). A comparative analysis of methamphetamine use: Black gay and bisexual men in relation to men of other races. *Addictive Behaviors, 33,* 83–93.

Halkitis, P. N., Kutnick, A. H., Borkowski, T., & Parsons, J. T. (2002, July). *Adherence to HIV medications and club drug use among gay and bisexual men*. Poster presented at the 14th International AIDS Conference, Barcelona, Spain.

Halkitis, P. N., Kutnick, A. H., Rosof, E., Slater, S., & Parsons, J. T. (2003). Adherence to HIV medications in a cohort of men who have sex with men: Impact of September 11th. *Journal of Urban Health: Bulletin of the New York Academy of Medicine, 80*, 161–166.

Halkitis, P. N., Moeller, R. W., Siconolfi, D., Jerome, R., Rogers, M., & Schillinger, J. (2008). Methamphetamine and poly-substance use among gym-attending gay and bisexual men in New York City. *Annals of Behavioral Medicine, 35*, 41–48.

Halkitis, P. N., Mukherjee, P. P., & Palamar, J. J. (2007). Multilevel modeling to explain methamphetamine use among gay and bisexual men. *Addiction, 102*(Suppl. 1), 76–83.

Halkitis, P. N., & Palamar, J. (2008). Multivariate modeling of club drug use initiation among gay and bisexual men. *Substance Use & Misuse, 43*, 871–879.

Halkitis, P. N., Palamar, J. J., & Pandey, M. P. (2007). Patterns of poly-club-drug use among gay & bisexual men: A longitudinal analysis. *Drug and Alcohol Dependence, 89*, 153–160.

Halkitis, P. N., Pandey, M. P., & Palamar, J. J. (2007). Multilevel modeling to explain methamphetamine use. *Addiction, 102*, 75–82.

Halkitis, P. N., & Parsons, J. T. (2002). Recreational drug use and HIV-risk sexual behavior among men frequenting gay social venues. *Journal of Gay & Lesbian Social Services, 14*, 19–38.

Halkitis, P. N., Parsons, J. T., & Stirratt, M. J. (2001). A double epidemic: Crystal methamphetamine drug use in relation to HIV transmission among gay men. *Journal of Homosexuality, 41*, 17–35.

Halkitis, P. N., Parsons, J. T., & Wilton, L. (2003a). Barebacking among gay and bisexual men in New York City: Explanations for the emergence of intentional unsafe behavior. *Archives of Sexual Behavior, 32*, 351–358.

Halkitis, P. N., Parsons, J. T., & Wilton, L. (2003b). An exploratory study of contextual and situational factors related to methamphetamine use among gay and bisexual men in New York City. *Journal of Drug Issues, 33*, 413–432.

Halkitis, P. N., & Shrem, M. (2006). Psychological differences between binge and chronic methamphetamine using gay and bisexual men. *Addictive Behaviors, 31*, 549–552.

Halkitis, P. N., Shrem, M. T., & Martin, F. W. (2005). Sexual behavior patterns of methamphetamine-using gay and bisexual men in New York City. *Substance Use & Misuse, 40*, 703–719.

Halkitis, P. N., Solomon, T. M., Moeller, R. W., Espinosa, L. S., Doig, S. R., & Homer, B. D. (2009). Methamphetamine use among gay, bisexual and non-identified men-who-have-sex-with-men: An analysis of daily patterns and contexts for use. *Journal of Health Psychology, 14*(2), 222–231.

Halkitis, P. N., & Warren, B. W. (2005, October). *Addressing the methamphetamine-sexual risk-taking link among MSM: Information exchange between science and prac-*

*tice*. Paper presented at the 4th International Conference on Urban Health, Toronto, Ontario, Canada.

Hall, W., Hando, J., Darke, S., & Ross, J. (1996). Psychological morbidity and route of administration among amphetamine users in Sydney, Australia. *Addiction, 91,* 81–87.

Halpern, J. H. (1999). Treatment of attention-deficit/hyperactivity disorder. *Journal of the American Medical Association, 281,* 1490–1491.

Hartel-Petri, R., Rodler, R., Schmeisser, U., Steinmann, J., & Wolfersdorf, M. (2005). Increasing prevalence of amphetamine and methamphetamine-induced psychosis. *Psychiatrische Praxis, 32,* 13–17.

Hasan, A., & Ciancio, S. (2004). Relationship between amphetamine ingestion and gingival enlargement. *Pediatric Dentistry, 26,* 396–400.

Hastings, G., Stead, M., & Webb, J. (2004). Fear appeals in social marketing: Strategic and ethical reasons for concern. *Psychology and Marketing, 21,* 961–986.

Hawkins, J. D., Catalano, R. F., & Miller, J. Y. (1992). Risk and protective factors for alcohol and early adulthood: Implications for substance abuse prevention. *Psychological Bulletin, 112,* 64–105.

Healthyplace. (2002). *Desoxyn, methamphetamine pharmacology.* Retrieved April 8, 2007, from http://www.healthyplace.com/Medications/desoxyn.htm

Hecht, F. M., Wang, L., Collier, A., Little, S., Markowitz, M., Margolick, J., et al. (2006). A multicenter observational study of the potential benefits of initiating combination antiretroviral therapy during acute HIV infection. *Journal of Infectious Diseases, 194,* 725–733.

Henry, J. A., & Hill, I. R. (1998, November 28). Fatal interaction between ritonavir and MDMA. *The Lancet, 352,* 1751–1752.

Heredia, C. (2003, May 4). Dance of death: Crystal meth fuels HIV. *San Francisco Chronicle.* Retrieved June 17, 2007, from http://www.sfgate.com/cgi=bin/article.cgi?f=/c/a/2003/05/04/MN281636.DTL&hw=Dance+of+Death+Crystal+meth+fuels+HIV&sn=001&sc=1000

Heston, L. L., & Heston, R. (1979). *The medical casebook of Adolph Hitler.* New York: Copper Square Press.

Higgins, S. T., Budney, A. J., Bickel, W. K., Hughes, J. R., Foerg, F., & Badger, G. (1993). Achieving cocaine abstinence with a behavioral approach. *American Journal of Psychiatry, 150,* 763–769.

Higgins, S. T., & Petry, N. M. (1999). Contingency management: Incentives for sobriety. *Alcohol Research & Health, 23,* 122–127.

Higgins, S. T., & Silverman, K. (1999). *Motivating behavior change among illicit-drug abusers: Research on contingency management interventions.* Washington, DC: American Psychological Association.

Hillhouse, M. P., Marinelli-Casey, P., Gonzalez, R., Ang, A., Rawson, R. A., & the Methamphetamine Treatment Project Corporate Authors. (2007). Predicting in-treatment performance and post-treatment outcomes in methamphetamine users. *Addiction, 102*(Suppl. 1), 84–95.

Hirshfield, S., Remien, R., & Chiasson, M. A. (2006). Crystal methamphetamine use among men who have sex with men: Results from two national online studies. In M. Wainberg, A. Kolodny, & J. Drescher (Eds.), *Crystal meth and men who have sex with men: What mental health care professionals need to know* (pp. 85–93). New York: Haworth Medical Press.

Hirshfield, S., Remien, R. H., Humberstone, M., Walavalka, I., & Chiasson, M. A. (2004). Substance use and high-risk sex among men who have sex with men: A national online study in the USA. *AIDS Care, 16,* 1036–1047.

Hirshfield, S., Remien, R. H., Walavalkar, I., & Chiasson, M. A. (2004). Crystal methamphetamine use predicts incident STD infection among men who have sex with men recruited online: A nested case-control study. *Journal of Medical Internet Research 6,* e41.

Ho, E., Karimi-Tabesh, L., & Koren, G. (2001). Characteristics of pregnant women who use Ecstasy (3, 4-methylenedioxymethamphetamine). *Neurotoxicology and Teratology, 23,* 561–571.

Hoffman, W. F., Moore, M., Templin, R., McFarland, B., Hitzemann, R. J., & Mitchell, S. H. (2006). Neuropsychological functioning and delay discounting in methamphetamine-dependent individuals. *Psychopharmacology, 188,* 162–170.

Holley, M. F. (2005). *Crystal meth: They call it 'ice'.* Mustang, OK: Tate Publishing.

Holmes-Lonergan, H. A. (2003). Understanding of affective false beliefs, perceptions of parental discipline, and classroom behavior in children from Head Start. *Early Education and Development, 14,* 29–46.

Homer, B. D., Solomon, T. M., Moeller, R. W., Macia, A., DeRaleau, L., & Halkitis, P. N. (2008). Methamphetamine abuse and impairment of social functioning: A review of the underlying neurophysiological causes and behavioral implications. *Psychological Bulletin, 134,* 301–310.

Hong, R., Matsuyama, E., & Nur, K. (1991). Cardiomyopathy associated with the smoking of crystal methamphetamine. *Journal of American Medical Association, 265,* 1152–1154.

Horner, B. R., & Scheibe, K. E. (1997). Prevalence and implications of attention-deficit hyperactivity disorder among adolescents in treatment for substance abuse. *Journal of the American Academy of Child and Adolescent Psychiatry, 36,* 30–36.

Howe, A. (1995). Methamphetamine and childhood and adolescent caries. *Australian Dental Journal, 40,* 340.

Hser, Y. I., Evans, E., & Huang, Y. C. (2005). Treatment outcomes among women and men methamphetamine abusers in California. *Journal of Substance Abuse Treatment, 28,* 77–85.

Huber, A., Ling, W., Shoptaw, S. J., Gulati, V., Brethen, P., & Rawson, R. (1997). Integrating treatments for methamphetamine abuse: A psychosocial perspective. *Journal of Addictive Disease, 16,* 41–50.

Huber, A., Lord, R., Gulati, V., Marinelli-Casey, P., Rawson, R., & Ling, W. (2000). The CSAT methamphetamine treatment program: Research design accommodations for "real world" application. *Journal of Psychoactive Drugs, 32,* 149–156.

Humphreys, K. (1999). Professional interventions that facilitate 12-step self-help group involvement. *Alcohol Research and Health, 23,* 93–98.

Hunter, J. (1999). Beyond risk: Refocus research on coping. *Journal of the Gay and Lesbian Medical Association, 3,* 75–76.

Iguchi, M. Y., Stitzer, M. L., Bigelow, G. E., & Liebson, I. A. (1988). Contingency management in methadone maintenance: Effects of reinforcing and aversive consequences on illicit polydrug use. *Drug and Alcohol Dependence, 22,* 1–7.

Illegal drugs: Speedy decline. (2008, May 3). *The Economist.* Retrieved January 26, 2009, from http://www.economist.com/world/unitedstates/displaystory.cfm?story_id=11293716

Institute of Medicine. (1998). *Bridging the gap between practice and research: Forging partnerships with community-based drug and alcohol treatment.* Washington, DC: National Academy Press.

Institute of Medicine. (2001). *Health and behavior: The interplay of biological, behavioral, and societal influences.* Washington, DC: National Academy Press.

Ireland, K., Southgate, E., Knox, S., Van de Ven, P., Howard, J., & Kippax, S. (1999). *Using and "the scene": Patterns and contexts of drug use among Sydney gay men, 7.* Sydney, Australia: National Centre in HIV Social Research.

Iritani, B. J., Hallfors, D. D., & Bauer, D. J. (2007). Crystal methamphetamine use among young adults in the USA. *Addiction, 102,* 1102–1113.

Irvin, J. E., Bowers, C. A., Dunn, M. E., & Wang, M. C. (1999). Efficacy of relapse prevention: A meta-analytic review. *Journal of Consulting and Clinical Psychology, 67,* 563–570.

Irvine, G. D., & Chin, L. (1991). The environmental impact and adverse health effects of the clandestine manufacture of methamphetamine. In M. Miller & N. Kozel (Eds.), *Methamphetamine abuse: Epidemiologic issues and implications* (pp. 33–46). Rockville, MD: National Institute on Drug Abuse.

Irwin, T. (2006). Strategies for the treatment of methamphetamine use disorders among gay and bisexual men. In M. Wainberg, A. Kolodny, & J. Drescher (Eds.), *Crystal meth and men who have sex with men: What mental health professionals need to know* (pp. 131–141). New York: Hawthorn Press.

Israel, J. A., & Lee, K. (2002). Amphetamine usage and genital self-mutilation. *Addiction, 97,* 1215–1218.

Itzhak, Y., & Ali, S. F. (2002). Behavioral consequences of methamphetamine-induced neurotoxicity in mice: Relevance to the psychopathology of methamphetamine addiction. *Annals of the New York Academy of Science, 965,* 127–135.

Iversen, L. (2006). *Speed, ecstasy, ritalin: The silence of amphetamines.* Oxford, England: Oxford University Press.

Ivo, M., Sekine, Y., & Mori, N. (2004). Neuromechanism of developing methamphetamine psychosis: A neuroimaging study. *Annals of the New York Academy of Sciences, 1025,* 288–295.

Jacobs, A. (2006, February 21). Battling H.I.V. Where sex meets crystal meth. *New York Times.* Retrieved November 20, 2007, from http://www.nytimes.com/2006/02/21/nyregion/21meth.html

Jacobsen, L. K., Southwick, S. M., & Kosten, T. R. (2001). Substance use disorders in patients with posttraumatic stress disorder: A review of the literature. *American Journal of Psychiatry, 158,* 1184–1190.

Jacquez, J. A., Koopman, J. S., Simon, C. P., & Longini, I. M., Jr. (1994). Role of the primary infection in epidemics of HIV infection in gay cohorts. *Journal of Acquired Immune Deficiency Syndromes, 7,* 1169–1184.

Jaeckel, E., Cornberg, M., Wedemeyer, H., Sanantonio, T., Mayer, J., Zankel, M., et al. (2001). Treatment of acute hepatitis C with interferon alfa-2b. *The New England Journal of Medicine, 345,* 1452–1457.

Jaffe, A., Shoptaw, S., Stein, J., Reback, C. J., & Rotheram-Fuller, E. (2007). Depression ratings, reported sexual risk behaviors, and methamphetamine use: Latent growth curve models of positive change among gay and bisexual men in an outpatient treatment program. *Experimental and Clinical Psychopharmacology, 15,* 301–307.

Jefferson, D. J. (2005, August 8). Americas's most dangerous drug. *Newsweek,* pp. 41–48.

Jernigan, T. L., Gamst, A. C., Archibald, S. L., Fennema-Notestine, C., Mindt, M. R., Marcotte, T. L., et al. (2005). Effects of methamphetamine dependence and HIV infection on cerebral morphology. *American Journal of Psychiatry, 162,* 1461–1472.

Jerome, R. (2007, February). *Methamphetamine use and HIV behaviors in black MSM.* Paper presented at the 2nd National Conference on Methamphetamine, HIV, and Hepatitis, Salt Lake City, UT.

Jerome, R., Halkitis, P. N., & Siconolfi, D. (2009). Club drug use, sexual behavior, and HIV seroconversion: A qualitative study on motivations of risky and protective drug and sex practices. *Substance Use & Misuse, 44,* 303–319.

Johnson, B., Wells, L., Roache, J., Wallace, C., Ait-Daoud, N., & Wang, Y. (2005). Isradipine decreases the hemodynamic responses of cocaine and methamphetamine: Results from two human laboratory studies. *American Journal of Hypertension, 18,* 813–822.

Johnson, D. (2005). *Meth: The home-cooked menace.* Center City, MN: Hazleden.

Jones, P. (2007). *METH: Don't even start: Resource Guide for Educators.* Phoenix, AZ: City of Phoenix.

Kalant, H., & Kalant, O. J. (1975). Death in amphetamine users: Causes and rates. *Canadian Medical Association Journal, 112,* 299–304.

Kalechstein, A., Newton, T., Longshore, D., Anglin, M., van Gorp, W., & Gawin, F. (2000). Psychiatric comorbidity of methamphetamine dependence in a forensic sample. *Journal of Neuropsychiatry, 12,* 480–484.

Kalechstein, A. D., Newton, T. F., & Green, M. (2003). Methamphetamine dependence is associated with neurocognitive impairment in the initial phases of abstinence. *Journal of Neuropsychiatry and Clinical Neurosciences, 15,* 215–220.

Kalichman, S. C., Cherry, C., & Browne-Sperling, F. (1999). Effectiveness of a video-based motivational skills-building HIV risk-reduction intervention for inner-city African American men. *Journal of Consulting and Clinical Psychology, 67,* 959–966.

Kamijo, Y., Soma, K., Nishida, M., Namera, A., & Ohwada, Y. (2002). Acute liver failure following intravenous methamphetamine. *Veterinary and Human Toxicology, 44,* 216–217.

Kandel, D., & Faust, R. (1975). Sequence and stages in patterns of adolescent drug use. *Archives of General Psychiatry, 32,* 923–932.

Kassebaum, G., & Chandler, S. M. (1994). Poly use and self control among men and women in prisons. *Journal of Drug Education, 24,* 333–350.

Kassutto, S., Maghsoudi, K., Johnston, M. N., Robbins, G. K., Burgett, N. C., Sax, P. E., et al. (2006). Longitudinal analysis of clinical markers following antiretroviral therapy initiated during acute or early HIV type I infection. *Clinical Infectious Diseases, 42,* 1024–1031.

Kaye, S., McKetin, R., Duflou, J., & Darke, S. (2007). Methamphetamine and cardiovascular pathology: A review of the evidence. *Addiction, 102,* 1204–1211.

Keane, T. M., Gerardi, R. J., Lyons, J. A., & Wolfe, J. (1988). The interrelationship of substance abuse and posttraumatic stress disorder: Epidemiological and clinical considerations. *Recent Developments in Alcoholism, 6,* 27–48.

Keegan, R. W. (2006, September 18). Screen test. *Time.* Retrieved May 5, 2007, from http://www.time.com/time/magazine/article/0,9171,1533424,00.html

Kellogg, S. H. (2003). On "Gradualism" and the building of the hard reduction-abstinence continuum. *Journal of Substance Abuse Treatment, 25*(4), 241–247.

Kellogg, S. H., & Kreek, M. J. (2005). Gradualism, identity, reinforcements, and change. *International Journal of Drug Policy, 16,* 369–375.

Kelly, B. C., Parsons, J. T., & Wells, B. E. (2006). Prevalence and predictors of club drug use among club-going young adults in New York City. *Journal of Urban Health, 83,* 884–895.

Khantzian, E. J. (1985). The self-medication hypothesis of addictive disorders: Focus on heroin and cocaine dependence. *American Journal of Psychiatry, 142,* 1259–1264.

Kilpatrick, D. G., Ruggiero, K. J., Acierno, R., Saunders, B. E., Resnick, H. S., & Best, C. L. (2003). Violence and risk of PTSD, major depression, substance abuse/dependence, and comorbidity: Results from the National Survey of Adolescents. *Journal of Consulting and Clinical Psychology, 71,* 692–700.

King, G., & Ellinwood, E. (1997). Amphetamine and other stimulants. In J. Lowenson, P. Ruiz, R. Millman, & J. Langrod (Eds.), *Substance abuse: A comprehensive textbook* (pp. 207–222). Baltimore: Williams & Wilkins.

Klasser, G., & Epstein, J. (2005). Methamphetamine and its impact on dental care. *Journal Canadian Dental Association, 71,* 759–762.

Klee, H. (1992). Sexual risk among amphetamine misusers: Prospects for change. In P. Aggleton, P. M. Davies, & G. Hart (Eds.), *AIDS: Rights, risks and reason* (pp. 77–84). London: The Falmer Press.

Klitzman, R. (2006). From "male bonding rituals" to "suicide Tuesday": A qualitative study of issues faced by gale male ecstasy (MDMA) users. *Journal of Homosexuality, 51,* 7–32.

Koffler, K. (2002, July/August). Life vs. meth. *POZ*, p. 42.

Kolecki, P. (1998). Inadvertent methamphetamine poisoning in pediatric patients. *Pediatric Emergency Care, 14*, 285–287.

Kosten, T. R., Rounsaville, B. J., & Kleber, H. D. (1986). A 2.5 year follow-up of depressions, life crises, and treatment effects on abstinence among opioid addicts. *Archives of General Psychiatry, 43*, 733–739.

Kurtz, S. P. (2005). Post-circuit blues: Motivations and consequences of crystal meth use among gay men in Miami. *AIDS and Behavior, 9*, 63–72.

Lampinen, T. M., Greatheart, M. S., Schilder, A. J., & Kowdley, K. K. (2007). Initiation of methamphetamine abuse during interferon treatment. *American Journal of Psychiatry, 164*, 1439.

Lampinen, T. M., McGhee, D., & Martin, I. (2006). Increased risk of "club" drug use among gay and bisexual high school students in British Columbia. *Journal of Adolescent Health, 38*, 458–461.

Langford, D., Adame, A., Grigorian, A., Grant, I., McCutchan, J. A., Ellis, R. J., et al. (2003). Patterns of selective neuronal damage in methamphetamine-user AIDS patients. *Journal of Acquired Immune Deficiency Syndromes, 34*, 467–474.

Lee, S. J. (2006). *Overcoming crystal meth addiction: An essential guide to getting clean.* New York: Marlowe & Company.

Lee, S. J., Galanter, M., Dermatis, H., & McDowell, D. (2003). Circuit parties and patterns of drug use in a subset of gay men. *Journal of Addictive Diseases, 22*, 47–60.

Leigh, B. C., & Stall, R. (1993). Substance use and risky sexual behavior for exposure to HIV: Issues in methodology, interpretation, and prevention. *American Psychologist, 48*, 1035–1045.

Lemonick, M. D. (2007, July 5). How we get addicted. *Time*. Retrieved August 13, 2008, from http://www.time.com/time/magazine/article/0,9171,1640436,00.html

Leshner, A. I. (1997, October 3). Addiction is a brain disease, and it matters. *Science, 278*, 45–47.

Lewis, L. A., & Ross, M. W. (1995). *A select body: The gay dance party subculture and the HIV/AIDS pandemic.* London: Cassell.

Liang, H., Wang, X., Chen, H., Song, L., Ye, L., Wang, S. H., et al. (2008). Methamphetamine enhances HIV infection of macrophages. *American Journal of Pathology, 172*, 1617–1624.

Lin, S., Ball, D., Hsiao, C., Chiang, Y., Ree, S., & Chen, C. (2004). Psychiatric comorbidity and gender differences of persons incarcerated for methamphetamine abuse in Taiwan. *Psychiatry and Clinical Neurosciences, 58*, 206–212.

Lineberry, T. W., & Bostwick, J. M. (2006). Methamphetamine abuse: A perfect storm of complications. *Mayo Clinical Proceedings, 81*, 77–84.

Logan, B. K., Fligner, C. L., & Haddix, T. (1998). Cause and manner of death in fatalities involving methamphetamine. *Journal of Forensic Science, 43*, 28–34.

London, E. D., Simon, S. L., Berman, S. M., Mandelkern, M. A., Lichtman, A. M., Bramen, J. et al. (2004). Mood disturbances and regional cerebral metabolic abnormalities in recently abstinent methamphetamine abusers. *Archives of General Psychiatry, 61,* 73–84.

Lorvick, J., Martinez, A., Gee, L., & Kral, A. H. (2006). Sexual and injection risk among women who inject methamphetamine in San Francisco. *Journal of Urban Health, 83,* 497–505.

Lynch, J., & House, M. A. (1992). Cardiovascular effects of methamphetamine. *Journal of Cardiovascular Nursing, 6,* 12–18.

Maheshwari, A., Ray, S., & Thuluvath, P. J. (2008). Acute hepatitis C. *The Lancet, 372*(9635), 321–332.

Mandell, W., Vlahov, D., Latkin, C., Oziemkowska, M., & Cohn, S. (1994). Correlates of needle sharing among injection drug users. *American Journal of Public Health, 84,* 920–923.

Mansergh, G., Colfax, G. N., Marks, G., Rader, M., Guzman, R., & Buchbinder, S. (2001). The Circuit Party Men's Health Survey: Findings and implications for gay and bisexual men. *American Journal of Public Health, 91,* 953–958.

Mansergh, G., Purcell, D. W., Stall, R., McFarlane, M., Semaan, S., Valentine, J., et al. (2006). CDC consultation on methamphetamine use and sexual risk behavior for HIV/STD infection: Summary and suggestions. *Public Health Reports, 121,* 127–132.

Mansergh, G., Shouse, R. L., Marks, G., Guzman, R., Rader, M., Buchbinder, S., et al. (2006). Methamphetamine and sildenafil (Viagra) use are linked to unprotected receptive and insertive anal sex, respectively, in a sample of men who have sex with men. *Sexually Transmitted Infections, 82,* 131–134.

Marcovitz, H. (2006). *Methamphetamine.* Farmington Hills, MI: Thomson Gale.

Marincovich, B., Castilla, J., del Romero, J., Garcia, S., Hernando, V., Raposo, M., et al. (2003). Absence of hepatitis C virus transmission in a prospective cohort of heterosexual serodiscordant couples. *Sexually Transmitted Infections, 79,* 160–162.

Marinelli-Casey, P., Domier, C. P., & Rawson, R. A. (2002). The gap between research and practice in substance abuse treatment. *Psychiatric Perspectives, 53*(8), 984–987.

Marlatt, G. A., & Gordon, J. R. (1985). *Relapse prevention: Maintenance strategies in the treatment of addictive behaviors.* New York: Guilford Press.

Martin, E. M., Pitrak, D. L., Weddington, W., Rains, N. A., Nunnally, G., Nixon, H., et al. (2004). Cognitive impulsivity and HIV serostatus in substance dependent males. *Journal of the International Neuropsychological Society, 10,* 931–938.

Martin, J. L., Dean, L., Garcia, M., & Hall, W. (1989). The impact of AIDS on a gay community: Changes in sexual behavior, substance use, and mental health. *American Journal of Community Psychology, 17,* 269–293.

Mason, A. P. (2004). *Methamphetamine labs.* Paper presented at the annual conference of the North Carolina Family-Based Services Association, Bowling Rock, NC.

Matoba, R. (2001). Cardiac lesions in methamphetamine abusers. *Nippon Hoigaku Zasshi, 55,* 321–330.

Matsumoto, T. (2000). Clinical features of recent methamphetamine abusers: Comparison between smoking abusers and injection abusers. *Seishin Shinkeigaku Zasshi, 102*, 498–513.

Matsumoto, T., Kamijo, A., Miyakawa, T., Endo, K., Yabana, T., Kisimoto, H., et al. (2002). Methamphetamine in Japan: The consequences of methamphetamine abuse as a function of route of administration. *Addiction, 97*, 809–817.

Matsumoto, T., Kamijo, A., Yamaguchi, A., Iskei, E., & Hirayasu, Y. (2005). Childhood histories of attention-deficit hyperactivity disorders in Japanese methamphetamine and inhalant abusers: Preliminary report. *Psychiatry and Clinical Neurosciences, 59*, 102–105.

Matsumoto, T., Miyakawa, T., Yabana, T., Iizuka, H., & Kishimoto, H. (2000). A clinical study of comorbid eating disorders in female methamphetamine abusers—The first report. *Clinical Psychiatry, 42*, 1153–1160.

Matsumoto, T., Yamaguchi, A., Asami, T., Kamijo, A., Iseki, E., Hirayasu, Y., et al. (2005). Drug preferences in illicit drug abusers with a childhood tendency of attention deficit/hyperactivity disorder: A study using the Wender Utah reading scale in Japanese prison. *Psychiatry and Clinical Neurosciences, 59*, 311–318.

Mattison, A. M., Ross, M. W., Wolfson, T., & Franklin, D. (2001). Circuit party attendance, club drug use, and unsafe sex in gay men. *Journal of Substance Abuse, 13*, 119–126.

Maude-Griffin, P. M., Hohenstein, J. M., Humfleet, G. L., Reilly, P. M., Tusel, D. J., & Hall, S. M. (1998). Superior efficacy of cognitive-behavioral therapy for urban crack cocaine abusers: Main and matching effects. *Journal of Consulting and Clinical Psychology, 66*, 832–837.

Mausbach, B. T., Semple, S. J., Strathdee, S. A., Zians, J., & Patterson, T. L. (2007). Efficacy of behavioral intervention for increasing safer sex behaviors in HIV-positive MSM methamphetamine users: Results from the EDGE study. *Drug and Alcohol Dependence, 87*, 249–257.

Maxwell, J. C. (2004). *Patterns of club drug use in the U.S., 2004: Ecstasy, GHB, ketamine, LSD, methamphetamine, rohypnol.* The Gulf Coast Addiction Technology Transfer Center, University of Texas at Austin. Retrieved October 12, 2007, from http://www.tcada.state.tx.us/research/ClubDrug2004.pdf

McBride, N. (2003). A systematic review of school drug education. *Health Education Research, 18*, 729–742.

McCann, U. D., Wong, D. F., Yokoi, F., Villemagne, V., Dannals, R. F., & Ricaurte, G. A. (1998). Reduced striatal dopamine transporter density in abstinent methamphetamine and methcathinone users: Evidence from positron emission tomography studies with [11C]WIN-35,428. *Journal of Neuroscience, 18*, 8417–8422.

McDermott, D. (1984). The relationship of parental drug use and parents' attitude concerning adolescent drug use to adolescent drug use. *Adolescence, 19*, 89–97.

McFall, M. E., Mackay, P. W., & Donovan, D. M. (1992). Combat-related posttraumatic stress disorder and severity of substance abuse in Vietnam veterans. *Journal of Studies on Alcohol, 53*, 357–363.

McKirnan, D. J., Ostrow, D. G., & Hope, B. (1996). Sex, drugs and escape: A psychological model of HIV-risk sexual behaviors. *AIDS Care, 8,* 655–669.

Meller, W. H., Rinehart, R., Cadoret, R. J., & Troughton, E. (1988). Specific familial transmission in substance abuse. *International Journal of Addiction, 10,* 1029–1039.

Meredith, C. W., Jaffe, C., Ang-Lee, K., & Saxon, A. J. (2005). Implications of chronic methamphetamine use: A literature review. *Harvard Review of Psychiatry, 13,* 141–154.

Midford, R., Munro, G., McBride, N., Snow, P., & Ladzinski, U. (2002). Principles that underpin effective school-based drug education. *Journal of Drug Education, 32,* 363–386.

Midwest High Intensity Drug Trafficking Area and The Iowa's Governor's Office on Drug Policy. (2008). *Life or meth: What's the cost? A methamphetamine education program facilitator's guide.* Retrieved July 12, 2008, from http://www.lifeormeth.org/Pages/methed/high/cd6/Facilitators_Guide.pdf

Miles, R. M., Stallings, M. C., Young, S. E., Hewitt, J. K., Crowley, T. J., & Fulker, D. W. (1998). A family history and direct interview study of the familial aggregation of substance abuse: The adolescent substance abuse study. *Drug and Alcohol Dependence, 49,* 105–114.

Miller, M. (1991). Trends and patterns of methamphetamine smoking in Hawaii. In M. Miller & N. Kozel (Eds.), *Methamphetamine abuse: Epidemiologic issues and implications* (pp. 73–83). Rockville, MD: National Institute on Drug Abuse.

Miller, M. A. (1997). History and epidemiology of methamphetamine abuse in the United States. In H. Klee (Ed.), *Amphetamine misuse* (pp. 113–133). Amsterdam: Harwood Academic Publishers.

Miller, M. A., & Coon, T. P. (2006). Delayed ischemic stroke associated with methamphetamine use. *Journal of Emergency Medicine, 31,* 305–306.

Miller, W. R. (1995). Increasing motivation for change. In R. K. Hester & W. R. Miller (Eds.), *Handbook of alcoholism treatment approaches: Effective alternatives* (pp. 89–104). Boston: Allyn & Bacon.

Miller, W. R., & Rollnick, S. (1991). *Motivational interviewing: Preparing people to change.* New York: Guilford Press.

Milne, D. (2003). Experts desperately seeking meth abuse prevention, treatment. *Psychiatric News, 38,* 12.

Molitor, F., Ruiz, J. D., Flynn, N., Mikanda, J. N., Sun, R. K., & Anderson, R. (1999). Methamphetamine use and sexual and injection risk behaviors among out-of-treatment injection drug users. *American Journal of Drug and Alcohol Abuse, 25,* 475–493.

Molitor, F., Truax, S. R., Ruiz, J. D., & Sun, R. K. (1998). Association of methamphetamine use during sex with risky sexual behaviors and HIV infection among non-injection drug users. *Western Journal of Medicine, 168,* 93–97.

Moon, D. G., Jackson, K. M., & Hecht, M. L. (2000). Family risk and resiliency factors, substance use, and the drug resistance process in adolescence. *Journal of Drug Education, 30,* 373–398.

Morgan, P., & Beck, J. E. (1997). The legacy and the paradox: Hidden contexts of methamphetamine use in the United States. In H. Klee (Ed.), *Amphetamine misuse: International perspectives on current trends* (pp. 135–162). Amsterdam: Harwood Academic Publishers.

Morgan, P., Beck, J. E., Joe, K., McDonnell, D., & Gutierrez, R. (1994). *Ice and other methamphetamine use: An exploratory study.* Bethesda, MD: National Institute on Drug Abuse.

Morgenstern, J., Blanchard, K. A., Morgan, T. J., Labouvie, E., & Hayaki, J. (2001). Testing the effectiveness of cognitive-behavioral treatment for substance abuse in a community setting: Within treatment and posttreatment findings. *Journal of Consulting and Clinical Psychology, 69,* 1007–1017.

Morgenstern, J., Labouvie, E., McCrady, B. S., Kahler, C. W., & Frey, R. M. (1997). Affiliation with alcoholics anonymous after treatment: A study of its therapeutic effects and mechanisms of action. *Journal of Consulting and Clinical Psychology, 65,* 768–777.

Morgenstern, J., & McCrady, B. S. (1992). Curative factors in alcohol and drug treatment: Behavioral and disease model perspectives. *British Journal of Addiction, 87,* 901–912.

Moriya, F., & Hashimoto, Y. (2002). A case of fatal hemorrhage in the cerebral ventricles following intravenous use of methamphetamine. *Forensic Science International, 129,* 104–109.

Morrow, S. L. (2000). First do no harm: Therapist issues in psychotherapy with lesbian, gay, and bisexual clients. In R. M. Perez, K. A. DeBord, & K. J. Bieschke (Eds.), *Handbook of counseling and psychotherapy with lesbian, gay, and bisexual clients* (pp. 137–156). Washington, DC: American Psychological Association.

Murphy, S. (2007, February). *Women and meth.* Panel presented at the 2nd National Conference on Methamphetamine, HIV, and Hepatitis, Salt Lake City, UT.

Nair, M. P., Mahajan, S., Sykes, D., Bapardekar, M. V., & Reynolds, J. L. (2006). Methamphetamine modulates DC-SIGN expression by mature dendritic cells. *Journal of Neuroimmune Pharmacology, 1,* 296–304.

Najavits, L. M., Gastfriend, M. D., Baber, J. P., Reif, S., Muenz, J. B., Frank, A., et al. (1998). Cocaine dependence with and without PTSD among subjects in the National Institute on Drug Abuse collaborative cocaine treatment study. *American Journal of Psychiatry, 155,* 214–219.

Najavits, L. M., Weiss, R. D., & Shaw, S. R. (1997). The link between substance abuse and posttraumatic stress disorder in women: A research review. *American Journal of Addictions, 6,* 273–283.

Nath, A., Maragos, W. F., Avison, M. J., Schmitt, F. A., & Berger, J. R. (2001). Acceleration of HIV dementia with methamphetamine and cocaine. *Journal of Neurovirology, 7,* 66–71.

National Congress of American Indians. (2007). *Methamphetamine in Indian country: An American problem uniquely affecting Indian country; creative tribal solutions.* Washington, DC: Author.

National Drug Intelligence Center. (2002). *Children at risk* (Publication No. 2002-L0424-001). Johnstown, PA: Author.

National Drug Intelligence Center. (2006, October). *National drug threat assessment 2007*. Retrieved March 22, 2007, from http://www.whitehousedrugpolicy.gov

National Institutes of Health. (1996, November). *Methamphetamine abuse, consequences and solutions; topics of a regional conference in San Francisco*. Rockville, MD: Author.

National Institute of Mental Health. (2006). *Anxiety disorders*. Retrieved September 11, 2007, from http://www.nimh.nih.gov/publicat/anxiety

National Institute on Drug Abuse. (1996). Stimulants. *Proceedings of the Community Epidemiology Work Group Public Health Service, NIDA, Vol. 1,* 61–71. Rockville, MD: Author.

National Institute on Drug Abuse. (1997). Methamphetamine abuse. *NIDA Capsules,* 1–2. Rockville, MD: Author.

National Institute on Drug Abuse. (1998). *Methamphetamine abuse and addiction research report series*. Retrieved November 21, 2007, from http://www.drugabuse.gov/ResearchReports/Methamph/methamph6.html

National Institute on Drug Abuse. (2002). *Methamphetamine: Abuse and addiction*. Rockville, MD: National Clearinghouse on Alcohol and Drug Information.

National Institute on Drug Abuse Research Report Series. (2006). *Methamphetamine abuse and addiction* (NIH Publication No. 06-4210). Washington, DC: U.S. Government Printing Office. Retrieved November 21, 2007, from http://www.nida.nih.gov/PDF/RRMetham.pdf

National Institute on Drug Abuse and University of Michigan. (2006). *Monitoring the future national survey results on drug use, 1975–2005, Volume ii: College students & adults ages 19–45*. Bethesda, MD: Author.

Nemoto, T., Operario, D., & Soma, T. (2002). Risk behaviors of Filipino methamphetamine users in San Francisco: Implications for prevention and treatment of drug use and HIV. *Public Health Reports, 117*(Suppl. 1), S30–S38.

New York City Department of Health and Mental Hygiene. (2004). Health bulletin: *Methamphetamine and HIV* (Publication No. 3). New York: Author.

New York Crystal Meth Anonymous. (2007). *New York Crystal Meth Anonymous Intergroup*. Retrieved November 21, 2007, from http://www.nycma.org

New York State Department of Health AIDS Institute. (2004). *HIV prophylaxis following occupational exposure*. Albany, NY: Author. Retrieved November 1, 2007, from http://www.hivguidelines.org

Newton, T. F., Kalechstein, A. D., Duran, S., Vansluis, N., & Ling, W. (2004). Methamphetamine abstinence syndrome: Preliminary findings. *The American Journal on Addictions/American Academy of Psychiatrists in Alcoholism and Addictions, 13,* 248–255.

Newton, T., Reid, M., De La Garza, R., Mahoney, J., III, Abad, A., Condos, R., et al. (2008). Evaluation of the effects of aripiprazole and methamphetamine in methamphetamine-dependent volunteers. *The International Journal of Neuropsychopharmacology, 11,* 1037–1045.

Newton, T. F., Roache, J. D., De La Garza, R., Fong, T., Wallace, C. L., Li, S., et al. (2006). Bupropion reduces methamphetamine-induced subjective effects and cue-induced craving. *Neuropsychopharmacology, 31,* 1537–1544.

Nina, C. M. (2007). *The relationship between ego functions and personality traits with drug of choice and degree of substance involvement among gay and bisexual male club drug users.* Unpublished doctoral dissertation, New York University.

North Carolina Department of Justice. (2004). *North Carolina methamphetamine summit: Final report.* Raleigh, NC: Author. Retried April 2, 2007, from http://www.ncdoj.com

North, C. S., Nixon, S. C., Shariat, S., Mallonee, S., Mcmillen, J. C., Spitznagel, E. L., et al. (1999). Psychiatric disorders among survivors of the Oklahoma City bombing. *The Journal of the American Medical Association, 25,* 755–762.

Numachi, Y., Ohara, A., Yamashita, M., Fukushima, S., Kobayashi, H., Hata, H., et al. (2007). Methamphetamine-induced hyperthermia and lethal toxicity: Role of the dopamine and serotonin transporters. *European Journal of Pharmacology, 572,* 120–128.

Obert, J., London, E., & Rawson, R. (2002). Incorporating brain research findings into standard treatment: An example using the Matrix Model. *Journal of Substance Abuse Treatment, 23,* 107–113.

Obert, J., McCann, M., Marinelli-Casey, P., Weiner, A., Minsky, S., Brethen, P., et al. (2000). The matrix model of outpatient stimulant abuse treatment: History and description. *Journal of Psychoactive Drugs, 32,* 157–163.

Oetting, E. R., Beauvais, F., & Edwards, R. W. (1985). *The American drug and alcohol survey.* Ft. Collins, CO: Rocky Mountain Behavioral Science Institute.

Oetting, E. R., Deffenbacher, J. L., Taylor, M. J., Luther, N., Beauvais, F., & Edwards, R. W. (2000). Methamphetamine use by high school students: recent trends, gender and ethnicity differences, and sue of other drugs. *Journal of Child & Adolescent Substance Abuse, 10,* 33–550.

Office of Applied Statistics. (2006a). *The DASIS report; methamphetamine/amphetamine treatment admissions in urban and rural areas: 2004.* Rockville, MD: Substance Abuse and Mental Health Services Administration.

Office of Applied Statistics. (2006b, February). *Treatment episode data sets (TEDS); highlights—2005.* Rockville, MD: Substance Abuse and Mental Health Services Administration.

Office of Applied Statistics. (2006c). Trends in methamphetamine/amphetamine admissions to treatment: 1993–2003. *The DASIS Report, 9.* Rockville, MD: Substance Abuse and Mental Health Services Administration.

Office of Applied Statistics. (2007, January 26). *The National Survey on Drug Use and Health report: Methamphetamine use.* Rockville, MD: Substance Abuse and Mental Health Services Administration.

Office of National Drug Control Policy. (2003). *Facts & figures: Methamphetamine.* Rockville, MD: Author. Retrieved April 6, 2007, from http://www.whitehousedrugpolicy.gov/drugfact/methamphetamine/index.html

Office of National Drug Control Policy. (2007). *ONDCP's 2007 anti-meth campaign*. Retrieved July 12, 2008, from http://www.methresources.gov/antimeth

Okuda, T., Ito, Y., Nakagawa, N., Hishinuma, T., Tsukamoto, H., Iwabuchi, K., et al. (2004). Drug interaction between methamphetamine and antihistamines: Behavioral changes and tissue concentrations of methamphetamine in rats. *European Journal of Pharmacology, 505*, 135–144.

Operario, D., Choi, K. H., Chu, P. L., McFarland, W., Secura, G. M., Behel, S., et al. (2006). Prevalence and correlates of substance use among young Asian Pacific Islander men who have sex with men. *Prevention Science, 7*, 19–29.

Orme, J., & Starkey, F. (1999). Young people's views on drug education in schools: Implications for health promotion and health education. *Health Education, 4*, 142–152.

Osborne, D. (2005). *Suicide Tuesday; gay men and the crystal meth scare*. New York: Carroll & Graf.

Ouimette, P. C., Finney, J. W., & Moos, R. H. (1997). Twelve-step and cognitive-behavioral treatment of substance abuse: A comparison of treatment effectiveness. *Journal of Consulting and Clinical Psychology, 65*, 230–240.

Oyler, J. M., Cone, E. J., Joseph, R. E., Jr., Moolchan, E. T., & Huestis, M. A. (2002). Duration of detectable methamphetamine and amphetamine excretion in urine after controlled oral administration of methamphetamine to humans. *Clinical Chemistry, 48*, 1703–1714.

Palamar, J., & Halkitis, P. N. (2006). A qualitative analysis of GHB use among gay men: Reasons for use despite potential adverse outcomes. *International Journal of Drug Policy, 17*, 23–28.

Parallax Center. (2007). *Our approach*. Retrieved November 21, 2007, from http://www.parallaxcenter.com/approach.html

Parsons, J. T., Halkitis, P. N., & Bimbi, D. (2006). Club drug use among young adults frequenting dance clubs and other social venues in New York City. *Journal of Child & Adolescent Substance Abuse, 15*, 1–14.

Partnership for a Drug-Free America. (2006). *Meth information and resource center*. Retrieved August 15, 2008, from http://www.drugfree.org/Portal/programs.html

Patterson, T. L., & Semple, S. J. (2003). Sexual risk reduction among HIV-positive drug-using men who have sex with men. *Journal of Urban Health, 80*, 77–88.

Patterson, T. L., Semple, S. J., Zians, J. K., & Strathdee, S. A. (2005). Methamphetamine-using HIV-positive men who have sex with men: Correlates of polydrug use. *Journal of Urban Health, 82*(Suppl. 1), i120–i126.

Paul, J. P., Stall, R., Crosby, G. M., Barrett, D., & Midanik, L. (1994). Correlates of sexual risk taking among gay male substance abusers. *Addiction, 89*, 971–983.

Paul, J. P., Stall, R., & Davis, F. (1993). Sexual risk for HIV transmission among gay/bisexual men in substance abuse treatment. *AIDS Education and Prevention, 5*, 11–24.

Paulus, M., Hozack, N., Lawrence, F., Brown, G., & Schuckit, M. (2003). Decision making by methamphetamine-dependent subjects is associated with error-rate-independent decrease in prefrontal and parietal activation. *Biological Psychiatry, 53*, 65–74.

Paulus, M. P., Hozack, N. E., Zauscher, B. E., Frank, L., Brown, G. G., Braff, D. L., et al. (2002). Behavioral and functional neuroimaging evidence for prefrontal dysfunction in methamphetamine-dependent subjects. *Neuropsychopharmacology, 26*, 53–63.

Penning, M., & Barnes, G. E. (1982). Adolescent marijuana use: A review. *International Journal of Addiction, 17*, 749–791.

Perez, A. Y., Kirkpatrick, M. G., Gunderson, E. W., Marrone, G., Silver, R., Foltin, R. W., et al. (2008). Residual effects of intranasal methamphetamine on sleep, mood, and performance. *Drug and Alcohol Dependence, 94*, 258–262.

Perz, J. F., Armstrong, G. L., Farrington, L. A., Hutin, Y. J., & Bell, B. P. (2006). The contributions of hepatitis B virus and hepatitis C virus infections to cirrhosis and primary liver cancer worldwide. *Journal of Hepatology, 45*, 529–538.

Petry, N. M., Pierce, J. M., Stitzer, M. L., Blaine, J., Roll, J. M., Cohen, A., et al. (2005). Effect of prize-based incentives on outcomes in stimulant abusers in outpatient psychosocial treatment programs: A national drug abuse treatment clinical trials network study. *Archives of General Psychiatry, 62*, 1148–1156.

Piazza, P. V., & Le Moal, M. (1996). Pathophysiological basis of vulnerability to drug abuse: Role of an interaction between stress, glucocorticoids, and dopaminergic neurons. *Annual Review of Pharmacological Toxicology, 36*, 359–378.

Plankey, M. W., Ostrow, D. G., Stall, R., Cox, C., Li, X., Peck, J. A., et al. (2007). The relationship between methamphetamine and popper use and risk of HIV seroconversion in the multicenter AIDS cohort study. *Journal of Acquired Immune Deficiency Syndromes, 45*, 85–92.

Plessinger, M. A. (1998). Prenatal exposure to amphetamines. Risk and adverse outcomes in pregnancy. *Obstetrics & Gynecology Clinics of North America, 25*, 119–138.

Potula, R., & Persidsky, Y. (2008). Adding fuel to the fire: Methamphetamine enhances HIV infection. *American Journal of Pathology, 172*, 1467–1470.

Premack, D., & Woodruff, G. (1978). Does the chimpanzee have a theory of mind? *Behavioural and Brain Sciences, 1*, 515.

Pritzker, D., Kanungo, A., Kilicarslan, T., Tyndale, R. F., & Sellers, E. M. (2002). Designer drugs that are potent inhibitors of CYP2D6. *Journal of Clinical Psychopharmacology, 22*, 330–332.

PRNewswire-USNewswire. (2007, September 13). *Meth project advertisements selected for national prevention campaign.* Retrieved July 12, 2008, from http://www.bio-medicine.org/medicine-news-1/Meth-Project-Advertisements-Selected-for-National-Prevention-Campaign-1213-1

Project Match Research Group. (1997a). Matching alcoholism treatments to client heterogeneity: Project MATCH posttreatment drinking outcomes. *Journal of Studies on Alcohol, 58*, 7–29.

Project Match Research Group. (1997b). Project MATCH secondary a priori hypotheses. *Addiction, 92,* 1671–1698.

Pu, C., & Vorhees, C. V. (1993). Developmental dissociation of methamphetamine-induced depletion of dopaminergic terminals and astrocyte reaction in rat striatum. *Brain Research, Developmental Brain Research, 72,* 325–328.

Quinn, T. C. (1997). Acute primary HIV infection. *Journal of the American Medical Association, 278,* 58–62.

Rabkin, J. (2006). HIV and mood disorders. *ACRIA Update, 15,* 1–5. Retrieved September 3, 2007, from http://www.acria.org/treatment/treatment_edu_summerupdate2006_mood.html

Rawson, R. A. (1998). *Treatment of stimulant abuse—Treatment improvement protocols.* Rockville, MD: Center for Substance Abuse Treatment, Department of Health and Human Services.

Rawson, R. A., Anglin, D., & Ling, W. (2002). Will the methamphetamine problem go away? *Journal of Addictive Diseases, 21,* 5–19.

Rawson, R. A., Gonzales, R., & Brethen, P. (2002). Treatment of methamphetamine use disorders: An update. *Journal of Substance Abuse Treatment, 23,* 145–150.

Rawson, R. A., Gonzales, R., Obert, J. L., McCann, M. J., & Brethen, P. (2005). Methamphetamine use among treatment-seeking adolescents in Southern California: Participant characteristics and treatment response. *Journal of Substance Abuse Treatment, 29,* 67–74.

Rawson, R. A., Gonzales, R., Pearce, V., Ang, A., Martinelli-Casey, P., Brummer, J., et al. (2008). Methamphetamine dependence and human immunodeficiency virus. *Journal of Substance Abuse Treatment, 35,* 279–284.

Rawson, R. A., & Huber, A. (1996, December). *The matrix model of stimulant abuse treatment.* Presentation at NIDA conference methamphetamine abuse, treatment and prevention, San Francisco, CA.

Rawson, R., Huber, A., Brethen, P., Obert, J., Gulati, V., Shoptaw, S., et al. (2002). Methamphetamine and cocaine users: Differences in characteristics and treatment retention. *Journal of Psychoactive Drugs, 32,* 233–238.

Rawson, R., Huber, A., Brethen, P., Obert, J., Shoptaw, S., & Ling, W. (2002). Status of methamphetamine users 2–5 years after outpatient treatment. *Journal of Addictive Diseases, 21*(1), 107–119.

Rawson, R. A., Marinelli-Casey, P., Anglin, M. D., Dickow, A., Frazier, Y., Gallagher, C., et al. (2004). A multi-site comparison of psychosocial approaches for the treatment of methamphetamine dependence. *Addiction, 99,* 708–717.

Rawson, R. A., McCann, M. J., Flammino, F., Shoptaw, S. J., Miotto, K., Reiber, C., et al. (2006). A comparison of contingency management and cognitive-behavioral approaches for stimulant-dependent individuals. *Addiction, 101,* 267–274.

Rawson, R. A., McCann, M., Shoptaw, S. J., Farabee, D., Reiber, C., & Ling, W. (2002). A comparison of contingency management and cognitive-behavioral approaches during methadone maintenance treatment for cocaine dependence. *Archives of General Psychiatry, 59,* 817–824.

Rawson, R. A., Shoptaw, S. J., Obert, J. L., McCann, M. J., Hasson, A. L., Marinelli-Casey, P. J., et al. (1995). An intensive outpatient approach for cocaine abuse treatment: The matrix model. *Journal of Substance Abuse Treatment, 12,* 117–127.

Reback, C. J. (1997). *The social construction of a gay drug: Methamphetamine use among gay and bisexual males in Los Angeles* (Contract No. 934270). Los Angeles: City of Los Angeles AIDS Coordinator's Office.

Reback, C., Cohen, A. J., Freese, T. E., & Shoptaw, S. (2002). Making collaboration work: Key components of practice/research partnerships. *Journal of Drug Issues, 32,* 837–848.

Reback, C. J., & Grella, C. E. (1999). HIV risk behaviors of gay and bisexual male methamphetamine users contacted through street outreach. *Journal of Drug Issues, 29,* 155–166.

Reback, C. J., Larkins, S., & Shoptaw, S. (2004). Changes in the meaning of sexual risk behaviors among gay and bisexual male methamphetamine abusers before and after drug treatment. *AIDS and Behavior, 8,* 87–98.

Reid, M. S., Palamar, J., Flammino, F., Mahoney, J. J., De La Garza, R., Newton, T., et al. (2006, June). *A double-blind, placebo-controlled assessment of aripiprazole effects on methamphetamine craving: Longitudinal and cue reactivity studies.* Poster session for The College on Problems of Drug Dependence 68th Annual Meeting, Scottsdale, AZ.

Rhodes, F., Wolitski, R. J., & Thornton-Johnson, S. (1992). An experiential program to reduce AIDS risk among female sex partners of injection-drug users. *Health and Social Work, 17,* 261–272.

Richards, J., & Brofeldt, B. (2000). Patterns of tooth wear associated with methamphetamine use. *Journal of Periodontology, 71,* 1371–1374.

Richards, J. R., Johnson, E. B., Stark, R. W., & Derlet, R. W. (1999). Methamphetamine abuse and rhabdomyolysis in the ED: A 5-year study. *American Journal of Emergency Medicine, 17,* 681–685.

Rippeth, J. D., Heaton, R. K., Carey, C. L., Marcotte, T. D., Moore, D. J., Gonzalez, R., et al. (2004). Methamphetamine dependence increases risk of neuropsychological impairment in HIV infected persons. *Journal of the International Neuropsychological Society, 10,* 1–14.

Riverside County Department of Environmental Conservation. (2005). *Riverside County drug endangered children program.* Retrieved April 3, 2007, from http://dec.co.riverside.ca.us

Robins, A. G., Dew, M. A., Davidson, S., & Penkower, L. (1994). Psychosocial factors associated with risky sexual behavior among HIV-seropositive men. *AIDS Education and Prevention, 6,* 483–492.

Robinson, T. E., & Berridge, K. C. (1993). The neural basis of drug craving: An incentive-sensitization theory of addiction. *Brain Research Reviews, 18,* 247–291.

Rogala, B., & Lopez-Zetina, J. (2008, October). *Methamphetamine use and sexual risk: A comparison of Mexican and Mexican-American women in the San Diego/Tijuana border region.* Paper presented at the 136th Meeting of the American Public Health Association, San Diego, CA.

Rogers, R., Everitt, B., Baldacchino, A., Blackshaw, A., Swainson, R., Wynne, K., et al. (1999). Dissociable deficits in the decision-making cognition of chronic amphetamine abusers, opiate abusers, patients with focal damage to prefrontal cortex, and tryptophan-depleted normal volunteers: Evidence for monoaminergic mechanisms. *Neuropsychopharmacology, 20,* 322–339.

Roll, J. M. (2007). Contingency management: An evidence-based component of methamphetamine use disorder treatments. *Addiction, 102*(Suppl. 1), 114–120.

Roll, J. M, Petry, N. M., Stitzer, M. L., Brecht, M. L., Peirece, J. M., McCann, M. J., et al. (2006). Contingency management for the treatment of methamphetamine use disorders. *American Journal of Psychiatry, 163,* 1993–1999.

Room, R., & Greenfield, T. (1993). Alcoholics Anonymous, other 12-Step movements and psychotherapy in the US population, 1990. *Addiction, 88,* 555–562.

Rosenbaum, D. P., & Hanson, G. S. (1998). Assessing the effects of school-based drug education: A six-year multilevel analysis of project D.A.R.E. (1998). *Journal of Research in Crime and Delinquency, 35,* 381–412.

Rosenberg, E. S., Altfeld, M., Poon, S. H., Phillips, M. N., Wilkes, B. M., Eldridge, R. L., et al. (2000, September 28). Immune Control of HIV-1 after early treatment of acute infection. *Nature, 407,* 523–526.

Rounsaville, B. J., Kosten, T. R., & Weissman, M. M. (1991). Psychiatric disorders in relatives of probands with opiate addiction. *Archives of General Psychiatry, 48,* 38–42.

Rubia, K., Overmeyer, S., Taylor, E., Brammer, M., Williams, S. C., Simmons, A., et al. (2000). Functional frontalisation with age: Mapping neurodevelopmental trajectories with fMRI. *Neuroscience and Biobehavioral Reviews, 24,* 13–19.

Rumbaugh, C. (1977). Small vessel cerebral vascular changes following chronic methamphetamine intoxication. In E. Ellinwood & M. Kilbey Jr. (Eds.), *Cocaine and other stimulants* (pp. 241–251). New York: Plenum Press.

Rumbaugh, C. L., Fang, H. C., Higgins, R. E., Bergeron, R. T., Segall, H. D., & Teal, J. S. (1976). Cerebral microvascular injury in experimental drug abuse. *Investigative Radiology, 11,* 282–294.

Sabol, K. E., Roach, J. T., Broom, S. L., Ferreira, C., & Preau, M. M. (2001). Long-term effects of a high-dose methamphetamine regimen on subsequent methamphetamine-induced dopamine release in vivo. *Brain Research, 892,* 122–129.

Sadek, J. R., Vigil, O., Grant, I., Heaton, R. K., & The HNRC Group. (2007). The impact of neuropsychological functioning and depressed mood on functional complaints in HIV-1 infection and methamphetamine dependence. *Journal of Clinical and Experimental Neuropsychology, 29,* 266–276.

Saini, T., Edwards, P., Kimmes, N., Carroll, L., Shaner, J., & Dowd, F. (2005). Etiology of xerostomia and dental caries among methamphetamine abusers. *Oral Health & Preventive Dentistry, 3,* 189–195.

Salo, R., Nurdahl, T., Possin, K., Martin, L., Gibson, D., Galloway, G., et al. (2002). Preliminary evidence of reduced cognitive inhibition in methamphetamine-dependent individuals. *Psychiatry Research, 111,* 65–74.

Sato, M. (1992). A lasting vulnerability to psychosis in patients with previous methamphetamine psychosis. *Annals of the New York Academy of Sciences, 654,* 160–170.

Savin-Williams, R. C. (2006). Who's gay? Does it matter? *Current Directions in Psychological Science, 15,* 40–44.

Schaiberger, P. H., Kennedy, T. C., Miller, F. C., & Petty, T. L. (1993). Pulmonary hypertension associated with long-term inhalation of "crank" methamphetamine. *CHEST, 104,* 614–616.

Schiorring, E. (1977). Changes in individual and social behavior induced by amphetamine and related compounds in monkeys and man. In E. H. Ellinwood Jr. & M. M. Kilbey (Eds.), *Cocaine and other stimulants* (pp. 481–522). New York: Raven.

Schulenberg, J. E., Sameroff, A. J., & Cicchetti, D. (2004). The transition to adulthood as a critical juncture in the course of psychopathology and mental health. *Development and Psychopathology, 16,* 799–806.

Schuster, M. A., Stein, B., Jaycox, L. H., Collins, R. L., Marshall, G. N., Elliott, M. N., et al. (2001). A national survey of stress reactions after the September 11, 2001, terrorist attacks. *The New England Journal of Medicine, 345,* 1507–1512.

Seal, D. W., & Agostinelli, G. (1994). Individual differences associated with high-risk sexual behaviour: Implications of intervention programmes. *AIDS Care, 6,* 393–397.

Sekine, Y., Iyo, M., Ouchi, Y., Matsunaga, T., Tsukada, H., Yoshikawa, E., et al. (2001). Methamphetamine-related psychiatric symptoms and reduced brain dopamine transporters studied with PET. *American Journal of Psychiatry, 158,* 1206–1214.

Sekine, Y., Ouchi, Y., Takei, N., Yoshikawa, E., Nakamura, K., Futatsubashi, M., et al. (2006). Brian serotonin transporter density and aggression in abstinent methamphetamine abusers. *Archives of General Psychiatry, 63,* 90–100.

Semple, S., Grant, I., & Patterson, T. (2004). Female methamphetamine users: Social characteristics and sexual risk behavior. *Women & Health, 40,* 35–50.

Semple, S., Patterson, T. L., & Grant, I. (2003). Binge use of methamphetamine among HIV-positive men who have sex with men: Pilot data and HIV prevention implications. *AIDS Education and Prevention, 15,* 133–147.

Semple, S. J., Patterson, T. L., & Grant, I. (2002). Motivations associated with methamphetamine use among HIV+ men who have sex with men. *Journal of Substance Abuse Treatment, 22,* 149–56.

Semple, S. J., Patterson, T. L., & Grant, I. (2004). The context of sexual risk behavior among heterosexual methamphetamine users. *Addictive Behaviors, 29,* 807–810.

Semple, S. J., Zians, J., Grant, I., & Patterson, T. L. (2005). Impulsivity and methamphetamine use. *Journal of Substance Abuse Treatment, 29,* 85–93.

Semple, S. J., Zians, J., Grant, I., & Patterson, T. L. (2006a). Methamphetamine use, impulsivity, and sexual risk behavior among HIV-positive men who have sex with men. *Journal of Addictive Diseases, 25,* 105–114.

Semple, S. J., Zians, J., Grant, I. & Patterson, T. L. (2006b). Sexual risk behavior of HIV-positive methamphetamine-using men who have sex with men: The role of partner serostatus and partner type. *Archives of Sexual Behavior, 35*, 461–471.

Senjo, S. R. (2007). The insidious allure of methamphetamine: Female patterns of purchasing, use, consequences of use, and treatment. In G. H. Toolaney (Ed.), *New research on methamphetamine abuse* (pp. 53–68). New York: Nova Science Publishers, Inc.

Senterfiti, J. W., Harawa, N. T., Whitfield, C., Kerndt, P. R., & Daar, E. (1998, February 4). *Study of acute early infections yields surprising risk profiles.* Paper presented at the Fifth Annual Conference of Retroviruses and Opportunistic Infections, Chicago, IL.

Sheridan, J., Bennett, S., Coggan, C., Wheeler, A., & McMillan, K. (2006). Injury associated with methamphetamine: A review of the literature. *Harm Reduction Journal*, 1–8.

Shoptaw, S. J., & Frosch, D. (2000). Substance abuse treatment as HIV prevention for men who have sex with men. *AIDS and Behavior, 4*, 193–203.

Shoptaw, S. J., Huber, A., Peck, J., Yang, X., Liu, J., Dang, J., et al. (2006). Randomized, placebo-controlled trial of sertraline and contingency management for the treatment of methamphetamine dependence. *Drug Alcohol Dependence, 85*, 12–18.

Shoptaw, S., Peck, J., Reback, C., & Rotheram-Fuller, E. (2003). Psychiatric and substance dependence comorbidities, sexually transmitted diseases, and risk behaviors among methamphetamine-dependent gay and bisexual men seeking outpatient drug abuse treatment. *Journal of Psychoactive Drugs, 35*, 161–168.

Shoptaw, S. J., Rawson, R., McCann, M., & Obert, J. (1994). The matrix model of outpatient stimulant abuse treatment: Evidence of efficacy. In S. Magura & S. Rosenblum (Eds.), *Experimental therapeutics in addiction medicine* (pp. 129–141). Binghamton, NY: Haworth Press.

Shoptaw, S., & Reback, C. J. (2006). Associations between methamphetamine use and HIV among men who have sex with men: a model for guiding public policy. *Journal of Urban Health, 83*, 1151–1157.

Shoptaw, S. J., & Reback, C. J. (2007a). Associations between methamphetamine use and HIV among men who have sex with men: A model for guiding public policy. *Journal of Urban Health, 83*, 1151–1157.

Shoptaw, S. J., & Reback, C. J. (2007b). Methamphetamine use and infectious disease-related behaviors in men who have sex with men: Implications for interventions. *Addiction, 102*(Suppl. 1), 130–135.

Shoptaw, S. J., Reback, C. J., Frosch, D. L., & Rawson, R. A. (1998). Stimulant abuse treatment as HIV prevention. *Journal of Addictive Diseases, 17*, 19–32.

Shoptaw, S. J., Reback, C. J., Peck, J., Yang, X., Rotheram-Fuller, E., Larkins, S., et al. (2005). Behavioral treatment approaches for methamphetamine dependence and HIV-related sexual risk behaviors among urban gay and bisexual men. *Drug and Alcohol Dependence, 78*, 125–134.

Shrem, M., & Halkitis, P. N. (2008). Methamphetamine abuse in the United States: Contextual, psychological, and sociological considerations. *Journal of Health Psychology, 13*, 669–679.

Siconolfi, D., & Moeller, R. W. (2007). Serosorting. *Bulletin of Experimental Treatments for AIDS (BETA), 19*, 45–49.

Sim, T., Simon, S. L., Domier, C. P., Richardson, K., Rawson, R. A., & Ling, W. (2002). Cognitive deficits among methamphetamine users with attention deficit hyperactivity disorder symptomatology. *Journal of Addictive Diseases, 21*, 75–89.

Simcha-Fagan, O., Gersten, J. C., & Langner, T. S. (1986). Early precursors and concurrent correlates of patterns of illicit drug use in adolescence. *Journal of Drug Issues, 16*, 7–28.

Simon, S., Domier, C., Carnell, J. C., Brethen, P., Rawson, R., & Ling, W. (2000). Cognitive impairment in individuals currently using methamphetamine. *The American Journal on Addiction, 9*, 222–231.

Simon, S., Domier, C., Sim, T., Richardson, K., Rawson, R., Huber, A., et al. (1999, June). *Cognitive correlates of chronic methamphetamine use.* Paper presented at the 61st annual meeting of College on Problems of Drug Dependence, Acapulco, Mexico.

Simon, S., Domier, C., Sim, T., Richardson, K., Rawson, R., & Ling, W. (2002). Cognitive performance of current methamphetamine and cocaine abusers. *Journal of Addictive Diseases, 21*, 61–74.

Simons, J. S., Gaher, R. M., Correia, C. J., & Bush, J. A. (2005). Club drug use among college students. *Addictive Behavior, 30*, 1619–1624.

Simons, J. S., Oliver, M. N. I., Gaher, R. M., Ebel, G., & Brummels, P. (2005). Methamphetamine and alcohol abuse and dependence symptoms: Associations with affect lability and impulsivity in a rural treatment population. *Addictive Behaviors, 30*, 1370–1381.

Singer, M. (1994). AIDS and the health crisis of the US urban poor: The perspective of critical medical anthropology. *Social Science & Medicine, 39*, 931–948.

Singer, M. (1996). A dose of drugs, a touch of violence and case of AIDS: Conceptualizing the SAVA syndemic. *Free Inquiry, 24*, 99–110.

Sinha, R. (2001). How does stress increase risk of drug abuse and relapse? *Psychopharmacology, 158*, 343–359.

Skinner, B. F. (1938/1966). *Behavior of organisms.* Acton, MA: Copley Publishing.

Smith, L. M., LaGassee, L. L., Derauf, C., Grant, P., Shah, R., Arria, A., et al. (2006). The infant development, environment, and lifestyle study: Effects of prenatal methamphetamine exposure, polydrug exposure, and poverty on intrauterine growth. *Pediatrics, 118*, 1149–1156.

Smith, L., Yonekura, M. L., Wallace, T., Berman, N., Kuo, J., & Berkowitz, C. (2003). Effects of prenatal methamphetamine exposure on fetal growth and drug withdrawal symptoms in infants born at term. *Journal of Developmental and Behavioral Pediatrics, 24*, 17–23.

Somlai, A. M., Kelly, J. A., McAuliffe, T. L., Ksobiech, K., & Hackl, K. L. (2003). Predictors of HIV sexual risk behaviors in a community sample of injection drug-using men and women. *AIDS and Behavior, 7*, 383–393.

Sommers, I., Baskin, D., & Baskin-Sommers, A. (2006). Methamphetamine use among young adults: Health and social consequences. *Addictive Behavior, 31*, 1469–1476.

Sorensen, J. L., Mascovich, A., Wall, T. L., DePhillippis, D., Bataki, S. L., & Chesney, M. (1998). Medication adherence strategies for drug abusers with HIV/AIDS. *AIDS Care, 10*, 297–312.

Southeast Missouri State University's Office of Continuing Education. (2007). *MEDFEL; meth education for elementary schools.* Retrieved July 13, 2007, from http://www6.semo.edu/coned/Medfels/medfels.htm

Stall, R., & Biernacki, P. (1986). Spontaneous remission from the problematic use of substances: An inductive model derived from a comparative analysis of the alcohol, opiate, tobacco, and food/obesity literatures. *The International Journal of the Addictions, 21*, 1–23.

Stall, R., Friedman, M., & Catania, J. A. (2007). Interacting epidemics and gay men's health: A theory of syndemic production among urban gay men. In R. J. Wolitiski, R. Stall, & R. O. Valdiserri (Eds.), *Unequal opportunity: Health disparities affecting gay and bisexual men in the United States* (pp. 251–274). New York: Oxford University Press.

Stall, R., Mills, T. C., Williamson, J., Hart, T., Greenwood, G., Paul, J., et al. (2003). Association of co-occurring psychosocial health problems and increased vulnerability to HIV/AIDS among urban men who have sex with men. *American Journal of Public Health, 93*, 939–942.

Stall, R., McKusick, L., Wiley, J., Coates, T., & Ostrow, D. (1986). Alcohol and drug use during sexual activity and compliance with safe sex guidelines for AIDS: The AIDS behavioral research project. *Health Education & Behavior, 13*, 359–371.

Stall, R., Paul, J. P., Greenwood, G., Pollack, L. M., Bein, E., Crosby, G. M., et al. (2001). Alcohol use, drug use and alcohol-related problems among men who have sex with men: The urban men's health study. *Addiction, 96*, 1589–1601.

Stewart, S. H., Pihl, R. O., Conrod, P. J., & Dongier, M. (1998). Functional associations among trauma, PTSD, and substance-related disorders. *Addictive Behaviors, 23*, 797–812.

Stotts, A. L., Schmitz, J. M., Rhoads, H. M., & Grabowski, J. (2001). Motivational interviewing with cocaine-dependent patients: A pilot study. *Journal of Consulting and Clinical Psychology, 69*, 858–862.

Strang, J., Griffiths, P., & Gossop, M. (1997). Heroin in the United Kingdom: Different forms, different origins, and the relationship to different routes of administration. *Drug and Alcohol Review, 16*, 329–337.

Strona, F. V., McCright, J., Hjord, H., Ahrens, K., Tierney, S., Shoptaw, S. J., et al. (2006). The acceptability and feasibility of the Positive Reinforcement Opportunity Project, a community-based contingency management methamphetamine treatment program for gay and bisexual men in San Francisco. *Journal of Psychoactive Drugs, 3*, 377–383.

Substance Abuse and Mental Health Services Administration. (2006). *Meth: America's homegrown drug epidemic.* Retrieved August 15, 2008, from http://family.samhsa.gov/talk/drugepi.aspx

Substance Abuse and Mental Health Service Administration. (2008). *Methamphetamine users in treatment.* Rockville, MD: Author. Retrieved July 27, 2008, from http://download.ncadi.samhsa.gov/prevline/pdfs/DASISRPT08-0117.pdf

Suwaki, H., Fukui, S., & Konuma, K. (1997). The history of methamphetamine abuse in Japan. In H. Klee (Ed.), *Amphetamine misuse: International perspectives on current trends* (pp. 200–214). Amsterdam: Harwood Academic.

Swalwell, C., & Davis, G. (1999). Methamphetamine as a risk factor for acute aortic dissection. *Journal of Forensic Sciences, 44,* 23–26.

Swan, N. (1996). Response to escalating methamphetamine abuse builds on NIDA-funded research. *National Institute on Drug Abuse Notes, 11,* 1, 5–6, 18–19.

Swanson, A. J., Pantalon, M. V., & Cohen, K. R. (1999). Motivational interviewing and treatment adherence among psychiatric and dually diagnosed patients. *Journal of Nervous and Mental Disorders, 187,* 630–635.

Swetlow, K. (2003, June). Children at clandestine methamphetamine labs: Helping meth's youngest victims (Publication No. NCJ-197590). *OVC Bulletin.* Retrieved April 7, 2007, from http://www.ojp.usdoj.gov/ovc/publications/bulletins/children/197590.pdf

Syme, L., & Syme, G. (1974). Group instability and the social response to methamphetamine. *Pharmacology, Biochemistry, and Behavior, 2,* 851–854.

Szuster, R. (1990). Methamphetamine in psychiatric emergencies. *Hawaii Medical Journal, 49,* 389–391.

Tallóczy, Z., Martinez, J., Joset, D., Ray, Y., Gácser, A., Toussi, S., et al. (2008). Methamphetamine inhibits antigen processing, presentation, and phagocytosis. *PloS Pathogens, 4,* 1–11.

Taylor, M. J., Alhassoon, O. M., Schweinsburg, B. C., Videen, J. S., Grant, I., & the HNRC Group. (2000). MR spectroscopy in HIV and stimulant dependence. *Journal of the International Neuropsychological Society, 6,* 83–85.

Thaithumayanon, P., Limpongsanurak, S., Praisuwanna, P., Punnahitanon, S. (2005). Perinatal effects of amphetamine and heroin use during pregnancy on the mother and infant. *Journal of the Medical Association of Thailand, 88,* 1506–1513.

Thompson, H. S. (1967). *Hell's Angels: A strange and terrible saga.* New York: Random House.

Tobler, N., & Stratton, J. (1997). Effectiveness of school based drug prevention programs: A meta analysis. *Journal of Primary Prevention, 18,* 71–128.

Tonigan, J. S., Toscova, R., & Miller, W. R. (1996). Meta-analysis of the literature on alcoholics anonymous: Sample and study characteristics moderate findings. *Journal of Studies on Alcohol, 57,* 65–72.

Tsai, C. C., Emau, P., Follis, K. E., Beck, T. W., Benveniste, R. E., Bischofberger, N., et al. (1998). Effectiveness of postinoculation (R)-9-(2-phosphonylmethoxy-propyl) adenine treatment for prevention of persistent simian immunodeficiency virus SIVmne infection depends critically on timing of initiation and duration of treatment. *Journal of Virology, 72,* 4265–4273.

Turner, J. M., Rider, A. T., Imrie, J., Copas, A. J., Edwards, S. G., Dodds, J. P., et al. (2006). Behavioural predictors of subsequent hepatitis C diagnosis in a UK clinic sample of HIV positive men who have sex with men. *Sexually Transmitted Infections, 82,* 298–300.

Ujike, H., & Sato, M. (2004). Clinical feature of sensitization to methamphetamine observed in patients with methamphetamine dependence and psychosis. *Annals of the New York Academy of Sciences, 1025,* 279–287.

U.S. Department of Health and Human Services. (2004). *National survey on drug use and health, 2002.* Ann Arbor, MI: Research Triangle Park, NC: Research Triangle Institute.

U.S. Department of Justice. (2007). *Meth awareness.* Washington, DC: Author. Retrieved May 5, 2007, from http://www.usdoj.gov/methawareness

U.S. Drug Enforcement Administration. (2005). *Fast facts about meth.* Retrieved April 1, 2007, from http://www.usdoj.gov/dea/pubs/pressrel/methfact03.html

U.S. Drug Enforcement Administration. (2006). *Maps of methamphetamine lab incidents.* Retrieved March 2, 2006, from http://www.usdoj.gov/dea/concern/map_lab_seizures.html

U.S. Sentencing Commission. (2006, June). *2005 sourcebook of federal sentencing statistics.* Retrieved May 5, 2007, from http://www.ussc.gov

Urbina, A. (2006). Medical complications of crystal methamphetamine. In M. Wainberg, A. Kolodny, & J. Drescher (Eds.), *Crystal meth and men who have sex with men* (pp. 49–55). Binghamton, NY: Haworth Medical Press.

Urbina, A., & Jones, K. (2004). Crystal methamphetamine, its analogues, and HIV infection: medical and psychiatric aspects of a new epidemic. *Clinical Infectious Diseases, 38,* 890–894.

Uys, J. D. K., & Niesink, R. J. M. (2005). Pharmacological aspects of the combined use of 3, 4-methylenedioxmethamphetamine (MDMA, ecstasy) and gamma-hydroxybutric acid (GHB): A review of the literature. *Drug and Alcohol Review, 24,* 359–368.

Valasquez, M. M., Maurer, G. G., Crouch, C., & DiClemente, C. C. (2001). *Group treatment for substance abuse: A stages-of-change manual.* New York: Guilford Press.

Varner, K., Ogden, B., Delcarpio, J., & Meleg-Smith, S. (2002). Cardiovascular responses elicited by the "binge" administration of methamphetamine. *Journal of Pharmacological and Toxicological Methods, 301,* 152–159.

Vik, P. W., & Ross, T. (2003). Research report methamphetamine use among incarcerated women. *Journal of Substance Use, 8*(2), 69–77.

Virmani, A., Binienda, Z. K., Ali, S. F., & Gaetani, F. (2006). Links between nutrition, drug abuse, and the metabolic syndrome. *Annals of the New York Academy of Science, 1074,* 303–314.

Virmani, A., Binienda, Z. K., Ali, S. F., & Gaetani, F. (2007). Metabolic syndrome in drug abuse. *Annals of the New York Academy of Science, 1122,* 50–68.

Vlahov, D., Galea, S., Ahern, J., Boscarino, J. A., Bucuvalas, J. G., & Kilpatrick, D. (2002). Increased use of cigarettes, alcohol, and marijuana among Manhattan, New York, residents after the September 11th terrorist attacks. *American Journal of Epidemiology, 155,* 988–996.

Vocci, F. (1996, May). *Medication development for methamphetamine-related disorders.* Paper presented at the meeting of the Methamphetamine Advisory Group to Attorney General Reno, Washington, DC.

Vocci, F. J., & Appel, N. M. (2007). Approaches to the development of medications for the treatment of methamphetamine dependence. *Addiction, 102*(Suppl. 1), 96–106.

Vocci, F., & Ling, W. (2005). Medications development: Successes and challenges. *Pharmacological & Therapeutics, 108*, 94–108.

Volkow, N., Chang, L., Wang, G., Fowler, J., Franceschi, D., & Sedler, M., et al. (2001). Loss of dopamine transporters in methamphetamine abusers recovers with protracted abstinence. *Journal of Neuroscience, 21*, 9414–9418.

Volkow, N. D. (2001). Drug abuse and mental illness: Progress in understanding comorbidity. *American Journal of Psychiatry, 158*, 1181–1183.

Volkow, N. D., Chang, L., Wang, G. J., Fowler, J. S., Ding, Y. S., Sedler, M., et al. (2001). Low level of brain dopamine D2 receptors in methamphetamine abusers: Association with metabolism in the orbitofrontal cortex. *American Journal of Psychiatry, 158*, 2015–2021.

Volkow, N. D., Chang, L., Wang, G. J., Fowler, J. S., Leonido-Yee, M., & Franceschi, D., et al. (2001). Association of dopamine transporter reduction with psychomotor impairment in methamphetamine abusers. *American Journal of Psychiatry, 158*, 377–382.

Volkow, N. D., Fowler, J. S., Wang, G. J., Hitzemann, R., Logan, J., Schlyer, D. J., et al. (1993). Decreased dopamine D2 receptor availability is associated with reduced frontal metabolism in cocaine abusers. *Synapse, 14*, 169–177.

Volkow, N. D., Wang, G. J., Fischman, M. W., Foltin, R. W., Fowler, J. S., Abumrad, N. N., et al. (1997, April 24). Relationship between subjective effects of cocaine and dopamine transporter occupancy. *Nature, 386*, 827–830.

von Mayrhauser, C., Brecht, M. L., & Anglin, M. D. (2002). Use ecology and drug use motivations of methamphetamine users admitted to substance abuse treatment facilities in Los Angeles: An emerging portfolio. *Journal of Addictive Diseases, 21*, 45–60.

Wainberg, M. L., Kolodny, A. J., & Drescher, J. (Eds.). (2006). *Crystal meth and men who have sex with men; what mental health care professionals need to know*. Binghamton, NY: The Haworth Medical Press.

Wako, E., LeDoux, D., Mitsumori, L., & Aldea, G. S. (2007). The emerging epidemic of methamphetamine-induced aortic dissections. *Journal of Cardiac Surgery, 22*, 390–393.

Waldorf, D., Murphy, S., Lauderback, D., Reinarman, C., & Marotta, T. (1990). Needle sharing among male prostitutes: Preliminary findings of the Prospero Project. *The Journal of Drug Issues, 20*, 309–334.

Wang, G. J., Volkow, N. D., Chang, L., Miller, E., Sedler, M., Hitzemann, R. J., et al. (2004). Partial recovery of brain metabolism in methamphetamine abusers after protracted abstinence. *American Journal of Psychiatry, 161*, 242–248.

Wang, G. J., Volkow, N. D., Fowler, J. S., Logan, J., Abumrad, N. N., Hitzemann R. J., et al. (1997). Dopamine D2 receptor availability in opiate-dependent subjects before and after naloxone-precipitated withdrawal. *Neuropsychopharmacology, 16*, 174–182.

Weiss, R. D., Griffin, M. L., Gallop, R. J., Najavits, L. M., Frank, A., Crits-Cristoph, P., et al. (2005). The effect of 12-step self-help group attendance and participation on drug use outcomes among cocaine-dependent patients. *Drug and Alcohol Dependence, 77*, 177–184.

Wermuth, L. (2000). Methamphetamine use: Hazards and social influence. *Journal of Drug Education, 3*, 423–433.

Westover, A. N., Nakonezny, P. A., & Haley, R. W. (2008). Acute myocardial infarction in young adults who abuse amphetamines. *Drug Alcohol Dependence, 96*, 49–56.

White, D., & Pitts, M. (1998). Educating young people about drugs: A systematic review. *Addiction, 93*, 1475–1487.

Wijetunga, M., Bhan, R., Lindsay, J., & Karch, S. (2004). Acute coronary syndrome and crystal methamphetamine use: A case series. *Hawaii Medical Journal, 63*, 8–13.

Wilens, T., Biederman, J., Mick, E., Farone, S., & Spencer, T. (1997). Attention deficit hyperactivity disorder is associated with early onset substance use disorders. *The Journal of Nervous and Mental Disease, 185*, 475–482.

Wills, T. A. (1985). Stress, coping, and tobacco and alcohol use in early adolescence. In S. Shiffman & T. A. Wills (Eds.), *Coping and substance use* (pp. 67–94). New York: Academic Press.

Wilsnack, S. C., Vogeltanz, N. D., Klassen, A. D., & Harris, T. R. (1997). Childhood sexual abuse and women's substance abuse: National survey findings. *Journal of Studies on Alcohol, 58*, 264–271.

Wilson, W. J. (1987). The truly disadvantaged: The inner city, the underclass, and public policy. Chicago: University of Chicago Press.

Witte, K., & Allen, M. (2000). A meta-analysis of fear appeals: Implications for effective public health campaigns. *Health Education & Behavior, 27*. 591–615.

Wohl, A. R., Johnson, D. F., Lu, S., Jordan, W., Beall, G., Currier, J., et al. (2002). HIV risk behaviors among African American men in Los Angeles County who self identify as heterosexual. *Journal of Acquired Immune Deficiency Syndrome, 31*, 354–360.

Wolkoff, D. (1997). Methamphetamine abuse: An overview for health care professionals. *Hawaii Medical Journal, 56*, 34–36.

Wolkoff, D., & Burns, J. (1997). Methamphetamine abuse: An overview for health care professionals. *Hawaii Medical Journal, 56*, 34–36.

Wong, W., Chaw, J. K., Kent, C. K., & Klausner, J. D. (2006). Risk factors for early syphilis among gay and bisexual men seen in an STD clinic: San Francisco, 2002–2003. *Sexually Transmitted Diseases, 32*, 458–463.

Woolard, J., Beilin, L., Lord, T., Puddey, I., MacAdam, D., & Rouse, I. (1995). A controlled trial of nurse counseling on lifestyle change for hypertensives treated in general practice: Preliminary results. *Clinical Experimental Pharmacology and Physiology, 22*, 466–468.

Woolverton, W. L., Ricaurte, G. A., Forno, L. S., & Seiden, L. S. (1989). Long-term effects of chronic methamphetamine administration in rhesus monkeys. *Brain Research, 486*, 73–78.

Wu, L. T., Schlenger, W. E., & Galvin, D. M. (2006). Concurrent use of methamphetamine, MDMA, LSD, ketamine, GHB, and flunitrazepam among American youths. *Drug and Alcohol Dependence, 84,* 102–113.

Xian, H., Chantarujikapong, S. I., Scherrer, J. F., Eisen, S. A., Lyons, M. J., Goldberg, J., et al. (2000). Genetic and environmental influences on posttraumatic stress disorders, alcohol and drug dependence in twin pairs. *Drug and Alcohol Dependence, 61,* 95–102.

Yeo, K. K., Wijetunga, M., Ito, H., Efird, J. T., Tay, K., Seto, T. B., et al. (2007). The association of methamphetamine use and cardiomyopathy in young patients. *American Journal of Medicine, 120,* 165–171.

Yu, Q., Larson, D., & Watson, R. (2003). Heart disease, methamphetamine and AIDS. *Life Sciences, 73,* 129–140.

Yu, Q., Zhang, D., Walston, M., Zhang, J., Liu, Y., & Watson, R. R. (2002). Chronic methamphetamine exposure alters immune function in normal and retrovirus-infected mice. *International Immunopharmacology, 2,* 951–962.

Zernike, K. (2006, January 18). Hospitals say meth cases are rising, and hurt care. *The New York Times.* Retrieved January 18, 2006, from http://www.nytimes.com/2006/01/18/national/18drug.html

Zetola, N. M., & Pilcher, C. D. (2007). Diagnosis and management of acute HIV infection. *Infectious Disease Clinics of North America, 21,* 19–48.

Zule, W. A., Costenbader, E., Coomes, C., & Wechsberg, W. M. (2007, November). *Emerging methamphetamine use in North Carolina.* Paper presented at the 135th Meeting of the American Public Health Association, Washington, DC.

Zule, W. A., Costenbader, E. C., Meyer, W. J., Jr., & Wechsberg, W. M. (2007). Methamphetamine use and risky sexual behaviors during heterosexual encounters. *Sexually Transmitted Diseases, 34,* 689–694.

Zweben, J., Cohen, J., Christian, D., Galloway, G., Salinardi, M., Parent, D., et al. (2004). Psychiatric symptoms in methamphetamine users. *American Journal of Addiction, 13,* 181–190.

# INDEX